Poul Gernes
I cannot do it alone
– want to join in?

Foreword

Poul Erik Tøjner
Director

Anders Kold
Head of Aquisitions and curator of this exhibition

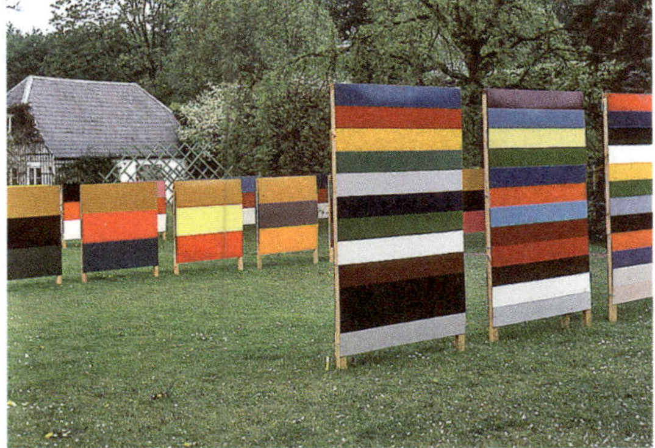

fig. 1 Poul Gernes' works in Louisiana's park at *Ung Dansk Kunst jubilæums-udstilling* in 1967

Poul Gernes (1925-1996) is one of the greatest Danish artists of the post-war generation, and Louisiana has long wished to shine a light on this impressive and insistent personality in Danish art. The past decade has seen growing international interest in Gernes, especially in Germany, while Louisiana's own engagement with the artist goes back to the mid-1960s. In 1967, Gernes was the chief organizer of Foreningen Ung Dansk Kunst's (The Association Young Danish Art) anniversary exhibition at the museum. That is when the iconic photographs of stripe paintings placed in the museum gardens were taken – one, "The Lottery Stripes" are in the museum's collection today. These were Systems paintings, based on random choices, and an anecdote even has it that Louisiana's founder, Knud W. Jensen, picked the colour scheme for one of them. Less than three years later, Gernes appeared in *Tabernakel*. A huge gamble in 1970 on Danish and international contemporary art, the exhibition challenged to the utmost the museum's – and modernism's – assumptions about what art and its materials could be: factory-fresh Citröen cars in the sculpture park, to take one example. The exhibition continues to enjoy mythical status in Danish art history, mainly because of the notorious horse slaughter carried out by Gernes' younger fellow artist Bjørn Nørgaard. Nearly half a century later, this catalogue also revisits *Tabernakel*, including how Gernes and the other three Danish artists ended up walking out in protest.

In the three and a half decades that followed, up to the artist's death in 1996, there was barely any interaction between Gernes and Louisiana. In the past decade, however, a series of acquisitions and donations has added to the collection considerably, fleshing out the story of Gernes and the still very present art of the 1960s. Gernes came out of the Constructivist tradition, also politically, giving his art a more robust intention than the contemporary Op Art. In the early 1960s he became a pivotal figure at Eks-skolen, Den Eksperimenterende Kunstskole (The Experimental Art School), in Copenhagen, whose core artists in one fell swoop came to dominate not only the art scene in their day but also later history writing with their views of art and society. New methods, new materials, a new view of the roles of art and the artist in society packed the agenda. You could say that Gernes made it out of that decade on the back of the large commission he got to decorate the new Herlev Hospital, then under construction. In turn, he also declined any contact with the art institutions, which he considered elitist and passé. For Gernes himself, and as he interpreted his times, the need lay in those situations where art came into touch with the rest of society, in public space. Whether he was right or wrong is not the premise of this exhibition, whatever you might think about this public linkage, even today. It is striking, however, that Gernes' many artistic devices, between buildings and people, have also positioned "Stripe Poul," as he was called, as a designer in his own right and a genius of scale. It is also striking how clearly his work expresses the period's pronounced criticism of capitalism and the new philosophy of the artwork. Witness his stripe paintings on Louisiana's beautiful, white walls, where his radical materiality and dislike of art as fetich nonetheless look like a million bucks. Louisiana's exhibition does not take the form of a retrospective and does not unfold in chronological order. Instead, it should be viewed as an exploration, with many very different rooms showcasing key characteristics of Gernes' work:

The very concrete approach to materiality and structure established in his Eks-skolen years from 1961-67. A goodbye to modernism's purity and exclusivity

Systems as a way of stripping a material of subjective choices and reaching for the universal. Unfolding a system as spatial potential

Art as a spatial experience – the great *Form Alphabet* – and as a fully integrated social practice, in a single-patient room from Herlev Hospital

The showdown with the figure of the artist as a mystical creative genius. Gernes disappears into the collective and reappears as someone else

The artwork as a monument of popular thought and agency.

Instead of tracking his oeuvre as a progressive, whole narrative, the exhibition can best be described as unfolding Gernes as a *Gesamtkunstwerk* – one big coherent whole: a mixture of attitudes, brushwork, circle strokes and hammer blows, systems and collages and a lifetime of aspiration to make life better and more beautiful with art. A sketch of a 1971 manifesto reads, "I cannot do it alone – Want to join in?" The statement has two sides. First, Gernes, insistent in everything he did, was actively trying to reach out to the people he saw his art as working for. Second, and this relates to the first point, his works, in keeping with 1960s ideas, then become a call to action, where the observer is not merely located at a remove, passively subjected to one-way communication. All the while, however, the works' presence, their form and impact, also makes us realize that most of his pictures, before they are anything else, are sensuous objects that affect us. And so, even though Gernes turned his back on Louisiana in 1970, pulling the plug on art institutions in general, the job of art institutions includes embracing and communicating such choices, as well. Only then will there be a possibility of everyone getting a little bit smarter. Want to join in?

ACKNOWLEDGMENTS
The exhibition above all is deeply indebted to the Gernes family for their invaluable support and encouragement. Aase Seidler Gernes, the artist's widow, has followed the project from a distance, while Ulrikka S. Gernes, their youngest daughter and manager of the Gernes Estate, generously and tirelessly has acted as a sparring partner and investigative unit throughout. Moreover, we would like to thank the following people for their help in the preparation of this exhibition: Bjørn Nørgaard, Kirsten Strømstad, Tania Ørum, Troels Andersen, Finn Thybo Andersen, Erik Steffensen, Anders Krüger, Hans Ulrich Obrist, Sir Paul Smith, Knud and Birgit Pontoppidan, Ursula Reuter Christiansen, Christine Buhl Andersen, Gitte Ørskou, Charlotte Sabroe, Ulrikke Neergaard, Maj-Britt Willumsen and the artist's gallery, Galleri Bo Bjerggaard. We are grateful to the lenders, institutional and private, who have generously shared their collections. Thanks also to the writers of the exhibition catalogue. Finally, a big thank you to the exhibition's sponsor, 15. Juni Fonden, for funding the project.

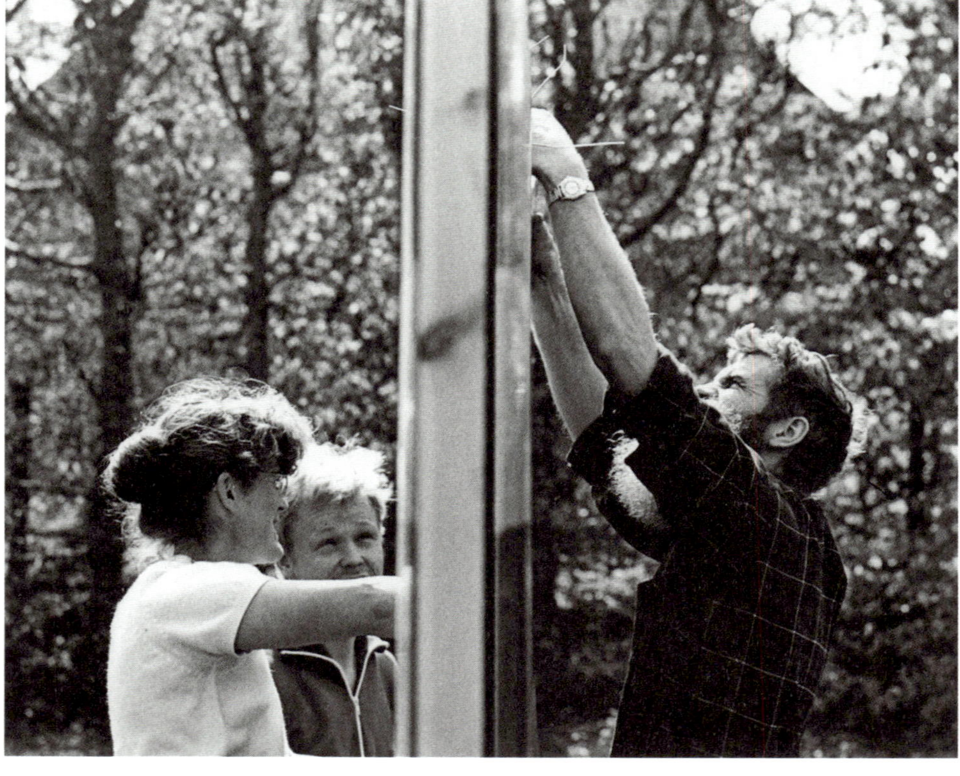
fig. 2

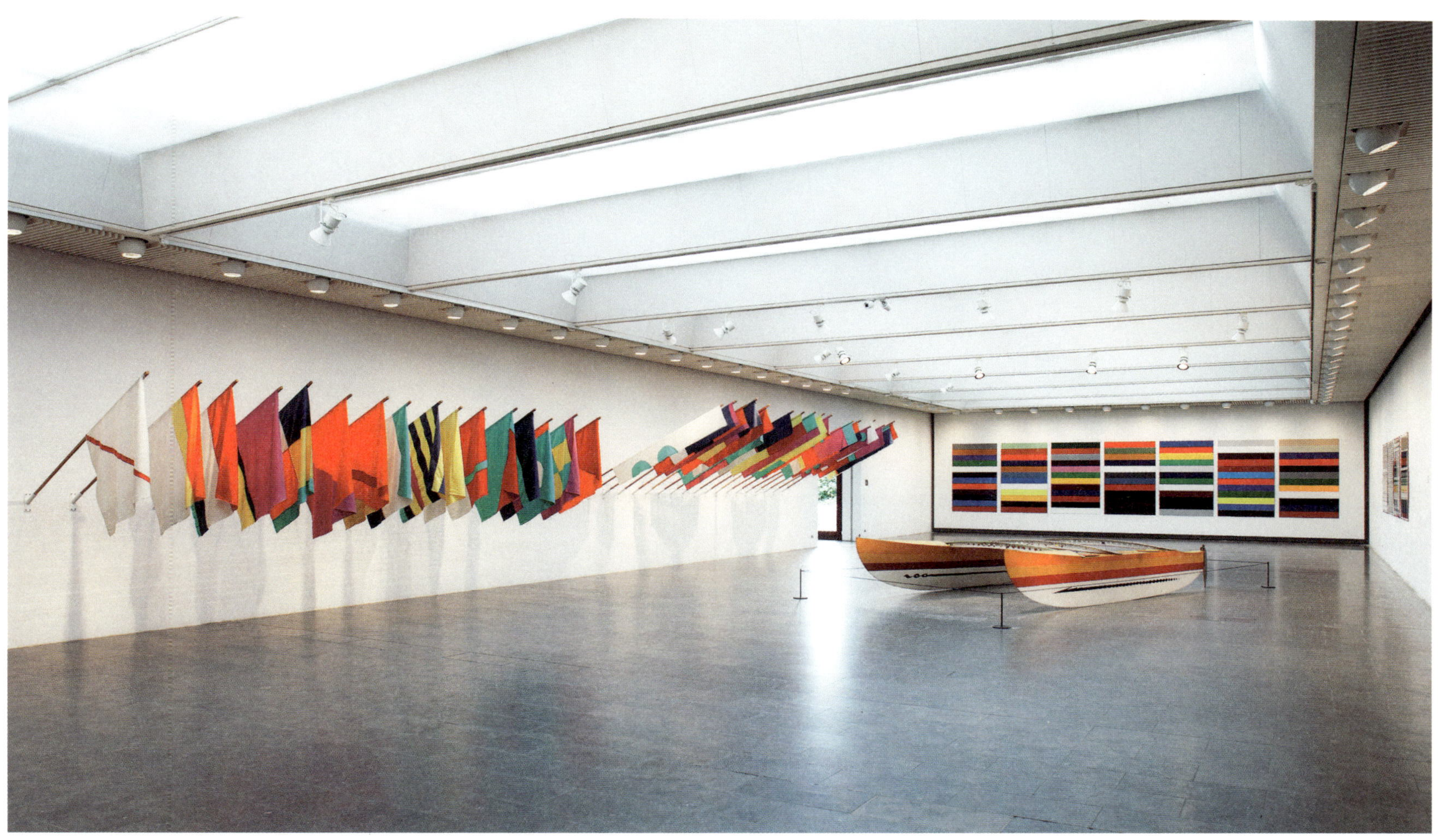

fig. 2   Peter Louis-Jensen with Poul and
          Aase Seidler Gernes at *Ung Dansk
          Kunst jubilæumsudstilling* in 1967

fig. 3   Installation view of works by Gernes
          in Louisiana's South Wing, 2013

fig. 1

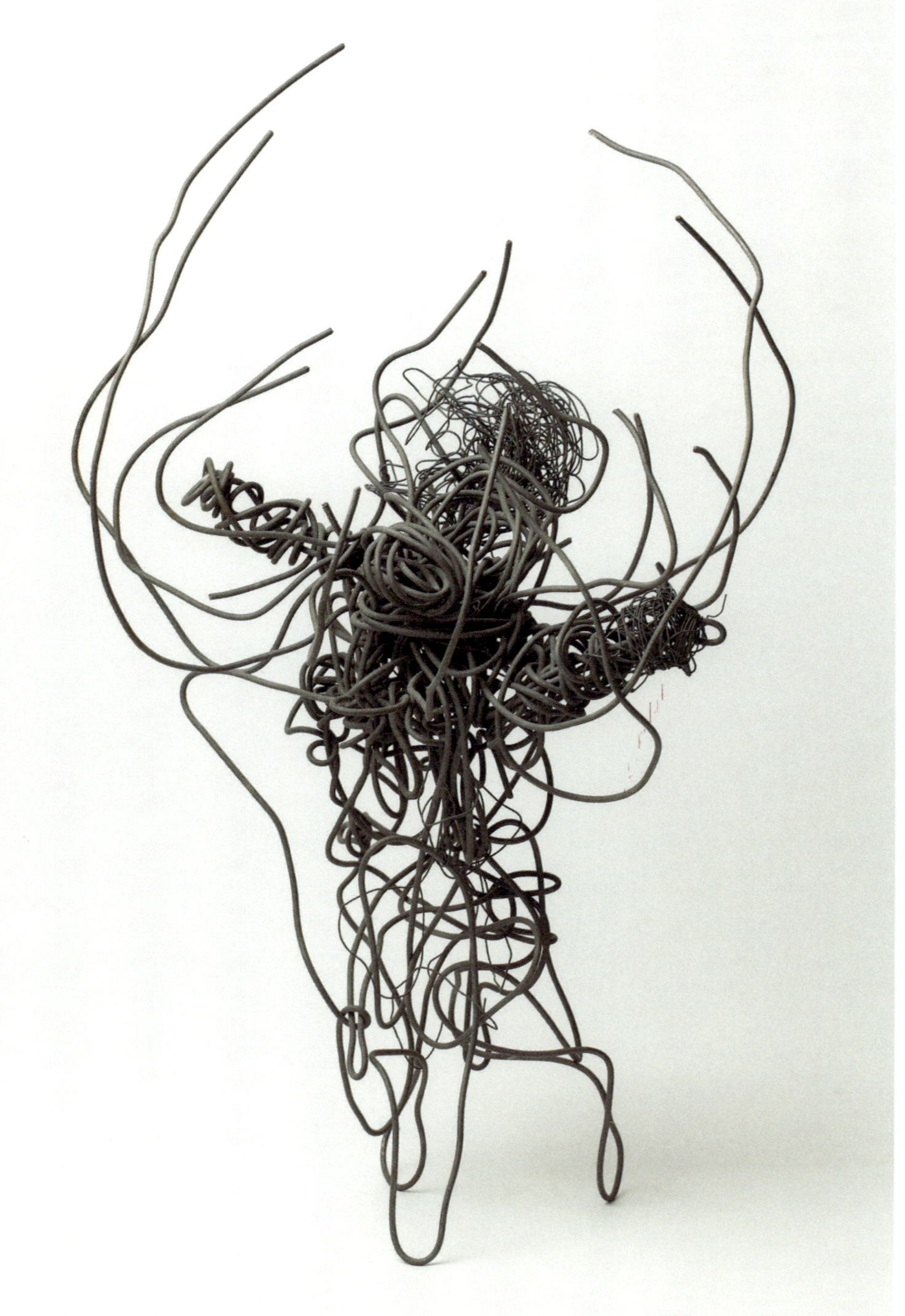

fig. 2

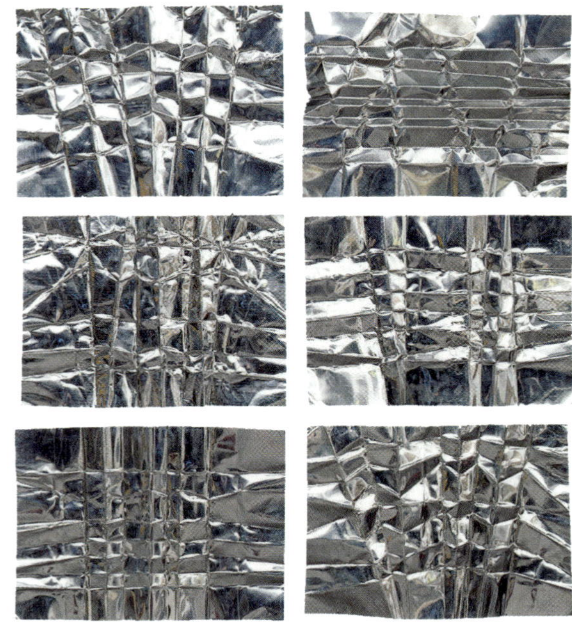

Poul Gernes
Between Matter and Method

By Helle Brøns

fig. 3

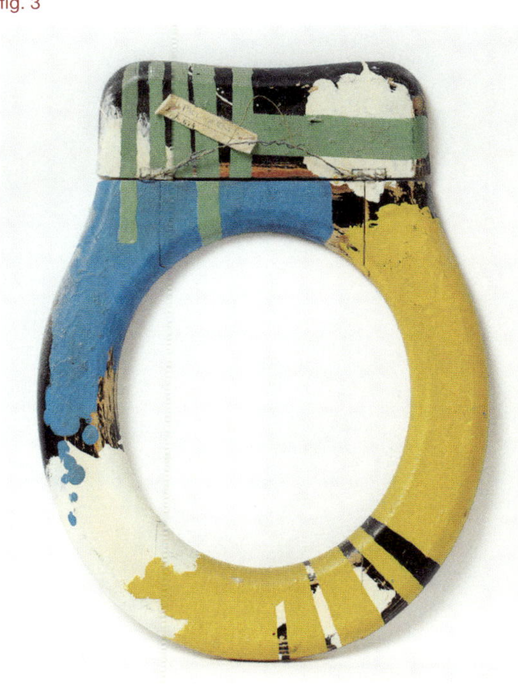

Ranging widely, the work of Poul Gernes is distinguished both by general stringency and by a number of apparent contradictions. On the one hand, the artist's work today can be seen as one long, coherent evolution – from his Concrete paintings in the 1950s to his collaborative experiments at Eks-skolen in the 1960s, his anonymous Minimalist paintings and his many commissions that moved art away from the individual work and into social space. On the other hand we have the contrasting trends in his oeuvre: razor-sharp, serial Systems paintings and quivering masses of jelly, rigorous conceptual works instructing the viewer in a social act and grungy junk sculptures, neo-realistic collages and minimalist works, pastel-coloured decorations of buildings and a film of the artist vomiting.

Gernes' different artistic expressions exist in a post-media situation, where the traditional boundaries between sculpture, painting and decoration are not maintained and conventional contradictions merge. For him, conceptual strategies and material excesses are not mutually exclusive; radically experimental, dogmatically moralizing elements and amazing banality mix. His personal authority and artistic impact go hand in hand with a desire to anonymize the artist-subject. While tight series of stripes and targets are what most people associate with Gernes, and what in recent years have won him international recognition,[1] this article will deal with the less clearly defined, and less discussed, material side of his production.[2] What did his use of cheap materials mean? What was his sensibility to his materials, and what sets it apart from other artistic use of found materials? How does his interest in art's materiality connect to his ideological and conceptual art view in specific works?

JUNK

As a co-founder, with art historian Troels Andersen, of Den Eksperimenterende Kunstskole (The Experimental Art School), known as Eks-skolen, in 1961, Gernes was in charge of teaching a course called "material experimentation." For the class, Gernes would bring in materials – often found at the junkyard – for him and his students to work with. The materials might include steel wire, wet paper, a toilet seat, an old gate or magazines – unpretentious, non-traditional materials, free of connotations to the established, "bourgeois" art that the school itself was a protest against. When the material was sheet metal, it was hammered round, heated or perforated with nails. Gernes himself made some simple, lovely reliefs by methodically folding a sheet of metal as many times as possible and then unfolding it again – *Untitled (6 Reliefs)*. According to Gernes, his "Material Experimentation" course aimed to "use objects inherently alien to picture-making to free the participants from inhibitions of a traditional and conventional nature" and to provide knowledge of the effects of different techniques and materials.[3] He insisted that his students be able to "work individually on collaborative assignments and collaboratively on individual assignments," i.e., the artists contributed their own unique ideas to the collaborative works and abandoned their personal patent on ideas and works.[4] From the beginning, the encounter with materials was both a tangible interaction and a method of freeing thought by sinking into matter. The material was a common matter bringing artists together, and the resulting thought-matter was common property, as well. Gernes emphasized the collective process rather than the finished works: "We didn't even have to make anything; we wanted to first find out together what the things we wanted to make should be used for. What art should be used for."[5]

One collective Eks-skolen project was a "positive demonstration" in November 1962, where, by one account, the artists built a pile of junk in Copenhagen's Kgs. Nytorv square, painted collaborative paintings and made prints. Moreover, they walked down the pedestrian shopping street Strøget, carrying coloured placards with no textual messages.[6] The happening should be viewed as a celebration of the raw, unpretentious material and colour's power to create joy. When one passerby wanted to know what they were demonstrating for, Gernes is said to have asked back, "Brother, isn't it a beautiful colour?"[7] The positive demonstration could also be seen as an implicit critique of the conventional art view, in which only materials such as marble, bronze and iron were worthy of art.[8]

Making art from junk and found objects is not Gernes' or Eks-skolen's invention, of course. A familiar avant-garde discipline, it had been cultivated by the Surrealists and Dadaists like Marcel Duchamp since the early 1900s. It was also a familiar practice in the Danish context: Henry Heerup made numerous "junk sculptures" in the 1940s, and Robert Jacobsen made his "dolls" from scrap metal in the 1950s when Albert Mertz also created junk assemblages. Unlike the above artists, Gernes' use of junk was neither figurative nor quaint but focused on a concrete, constructive and methodical – sometimes brutal – treatment of the material itself.

Because the most important thing was the process, a lot of the experiments ended up back on the scrapheap, though it also resulted in a number of individual works by Gernes. One, *Untitled ("Large Scrap Sculpture")* from c. 1963, is a jumble of different kinds of scrap metal – a lid, brackets, plates, broken tools and wire – crammed into a big metal basket. The work upends the medium of sculpture. In traditional sculptures, forms are most often composed around a central core and held together in harmonious balance as if by a natural inner force. In Gernes' sculpture, there is no inner cohesion and the elements are simply held together by the metal basket. The sculpture is brutally unsentimental in its use of materials. Only the consistency of their treatment, the material cohesion and the art-institutional context imply that this is art, not a trashcan.

In the 1950s, Gernes designed chairs, lamps and other utilitarian objects. He had an eye for the transformation that occurs when a designed, functional object is thrown out and turned into garbage, reverting to an existence as material. Presenting the discarded objects of consumer society as art implies a criticism of consumer culture as a whole, indicating artistic value as an alternative to commodity society's single-minded focus on economic value. Gernes' art remains in the everyday sphere, where the inherent power of things and the self-organization of objects are perceived as the dominant system.

Untitled ("The Cloth Ball") from 1962 is structured in the same way as the scrap sculpture, only it consists of a motley pile of old clothes tied together with a clothesline. The works contains clear signals of daily life in the modern world, where clothes are discarded when fashions change, and the viewer can directly relate to the material with her body. If clothes make the man, this bundle gathers a number of potential identities. Gernes himself consistently wore white craftsman trousers, signalling his solidarity with the workingman. The clothes bundle's shape approaches the basic geometric shape of a sphere, but, as Mikkel Bogh has put it, it is "made from the stuff of its time," marked by transience and tied to the social – unlike imperishable bronze which rings with timeless eternity.[9] The sculpture thus unites the geometric ideal with everyday materials.

Gernes' material experiments continued in 1962 and 1963 with bicycle handlebars, washing machines, fruit crates and paint buckets. The objects in the relief with colour samples on spools and plasctic cups (1962-63) compose a structure of circular forms, similar to the ones Gernes was using in his paintings, but here it is made up, in part, by the plastic buckets that once contained the paint. It is at once raw material, artwork and remnant of the process, reflecting Gernes' striving for an art that is "straightforward without holding anything back, without trying to be smug, clever or overly intellectual."[10] Even as Gernes was working to democratize art, for instance by using cheap materials, his works were not always perceived as such. As often happens when an artist tries to make "art for the people," "the people" were not particularly interested and did not necessarily feel they were being addressed.

DESTRUCTION

Materials were also challenged and tested by destructive methods. In one instance, Gernes burned a board of soft masonite along the edges, changing the material's colour, texture, shape and smell. The traces of the destructive process demonstrated certain basic qualities of the material and created interesting visual effects where the singed, blackened parts met the wood-coloured parts.

Gernes also applied his material experimentation to printmaking, cranking up the format to the largest possible size. One of his most iconic treatments of printmaking materials is seen in his *Blows with a Hammer* series. Metal plates were prepared on both sides with a coating of resin varnish, Gernes then knocked the varnish off with a hammer and the plates were etched. Printing ink remained in the etched areas. The works are experienced as direct impressions of the very act of destruction and the measured disintegration of the material. In places, Gernes punched holes in the plate with the hammer, which show up as white "holes" in the print. It is important to note that he did not just pound away in uncontrolled destruction. On the contrary, it was a completely systematized process, which is reflected in laconic titles, such as *Five Blows with a Hammer*, *10 Blows with a Hammer* and *100 Blows with a Hammer*. Although the works, in their materiality, might resemble the expressive prints of Asger Jorn, they are not expressive outpourings of emotion but systematic documentations of the impact of the hammer on the material. Moreover, Gernes printed both sides of the plates, sometimes in both the horizontal and the vertical formats,[11] and so the process was, in a manner of speaking, documented frontwards and back.

In another radical method of attacking printing plates, Gernes placed a prepared plate on the street and let it be run over by a bus, leaving tire marks on the surface, along the long dimension,

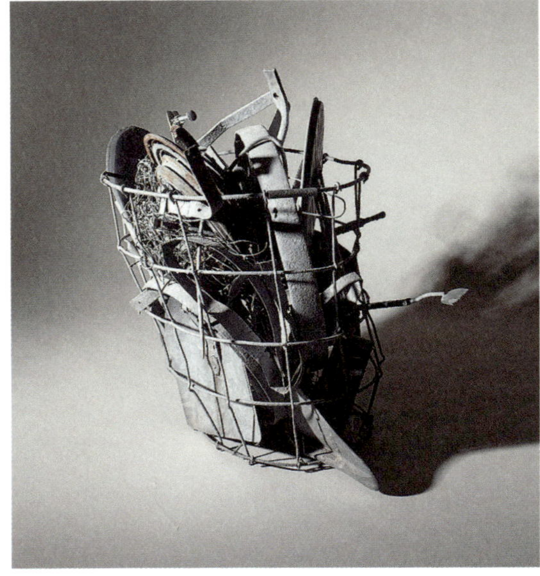

fig. 4

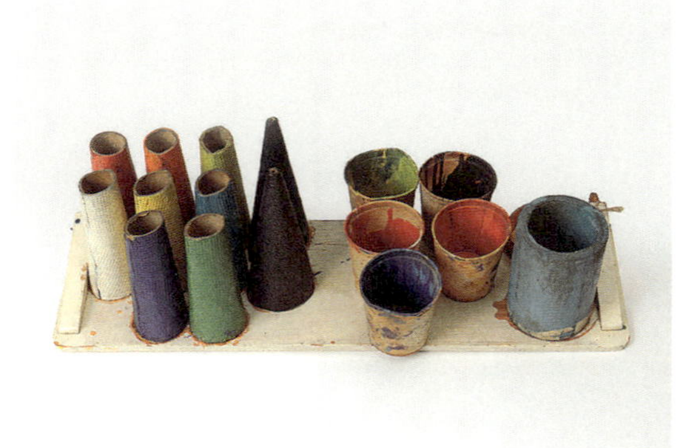

fig. 5

fig. 6

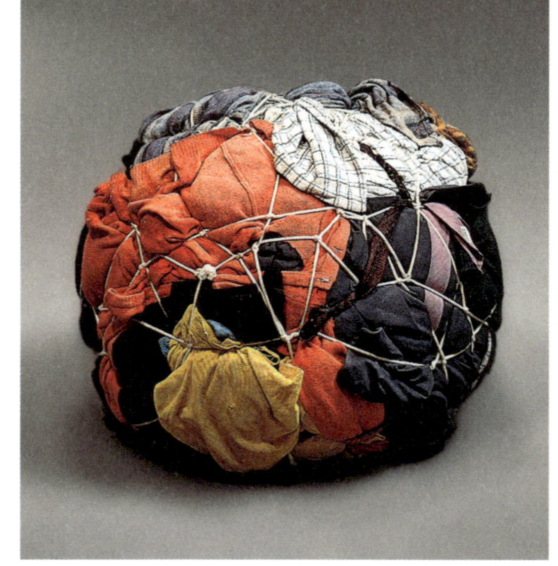

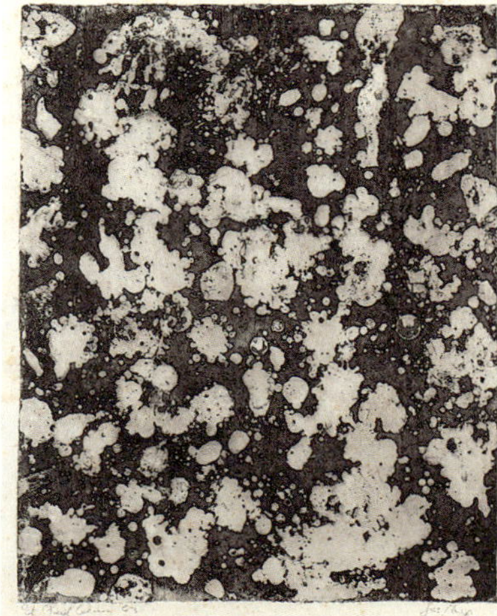

fig. 7

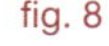
fig. 8

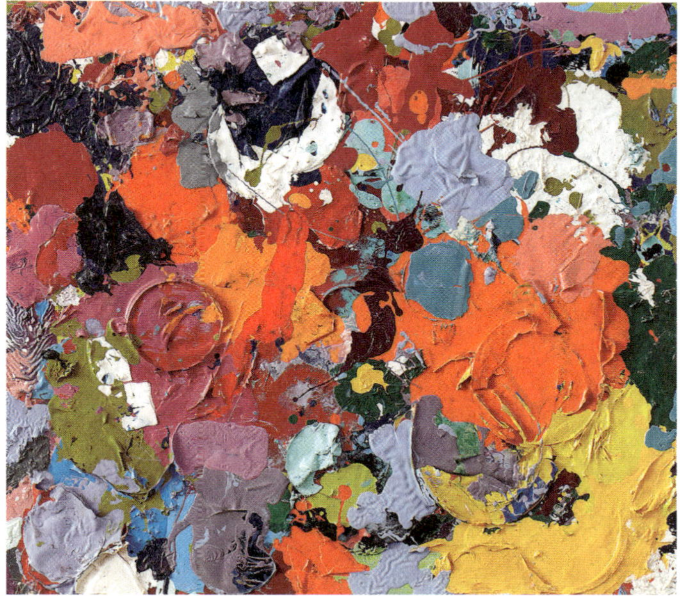

fig. 9

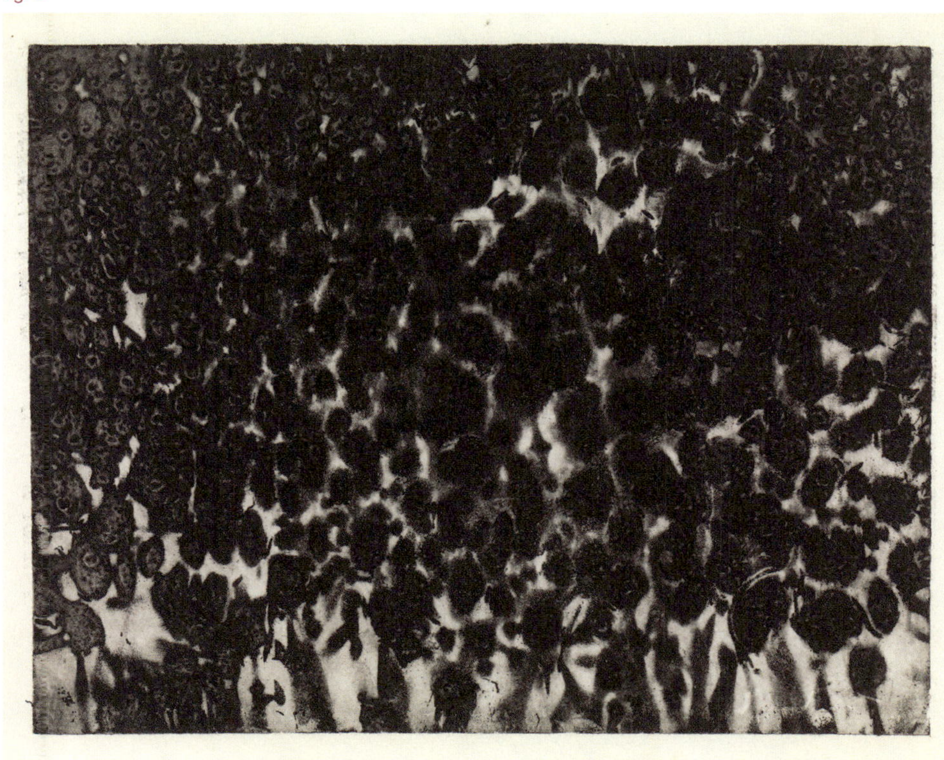

and these were then etched and printed. Here, too, one might be reminded of Asger Jorn's ceramic relief at Århus Statsgymnasium, which was made in part by running a motor scooter through the clay. But while Jorn's partially figurative relief is an excess of material effects, Gernes starts from a conceptual and simple methodical device. In the title, "Tyre Imprint from Bus 29 at Kgs. Nytorv" (1962, see p. 78), Gernes' prosaic, documenting approach is underscores – entirely removed from the artist's hand and personal expression. The work is an unsentimental imprint of a banal slice of everyday life, with no symbolic layers or aestheticizing efforts.

A 1963 series of aquatints, in their overwhelming, uncontrolled materiality, is likewise reminiscent of Jorn's drip paintings and the spontaneously abstract, so-called Informalist art to which Gernes otherwise saw himself as being in direct opposition.[12]

By occasionally surrendering to matter, Gernes radicalized efforts, also found in Jorn's art, to lose control of the work, abandoning the role of the active artist-subject shaping passive matter and instead letting the work be structured by matter's own design. In the name of anonymity, the artist-subject is dissolved in the material. Or, in the words of Gernes' Eks-skolen colleague Per Kirkeby, "Materiality conquers the 'immoral' fixation on the person."[13]

PAINTING MATTER

Gernes' painting in the early 1960s was characterized by the same interplay of materiality and method as his sculpture and printmaking. Having started out, in the 1950s, by making constructivist paintings consisting of lines in vertical and horizontal bands, he now dissolved structure entirely, producing a number of unruly, textural "glob paintings" with no form of compositional structure: no figures, no composition, no rhythmic brushwork or expressive gestures, no balanced colour scheme or dominant formations. Just an "all-overness" of enamels that have apparently been randomly dripped, wiped or poured on the canvas and, as they dried, have wrinkled or flaked, sometimes bearing imprints of objects placed in the wet paint. The painting is drained of the artist's personal expression. The paint above all appears as matter – importantly not oil on canvas but cheap enamel and house paint on masonite.

Gernes defined this as a "ground zero for painting, where it becomes doubtful whether it's possible to make pictures."[14] In the mid-1960s, he was at a crossroads between textural and structural paintings, which is best illustrated by an often cited experiment in 1962. In her important book on Gernes, *Der er dejligt i Danmark* (It is Beautiful in Denmark) (1971), art librarian Jane Pedersen describes how the artist had in front of him two boards marked with a chessboard pattern. One painting he coloured in using his subjective, aesthetic judgement, while the order of colours in the other was random. Every time he had used a colour, he wiped off the brush, without really looking, on a third painting placed behind him. Thus, Gernes ranges across all three of these contrasting artistic approaches in one and the same process. Pedersen describes how the three paintings become "symbolic of a situation where he is testing the different possibilities to find out which way he has to go. In the textural works, he has freed himself from the last vestiges of an ego-centred composition. In the random choice of colours, he has freed himself from his own subjective choice. The unconscious choice proved to be significantly more interesting, because in it constellations emerged that were impossible to imagine in advance. From this point on, he switches to employing anonymous non-textured structures that would soon be pointing beyond the individual painting to a greater totality."[15] Thus, both textural and pure structural painting could be used as tactics for creating resistance to meaning and pushing painting past subjectivity, which Gernes considered "mental masturbation."[16]

From 1965, Gernes concentrated on Systems paintings of simple and anonymous structures, such as stripes, check patterns, circles or letters, in enamel with no textural effects. Still, the Systems paintings were never as slick or pure in their look as American Hard Edge painting or Pop Art's industrial surface perfection, despite their similarity to artists such as Kenneth Noland, Morris Louis, Frank Stella and Jasper Johns. Gernes' paintings clearly have a handmade look about them and material remains offer some textural pushback even in his hard-edged paintings. For example, in his series *Untitled (Vertical and Horizontal Stripes in Four Squares)* (1963) each work consists of 32 stripes, all of which are monochrome except for a single stripe in a dirty and uneven, mixed colour with a pronounced texture. Another example is a painting of the letter Z, in which the paint, as the artist Claus Carstensen has noted, is filled with hair (see detail p. 61) – dog hairs and hairs from Gernes' own beard – in such a volume that he must have decided to include them. At any rate, he clearly could not have cared less about getting a clean, slick surface. Moreover, the letter is reversed and one of the stripes has not been coloured in completely. Carstensen sees the work as a typical example of what he calls Danish "kitchen-counter minimalism," where dust, hair and breadcrumbs end up in the painting.[17]

This does not mean that Gernes' Systems painting is just a cheap, slack version of the American kind, but that it should also be considered in terms of a Danish tradition, where a fondness for the banal, the popular and folk art can be traced in artists like Jorn and Heerup, just as the Danish traditions of the cooperative movement, folk high-schools and collectivism likely also play a part in his later relocation of art into social space.

Among the members of Eks-skolen, as Tania Ørum described in *De eksperimenterende tressere* (The Experimental Sixties), there was an ongoing discussion of the relationship between "the pure" and "the impure" in art. "The pure" referred to formal entities, Minimalism, Systems painting and the cool, concrete, conceptual side of art. "The impure" was the dirty, the expressive and the material, as well as connotations and content pointing out into the real world. As Hans-Jørgen Nielsen put it, the artists were striving to "hit the point in an artwork where it teeters between pure and impure. Where a pure endeavour is already impure or an impure endeavour is already also pure. The artwork should be pure in an impure way or impure in a pure way."[18] Especially in the 1960s, Gernes' work is nurtured by this basic tension between pure and impure, structure and texture, method and matter. A pile of dirty laundry becomes pure in its aspiration for the purity of the sphere, a pure concept of a certain number of hammer blows gets an impure, expressive look, a pure letter painting with simple systematic stripes gets an impure, hairy surface.

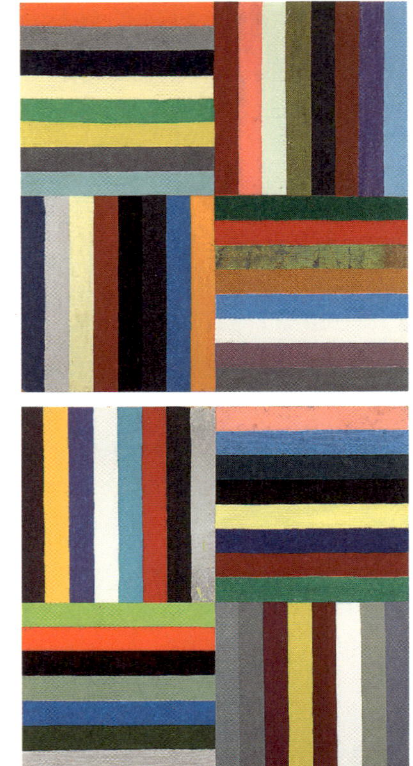

fig. 10

fig. 11

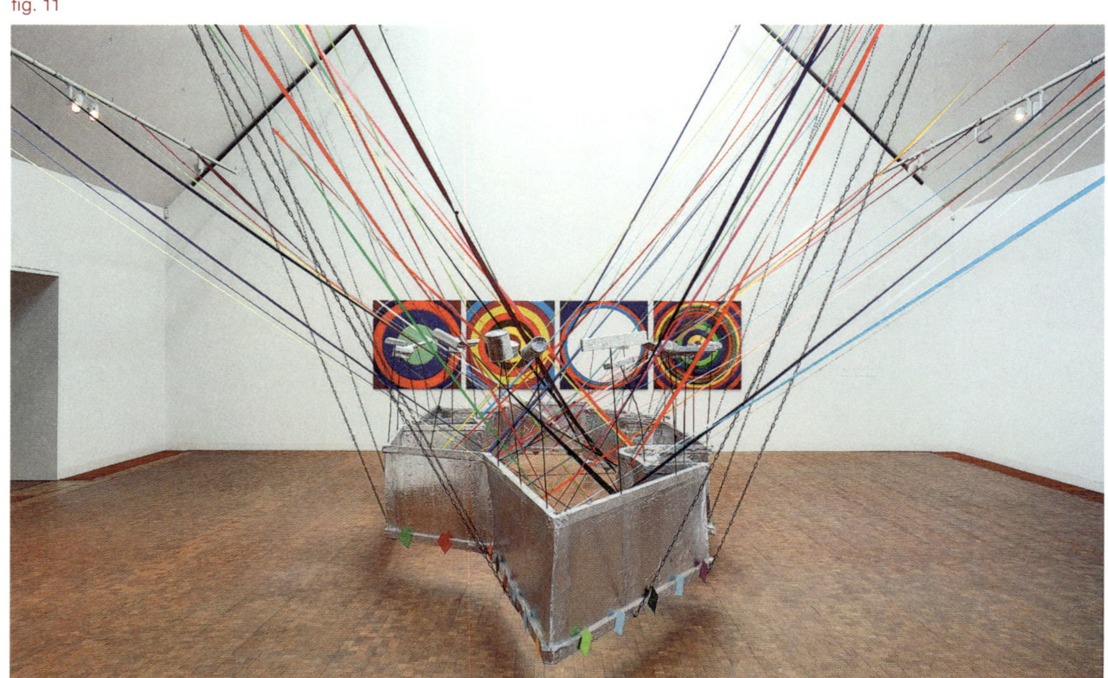

fig. 12

fig. 10 Untitled, (Vertical and horizontal stripes in four squares), 1963
Oil on masonite, 160 × 160 cm
Private Collection
(not in the exhibition)

fig. 11 Untitled ("The Dream Ship"), 1968
Installation, mixed media
Installation view from
Sorø Kunstmuseum, 2015

fig. 12 Untitled (Z), 1965
(The Alphabet Series)
Enamel paint and hair on masonite,
160 × 130 cm

fig. 13 Gernes works on plaster cakes,
Copenhagen, 1977-78

fig. 14 Stills from *Vomit Film*, 1963
Filmed by Den Eksperimenterende
Kunstskole
Duration: 4:44 min.

fig. 15 Installation view from the exhibition
Behind at Galerie Ben Kaufmann,
Berlin, 2007

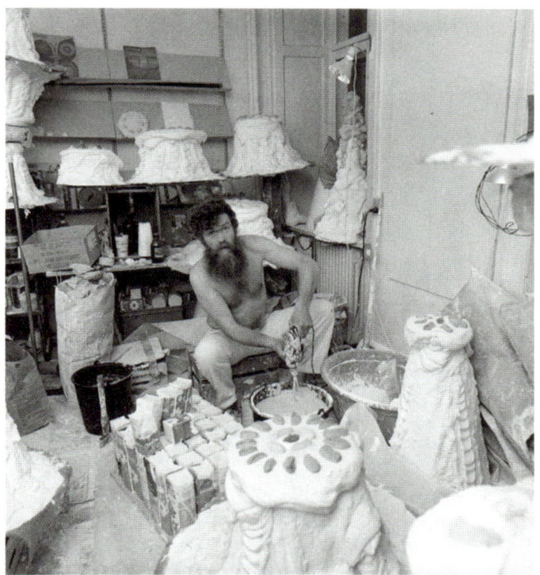
fig. 13

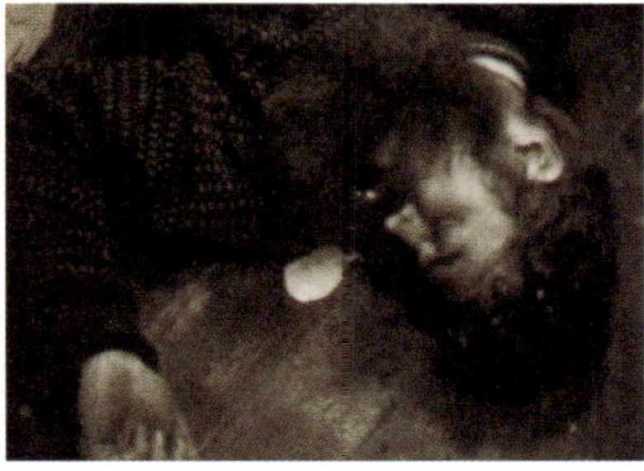
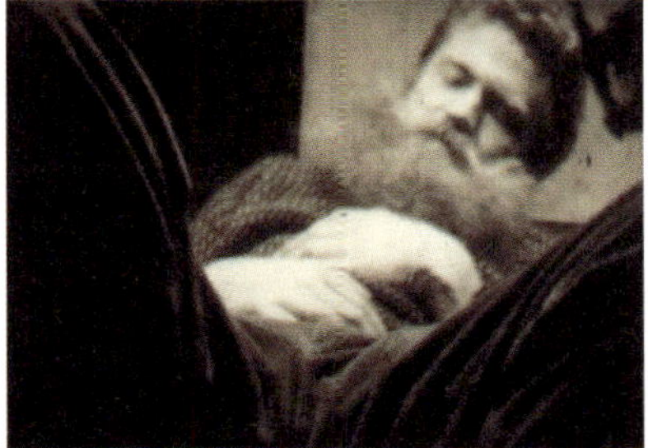
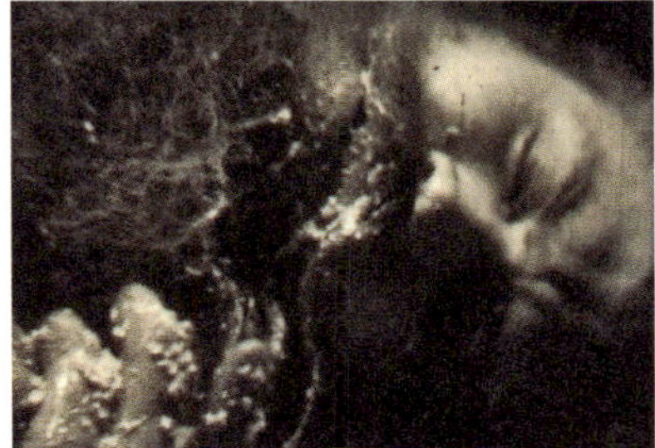
fig. 14

fig. 15
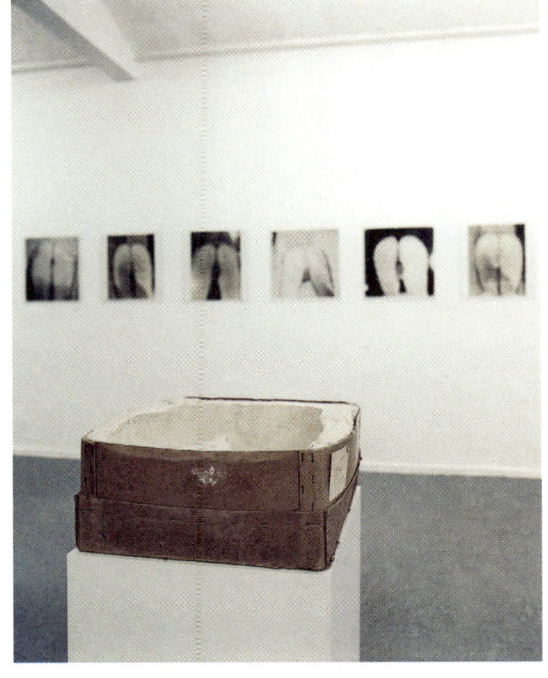

As he moved further towards a pure expression without the associative charm of the impure, impurities popped up in other connections and on another level, for instance when his pure public decorations became a framework for impure, everyday-infected life.[19]

BODY

The tension between the pure and the impure is also reflected by other traditional paired opposites, such as mind and body, ideal and material, reason and emotion, masculine and feminine. Gernes' work is configured as what is typically defined as "masculine," in its strict systems and discipline, monumental dimensions and aggressively executed hammer prints – all created within Eks-skolen's distinctly male-dominated "brotherhood," where the tone of collaboration was tough. But parallel to this are periodic emissions of what is generally linked to the "feminine," including material excesses in plaster, second-hand clothes, materially shapeless paintings and the bodily abject.[20]

Gernes incorporates the body into his work in many different ways. For one, in the "pure" sculptures, as an alphabet of forms, and in the cool, striped spatial decorations, where the visitor has to experience the sculptures with her senses, feeling the effects of scale, form, mass, colour and material on her body. Elsewhere, the body is incorporated in more "impure" ways. The *Vomit Film* (1963) famously shows Gernes vomiting for five long, painful minutes, while groping around on the floor, smearing his clothes, face, hands and beard. During the shoot, he periodically filled his mouth with oatmeal, though the film only includes shots of him vomiting and spitting out. The session was filmed from several different angles and the footage was edited together. The result is a violently repulsive expression, where the viewer loses her sense of temporal and physical context and cannot help but feel nauseous herself. The film can be seen as a provocative, ironic comment on the expressionist idea of the artist pouring out his inner self.

While the vomit film shows us the inside of the artist, *Untitled ("Ass")* from 1967 presents us with his backside. The sculpture is a self-portrait of sorts, but instead of his face he shows us his bare behind. A negative version of classic, white plaster figures, the work completely inverts the sculptural ideal. Traditionally, the art consisted in making the cold, hard body of the sculpture resemble a living body with convincing details like veins, locks of hair or the softness of a breast. In the plaster ass, the resemblance is entirely too overwhelming, revealing skin blemishes and hair, strands of which are still stuck in the plaster here and there (see detail p. 63). The idea of the artist's imprint on the work has been cultivated as a kind of proof in art, for example in the notion that the Veil of Veronica bears the true image of Jesus after he pressed the cloth to his face. The plaster ass mocks that notion in a scatological and impure rhetoric – for Gernes, art should not be too high and mighty. As a viewer, one feels an impulsive desire to test how the plaster cast matches one's own behind, a bodily identification conveying an interesting sculptural play of positive and negative, square and curved, hard and soft, smooth and hairy.

The plaster ass was followed by *Untitled ("Behind")* (1969), a series of 10 nude behinds photographed from below through the plate of glass they are sitting on. In these simple black and white, over-exposed images, the buttocks rise up as round, white forms that, at a distance, almost look like halved apples with genitals for cores. The impure subject matter is here combined with a serial method and a pure aesthetics that is far from pornographic. Gernes himself saw the images as monumental and beautiful, and although he acknowledged their element of irony, he did not consider it to be central.[21] The central element, rather, was the anonymizing, democratizing gesture with which he put the models on a par with each other. The works can be viewed as anonymous portraits satirizing individualism. The series came into being at Charlottenborg's *Festival 200* exhibition in 1969, where Gernes had put up a studio and invited visitors to have their backsides immortalized.[22] The social situation around the photographs and the inclusion of the visitors in the creation of the work is a big part of their point.

The idea that the moral core of art was facilitating human communities and social relations was the reason why Gernes also contributed to *Festival 200* with a makeshift public bath, offering visitors to take a sauna and a bath. Today, very few museum visitors would likely be persuaded to undress, but in 1969 the bath was very popular, and because the exhibition fell during a hot period of summer, the bath was eagerly used by the audience – including workers from the B&W shipyard who had discovered that it was less expensive than the local public bath.[23] As Pedersen notes, the bath presented "the sculptural object totally assimilated into an everyday situation that established a human community between those who, together, stood under the showers or sat in the sauna."[24] Nudity here was a marker of naturalness, community and gender equality. Unlike most nude bodies in art, these ones were not painted, chiselled in marble or cast in plaster. Gernes' material was real, living bodies.

EVERYDAY UTOPIA

The movement in Gernes' art away from the production of objects to the establishment of spatial, social situations is evident in his huge installational sculpture *Untitled ("The Dream Ship")*, which hung in the lobby of Charlottenborg for the 1968 Spring Exhibition. The work consists of a frame of masonite sheets shaped like an oddly angular vessel and wrapped in tinfoil. The construction is suspended on metal chains and a wealth of silk ribbons extending from the body of the ship to the ceiling. Occupying the entire room, the ship blocks the visitor's view and mobility. Different objects are stuck in the "gunwale," their shapes revealing them to be old tin cans, paper-towel rolls and other packaging. *The Dream Ship* is at once overwhelming and down to earth: a monumental sculpture made from cheap everyday materials, whose humbleness feels like a democratizing gesture. Unlike works like the scrap sculpture and the cloth ball with their closed sculptural forms, the floating structure is open and airy, signalling transience, freedom and tinfoil-glittering fantasy travel. The humble materials evoke a dream of turning around the ship, picking everyone up and sailing society towards Utopia.

While the systems paintings are drained of symbolic content, *The Dream Ship* fosters illusion in a way that mixes Disney fantasy and everyday packed-lunch dreams. It is connotations such as these that gave rise to the title, *The Dream Ship*, which did not appear in the contemporary reviews. At the time, the work was referred to as "the hanging sculpture," "the silver ship," "ship of fools" and "the boat."[25] *The Dream Ship* has aptly been described as a "post-Minimalist" work,[26] and it did indeed herald a turning point, after which Gernes left behind the systems works and moved art out among people in everyday spaces.

The same year – in 1968 – for the *Anonymiteter* exhibition at Lunds konsthall, Gernes developed an interactive conceptual work instructing visitors to go out in the street and say hello for him to every tenth person of the opposite sex, give that person a small amount of money, determined by a specific system, and possibly talk about the exhibition.[27] Another, more radical, initiative to move art into the social sphere was firmaet Hjælp (the firm Help), which he and his housemates at their commune in Humlebæk founded in 1972. As part of a resocializing plan for recovering drug addicts, firmaet Hjælp undertook to decorate four summer camps together with the addicts. Everyone was subject to the same discipline, including communal sleeping times in a common room, shared work, cultural events, common readings aloud and possibly fishing. Although Gernes did not directly frame these projects as art, they dovetailed with the moral turn his art was taking, where life itself became the material of his art.

Gernes' own life and lifestyle in many ways merge with his work. Nonetheless, as energetically as he aspired to deindividualization in his art, he stood out as distinctly as a person with enormous authority, and many of the collaborative activities in actuality ended up taking place on his terms. Although many of his works and commissions, undertaken in the name of community and anonymity, were executed by and with his family, housemates and students, and many patterns and colour combinations were created in collaboration with his wife, the artist and textile designer Aase Seidler Gernes, they bear only his name. Moreover, stripes and flowers that, in principle, were supposed to be completely anonymous could be identified as most successful when Aase or he had wielded the brush. Personal expression crept in. Despite his enormous respect for Gernes, the Danish artist Bjørn Nørgaard has said that "the problem with Poul's programme is that his entire artistic work refutes his thesis."[28] While that is putting it a bit bluntly, it is paradoxical that Gernes' stripe paintings today have become just as powerful a brand as Paul Smith striped socks. At any rate, what remains is a radical artist who had a mission with his art, pushing it past the existing boundaries and investing himself in the process. A conceptual and experimental artist who demonstrated that systems and sensuousness, repetition and experiment, stripes and texture, method and matter, are not mutually exclusive but can be embraced in one and the same move.

Helle Brøns (b. 1973) is Ph.D. in art history and Curator at Sorø Kunstmuseum. Her research concentrated on gender, matter and popular culture in Asger Jorn's art, and she has published a book and numerous articles about Jorn and generally about both avant-garde and contemporary art.

1   E.g., a large retrospective exhibition was first shown at Deichtorhallen, Hamburg, in 2010, then divided into two parts, shown at and Lunds Konsthall; in 2007, a major selection of his works was shown at *Documenta* XII in Kassel; in 2004, works by Gernes were included in the exhibition *Minimalism and After III, Neuerwerbungen/New Acquisitions* at Daimler Contemporary, Berlin; in 2002, Kunstverein Braunschweig in Germany showed a solo exhibition; and, in 2001, the German artist Cosima von Bonin mounted a Gernes homage exhibition entitled *Bruder Poul sticht in See* at Hamburger Kunstverein.

2   The following description of Gernes' work draws on the most significant contributions to the literature on Gernes made by Jane Pedersen (*Der er dejligt i Danmark*, 1971), Troels Andersen (countless articles and the book *Ex-skolen. Eksperiment, kunst, skole*, 2010), Tania Ørum (*De eksperimenterende tressere*, 2009), Mikkel Bogh (*Ny dansk kunsthistorie*, Vol. 9, 1996) and Lars Morell (*Broderskabet. Den eksperimenterende kunstskole*, 2009 and *Det grafiske eksperiment. Gernes' tryk*, 2005).

3   Gernes, note, 15 Nov. 1961, cited in Troels Andersen, *Ex-skolen. Eksperiment, kunst, skole, 1961-69*. Museum Jorn, 2010, p. 13.

4   Ibid.

5   Lars Morell, *Broderskabet. Den eksperimenterende kunstskole 1961-69*. Thanning & Appel, 2009, p. 67.

6   Mikkel Bogh, *Geometri og bevægelse. Ny dansk kunsthistorie*, Vol. 9. Kunstbogklubben, Forlaget Palle Fogtdal, 1996, p. 98.

7   Synne Rifbjerg, "'Broder, er det ikke en smuk farve?' Uddrag af to samtaler med Gernes' disciple fra 'Broderskabet Eks-skolen', Per Kirkeby og Bjørn Nørgaard," in *Weekendavisen*, 15 June 2001, Kultur, p. 1.

8   According to Troels Andersen, it was perceived that way by the academy, while he emphasizes that the primary target group was people in the streets. Andersen is cited in Tania Ørum, *De eksperimenterende tressere. Kunst i en opbrudstid*. Gyldendal, 2009, p. 217.

9   Mikkel Bogh, op. cit., p. 92.

10   Gernes, cited in Erik Steffensen, *Invitation til en kop mælk – og alt godt fra Poul Gernes*. Nordjyllands Kunstmuseum 2001, p. 6.

11   For a thorough treatment of Gernes' prints, see Lars Morell, *Det grafiske eksperiment. Gernes' tryk 1943-1996*. Thanning & Appel, 2005.

12   The aquatint printmaking process is described in Morell, 2005.

13   Per Kirkeby, "Per og Bjørn om Poul," in *Poul Gernes på Sophienholm*, 1980, n.p.

14   Jane Pedersen, *Der er dejligt i Danmark*. Borgen, 1971, p. 55.

15   Ibid., p. 62.

16   Ibid., p. 45.

17   Conversation with Claus Carstensen, 10 March 2016.

18   Hans-Jørgen Nielsen, cited in Ørum, 2009, p. 110.

19   Among Gernes' 100 or so commissions to decorate buildings, we can mention Herlev Hospital (1970-76), the Panum Building (1981), the Rebæk Søpark Dormitory (1984), City Hall Horsens (1985-86), Palads Cinema and Ordrup Gymnasium (1989), and Gurrebunkeren (1992). See, e.g., Hornung, Peter Michael and Ulrikka S. Gernes, *Farvernes medicin. Poul Gernes og Amtssygehuset i Herlev*. Borgens Forlag, 2003. Finn Thybo Andersen is preparing for publication a thoroughly illustrated catalogue raisonné of Gernes' commissions.

20   See, e.g., Mira Schor, *Wet: On Painting, Feminism, and Art Culture*. Duke University Press, 1997; Jane Blocker, *What the Body Cost: Desire, History, and Performance*. University of Minnesota Press, 2004; and Rune Gade (ed.), *Maskuliniteter – køn og kunst*. Informations forlag, 2001.

21   Pedersen, 1971, p. 72-74.

22   Tania Ørum, "En plats för ömsesidig acceleration," in *Poul Gernes,* Swedish insert for the exhibition catalogue for Deichtorhallen Hamburg, Malmö Konsthall and Lunds konsthall, 2011, p. 30.

23   Charlotte Bagger Brandt, "Værker der virker," exhibition folder for the exhibition of the same name at Charlottenborg, 2009.

24   Pedersen, op. cit., p. 100.

25   Pedersen, 1971, p. 98; Henning Christiansen, "4 danske kunstnere," in *Tabernakel,* Louisiana Revy, Vol. 10, No. 3, 1970, p. 37; Troels Andersen, *Eksempler og motiver. Artikler om dansk kunst i det 20. århundrede*. Borgen, 1988, p. 175.

26   Ørum, 2011, p. 30.

27   Pedersen, 1971, p. 68.

28   Bjørn Nørgaard, "Jeg ved ikke om man nogensinde bliver sig selv," in Steffensen, 2001, p. 19.

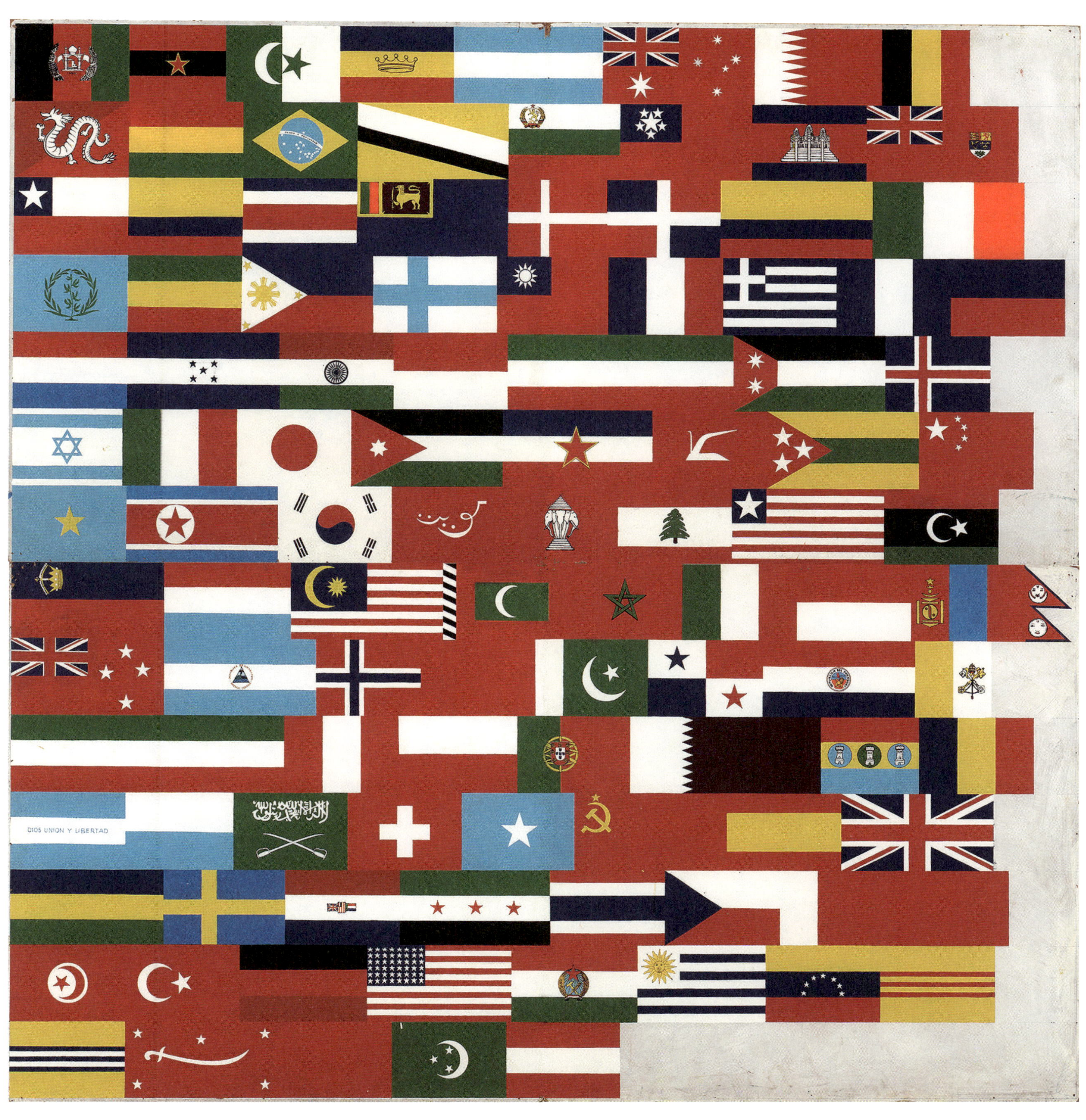

Untitled ("Flag Painting"), 1965
Enamel on masonite, 4 parts,
total 244 × 244 cm

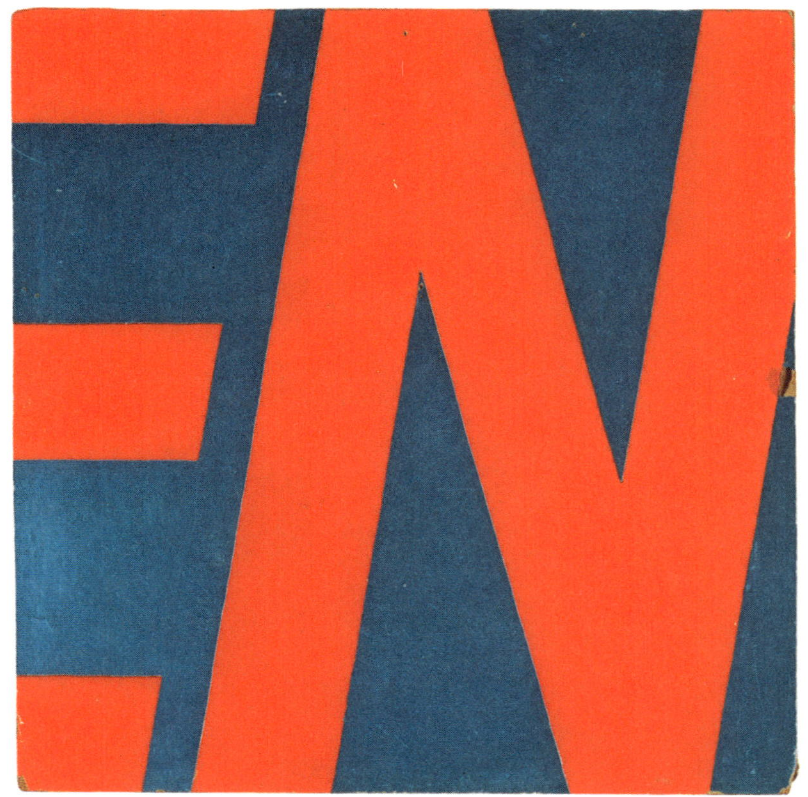

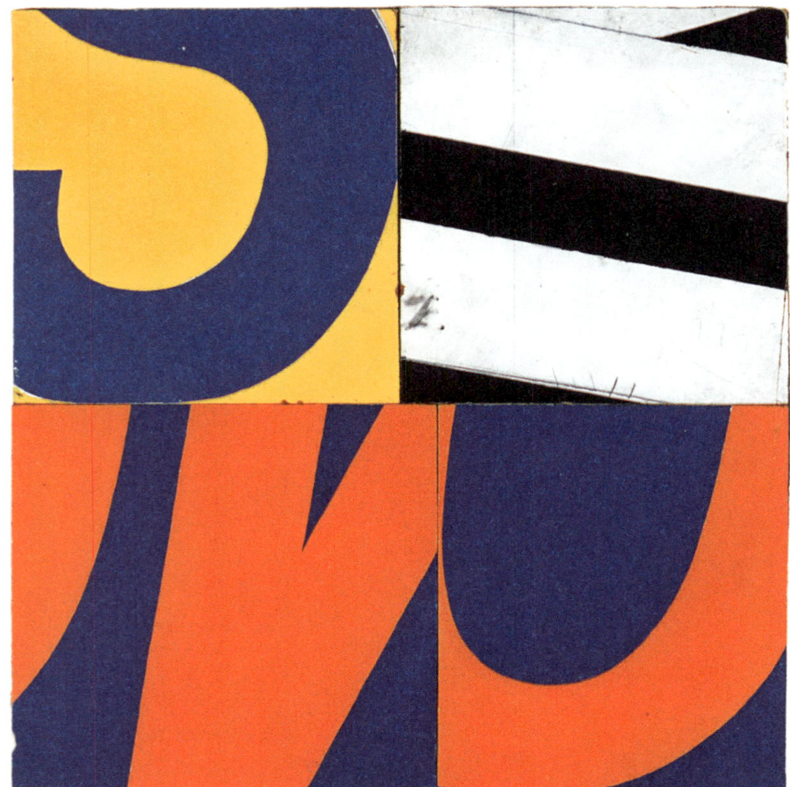

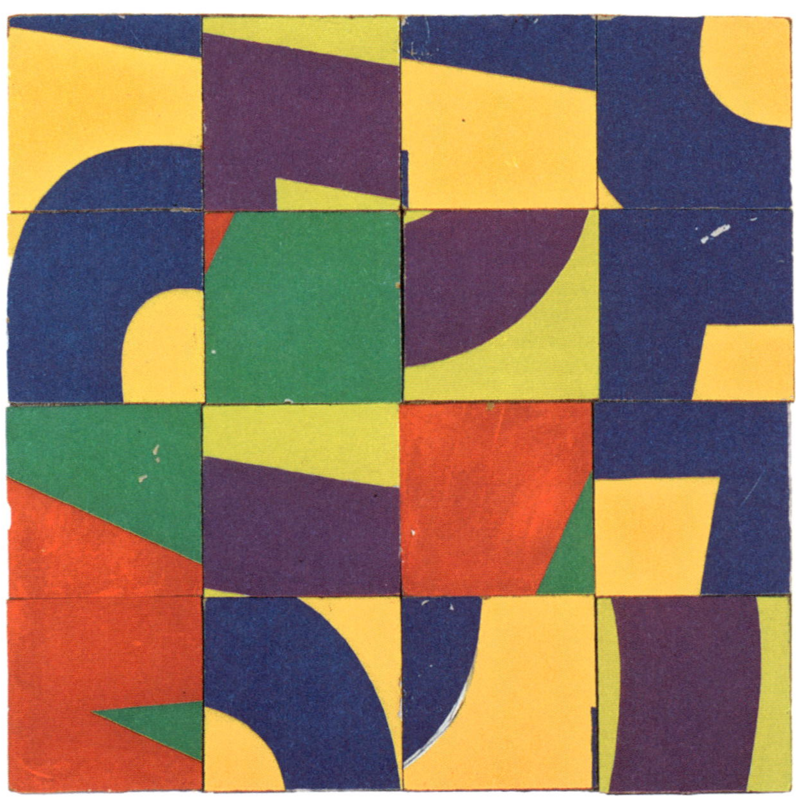

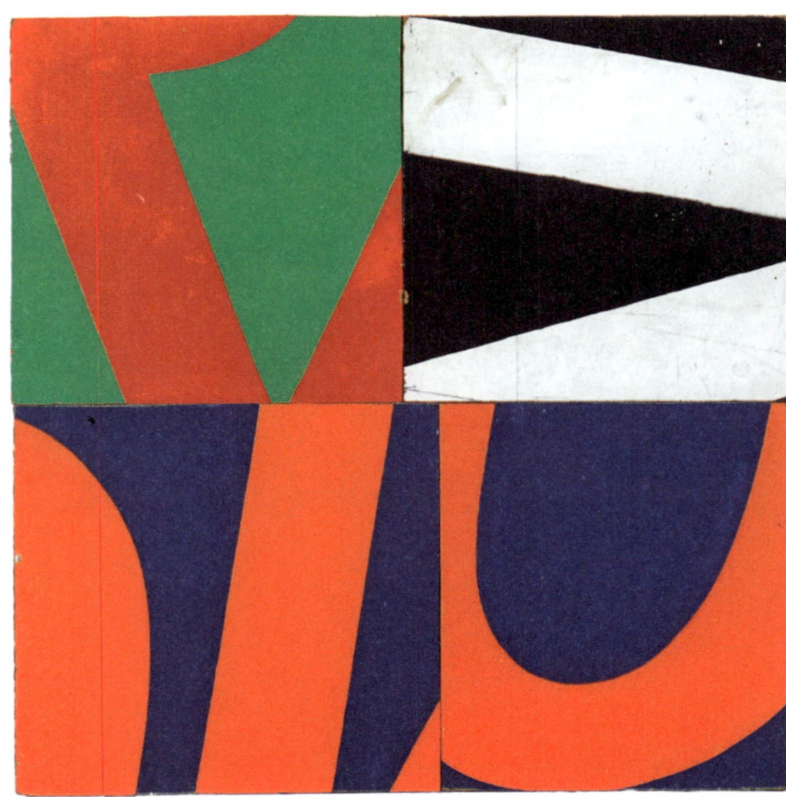

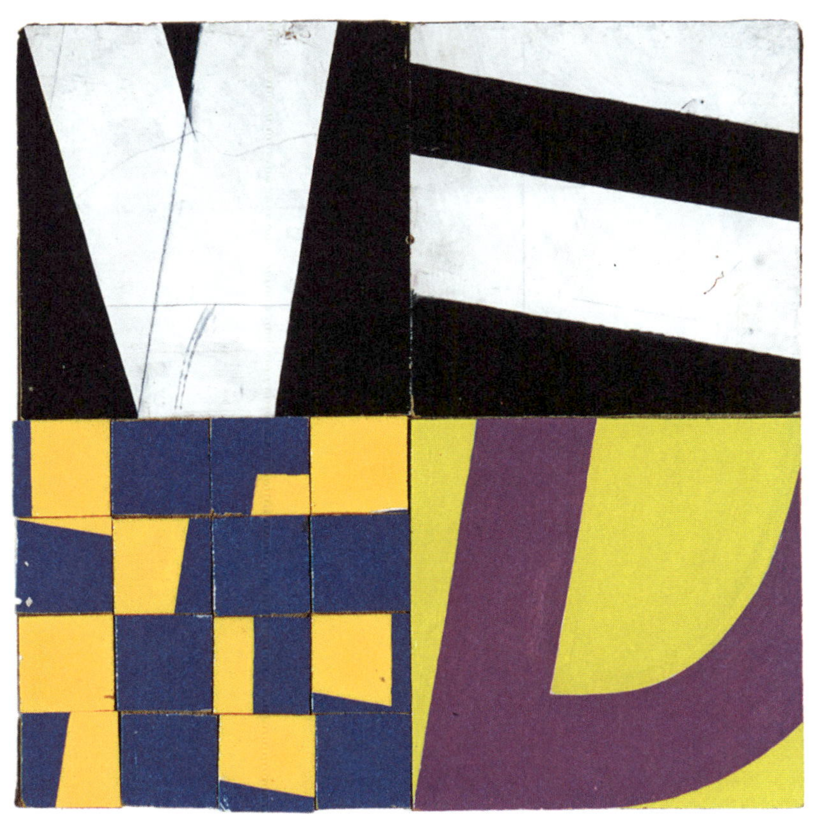

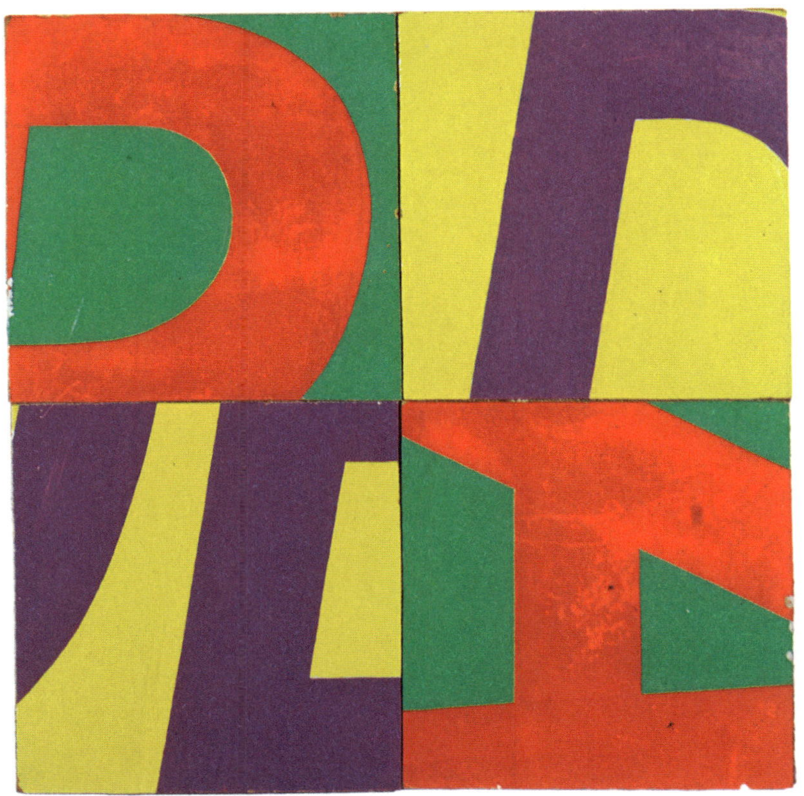

56

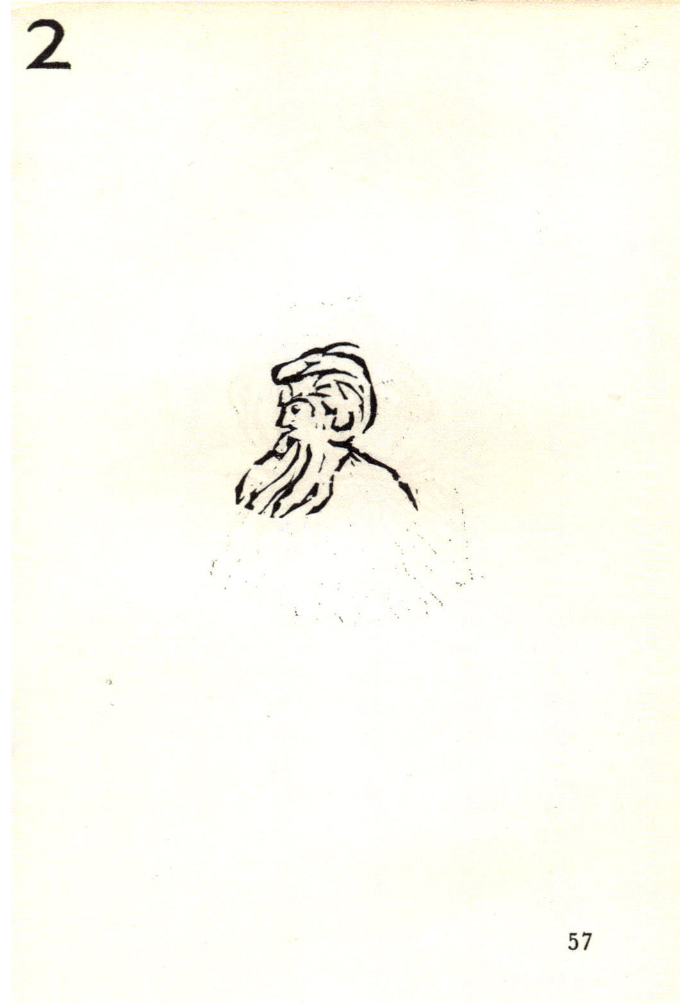

57

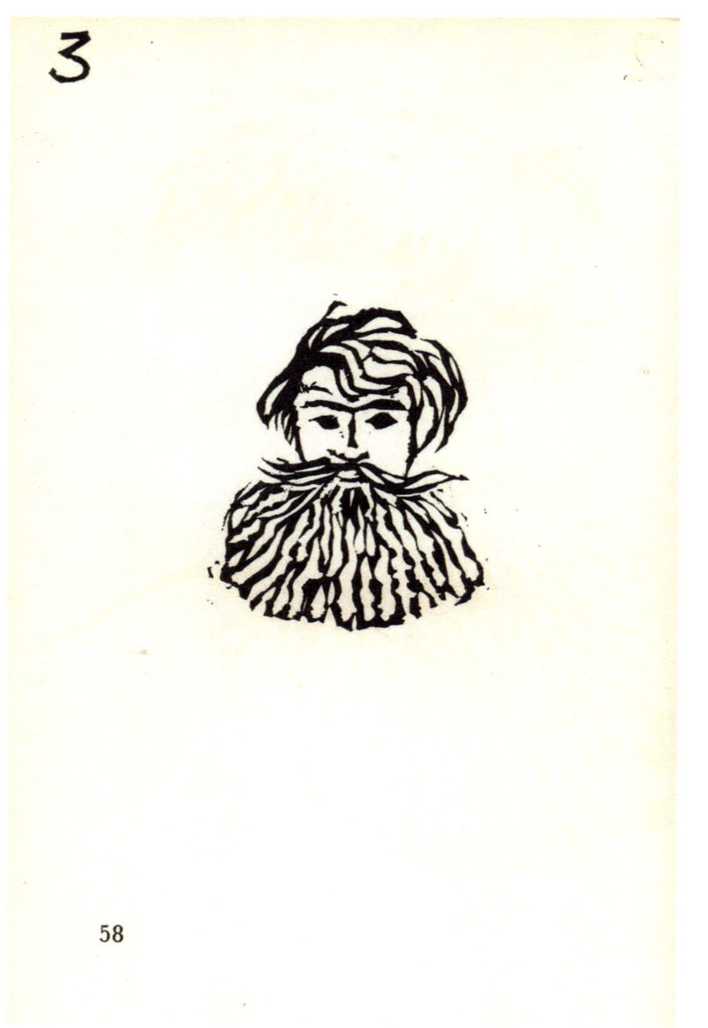

58

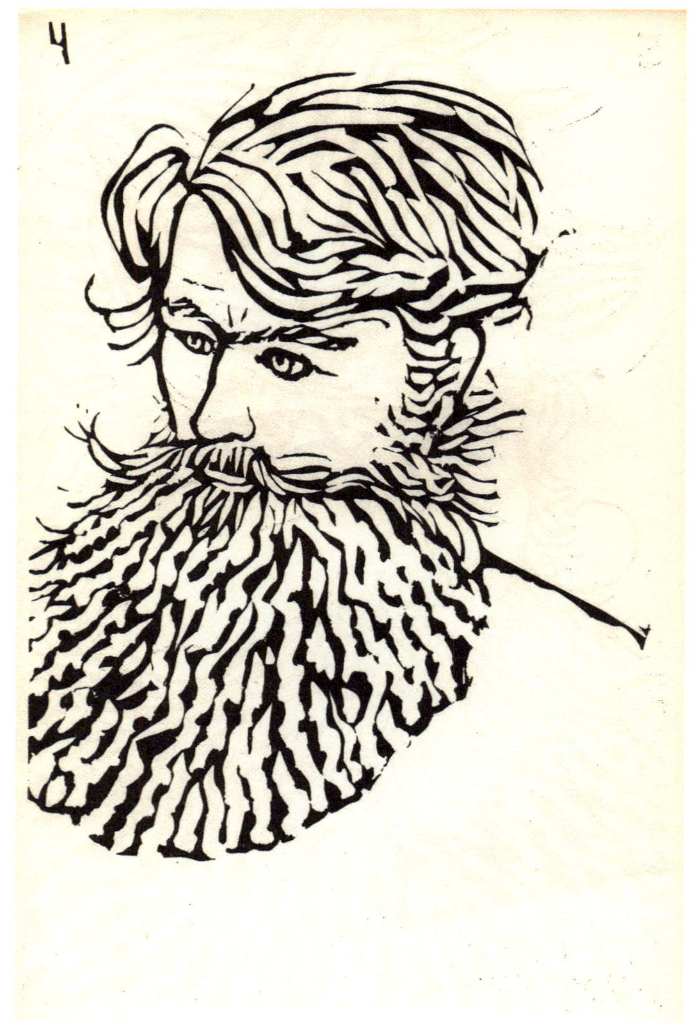

Self Portrait (1-16), 1965
Linocut, 16 parts,
each 24 × 16 cm

18

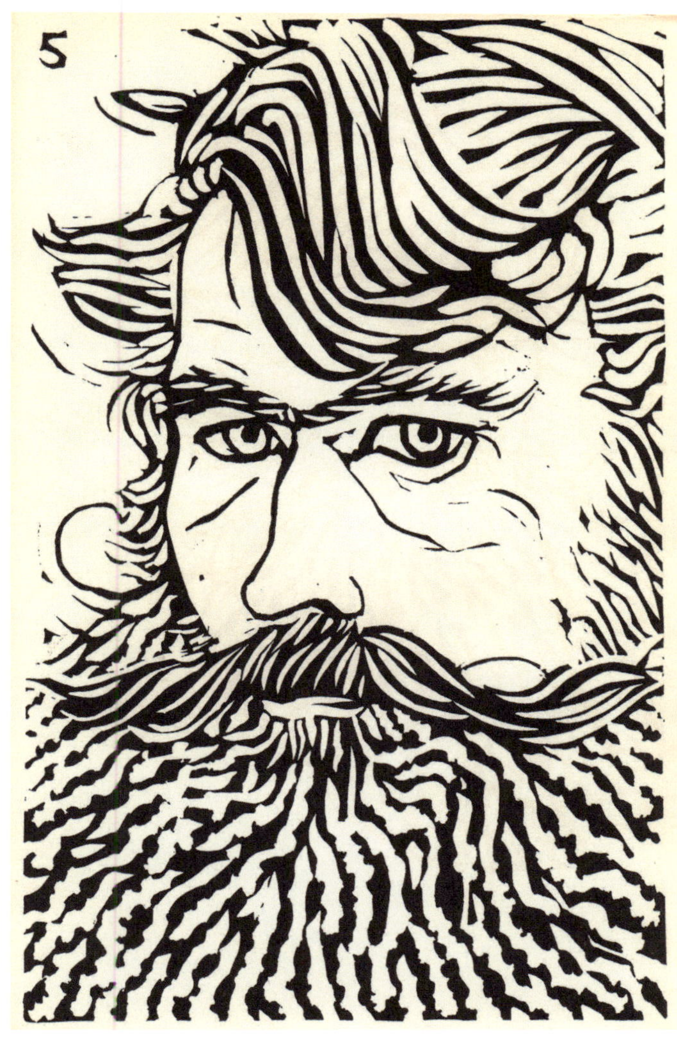

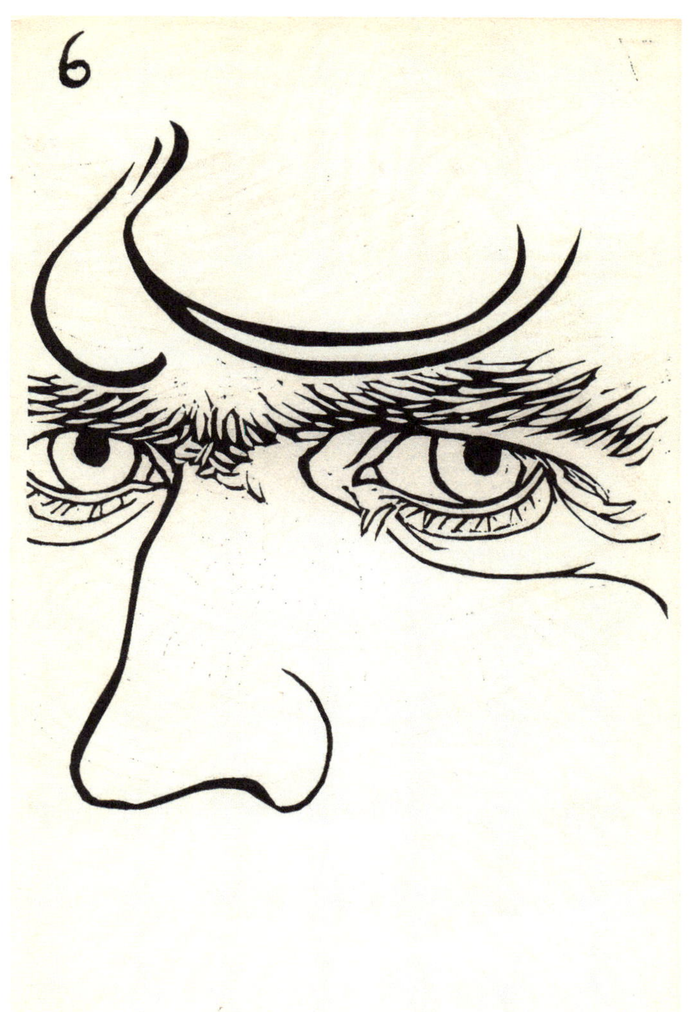

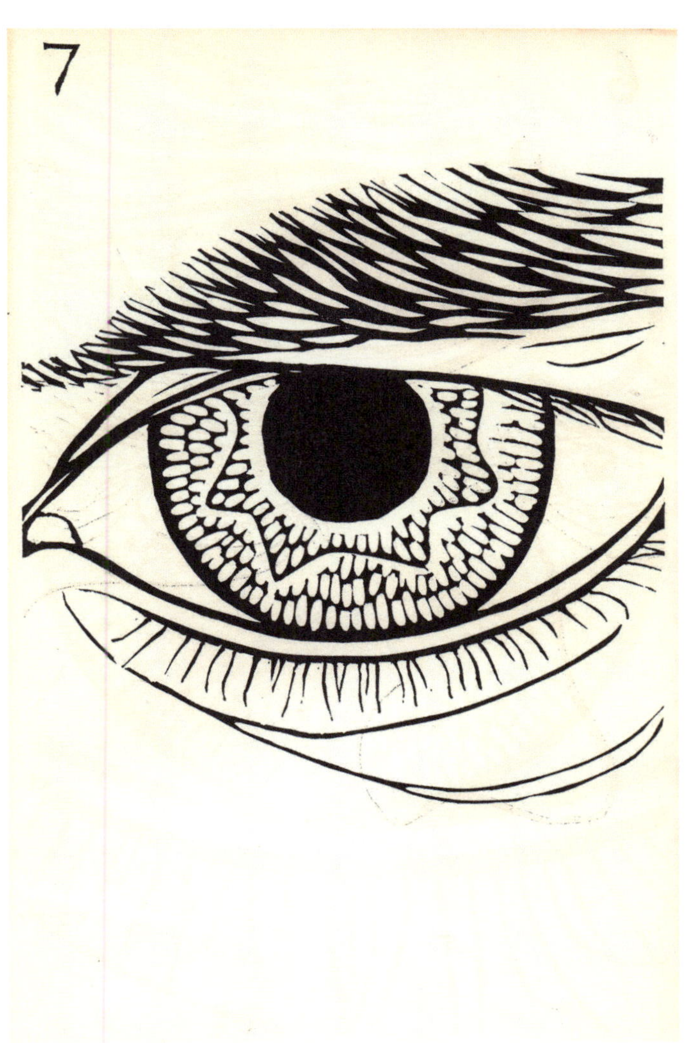

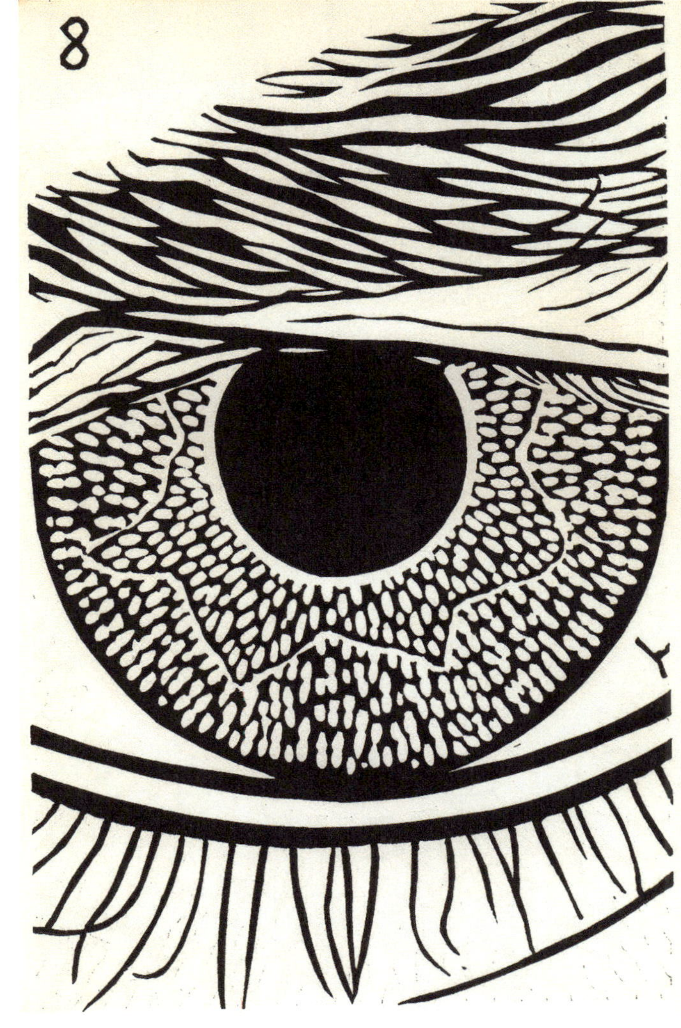

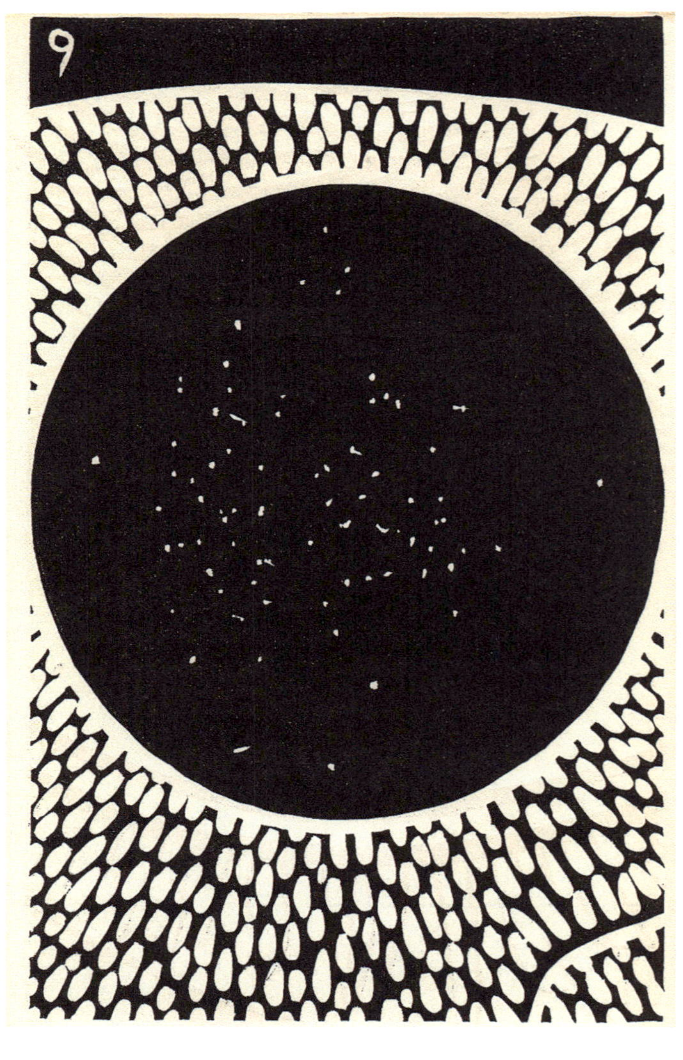

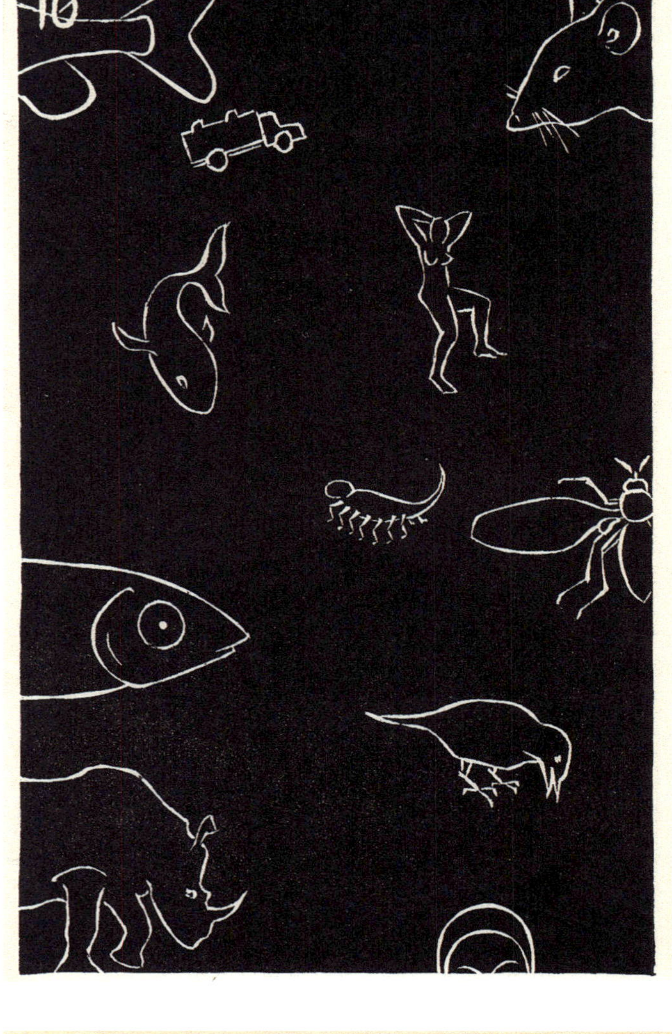

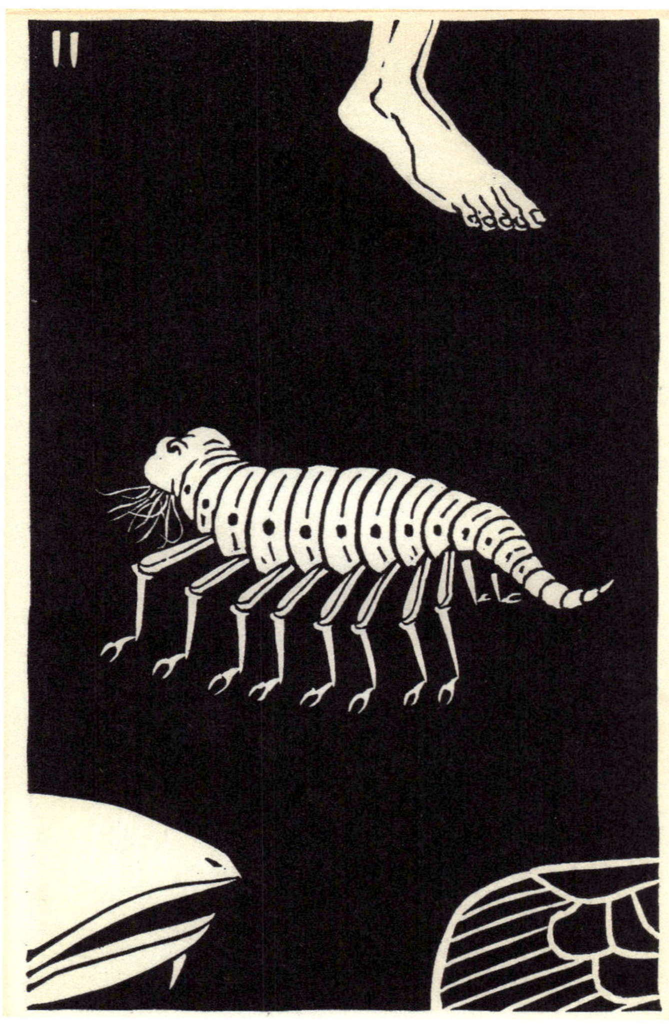

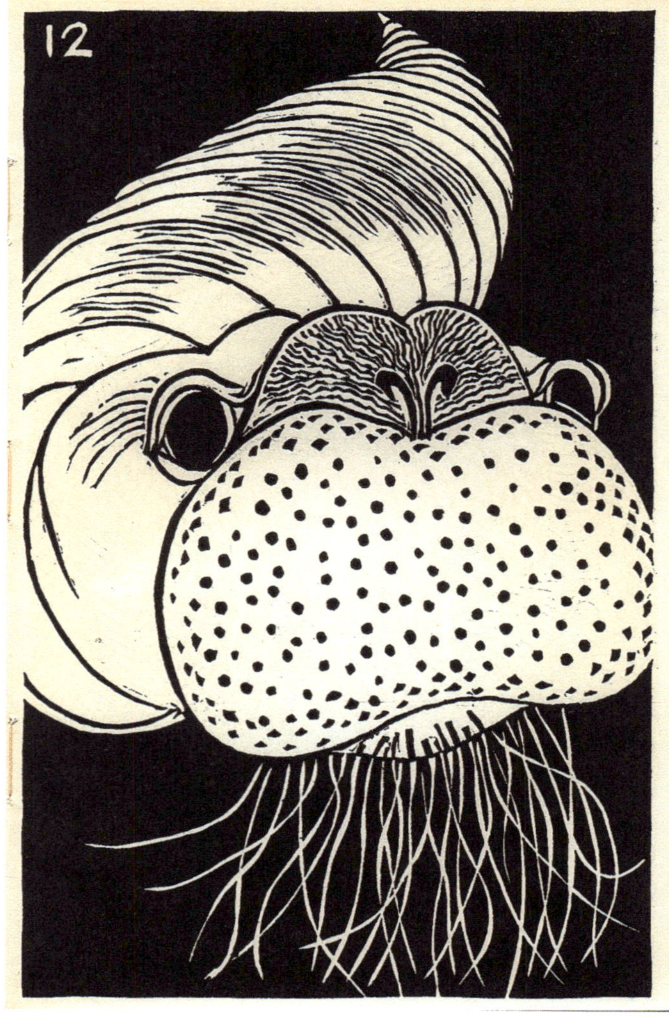

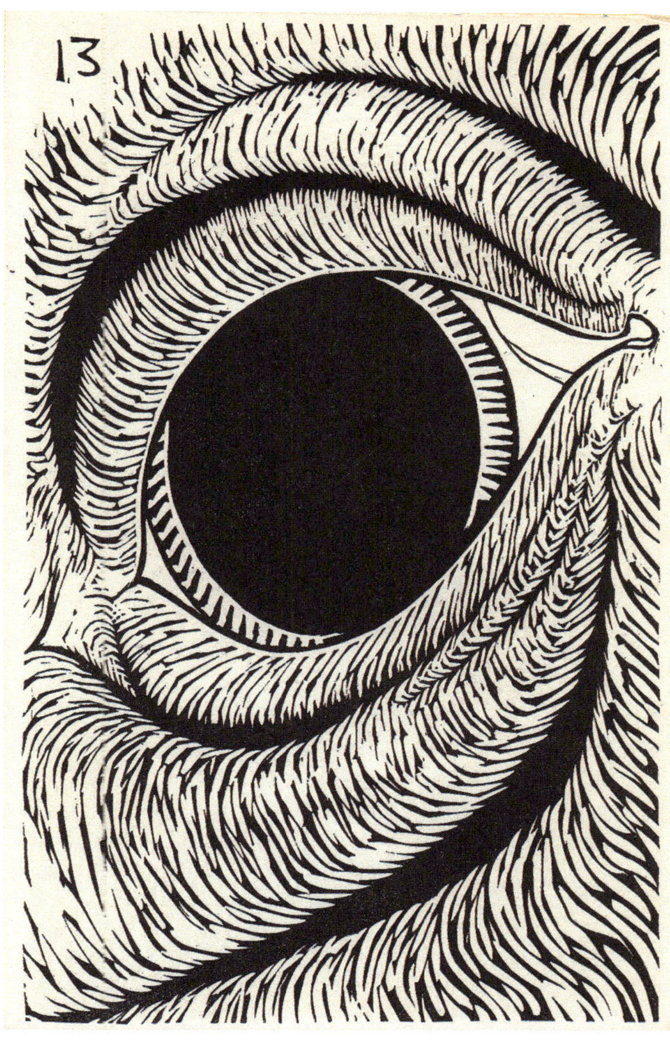

13

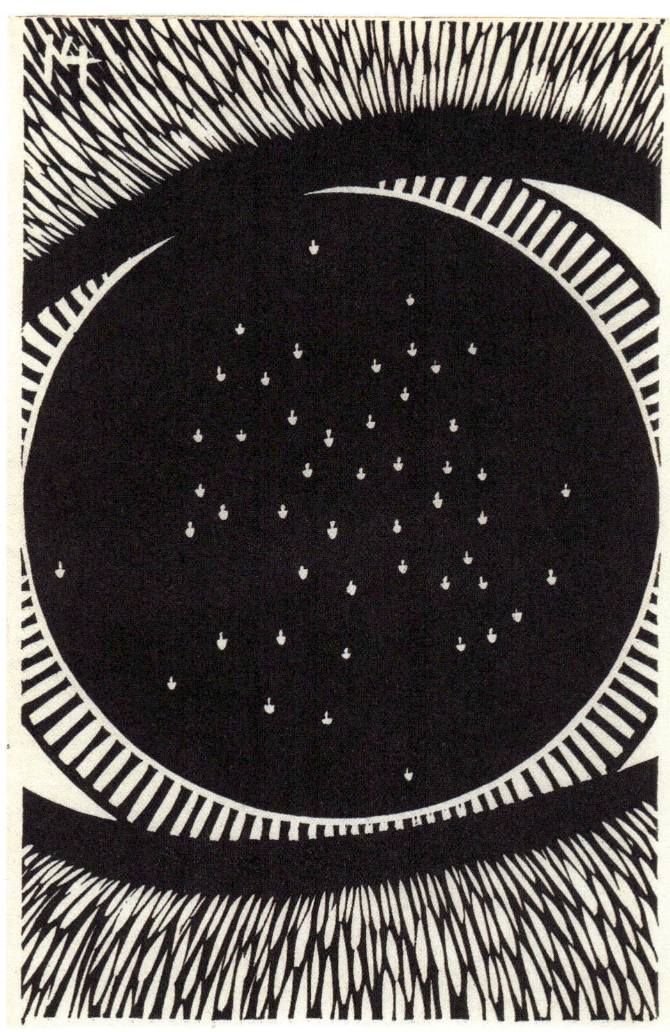

14

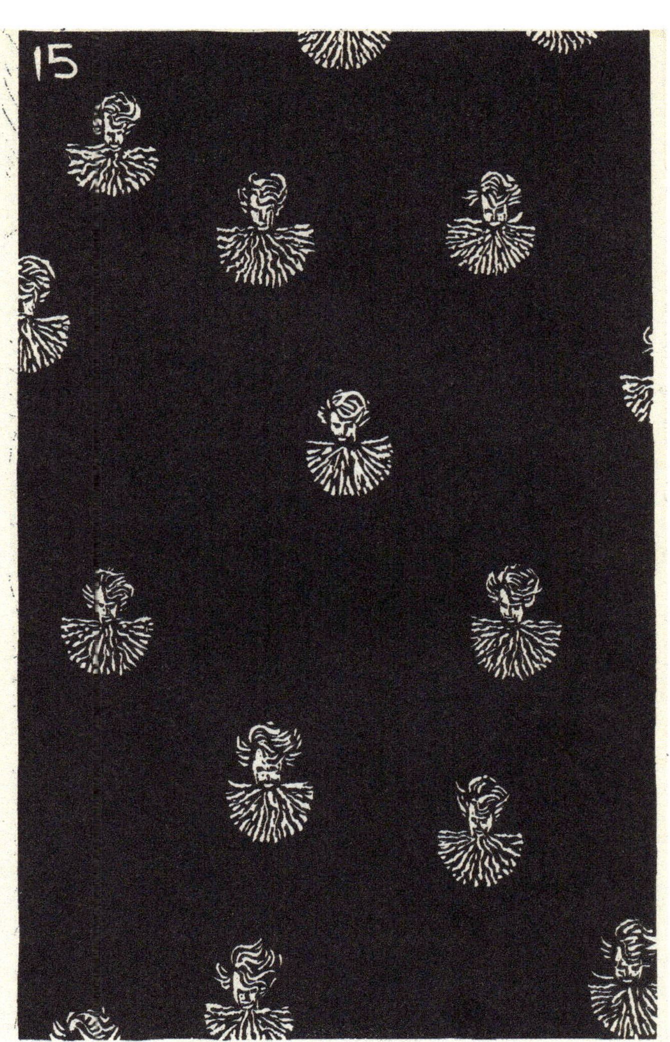

15

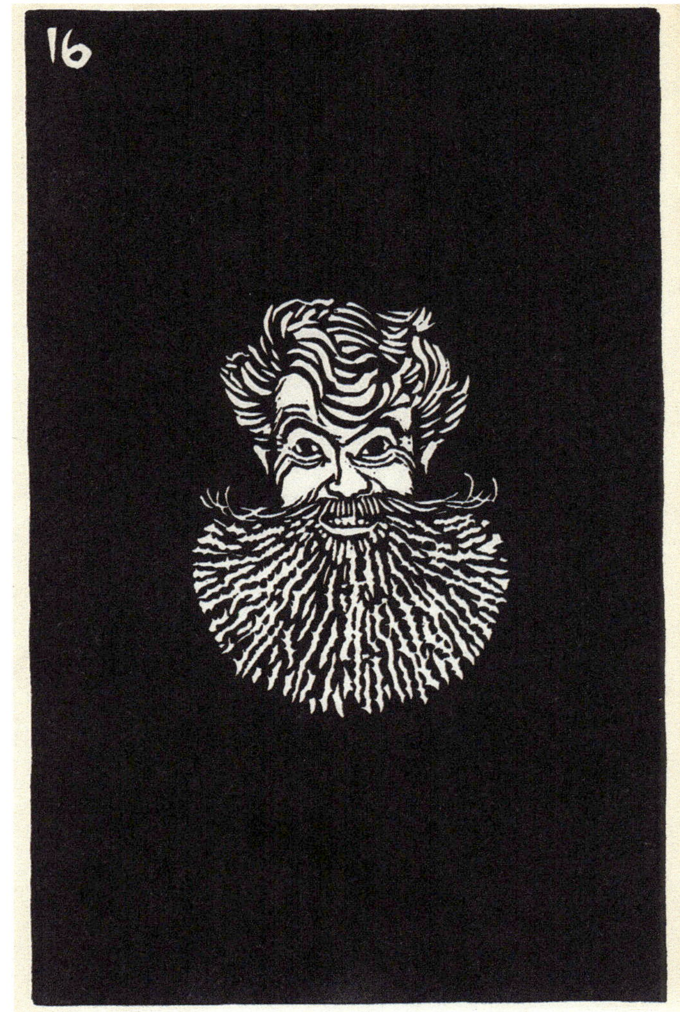

16

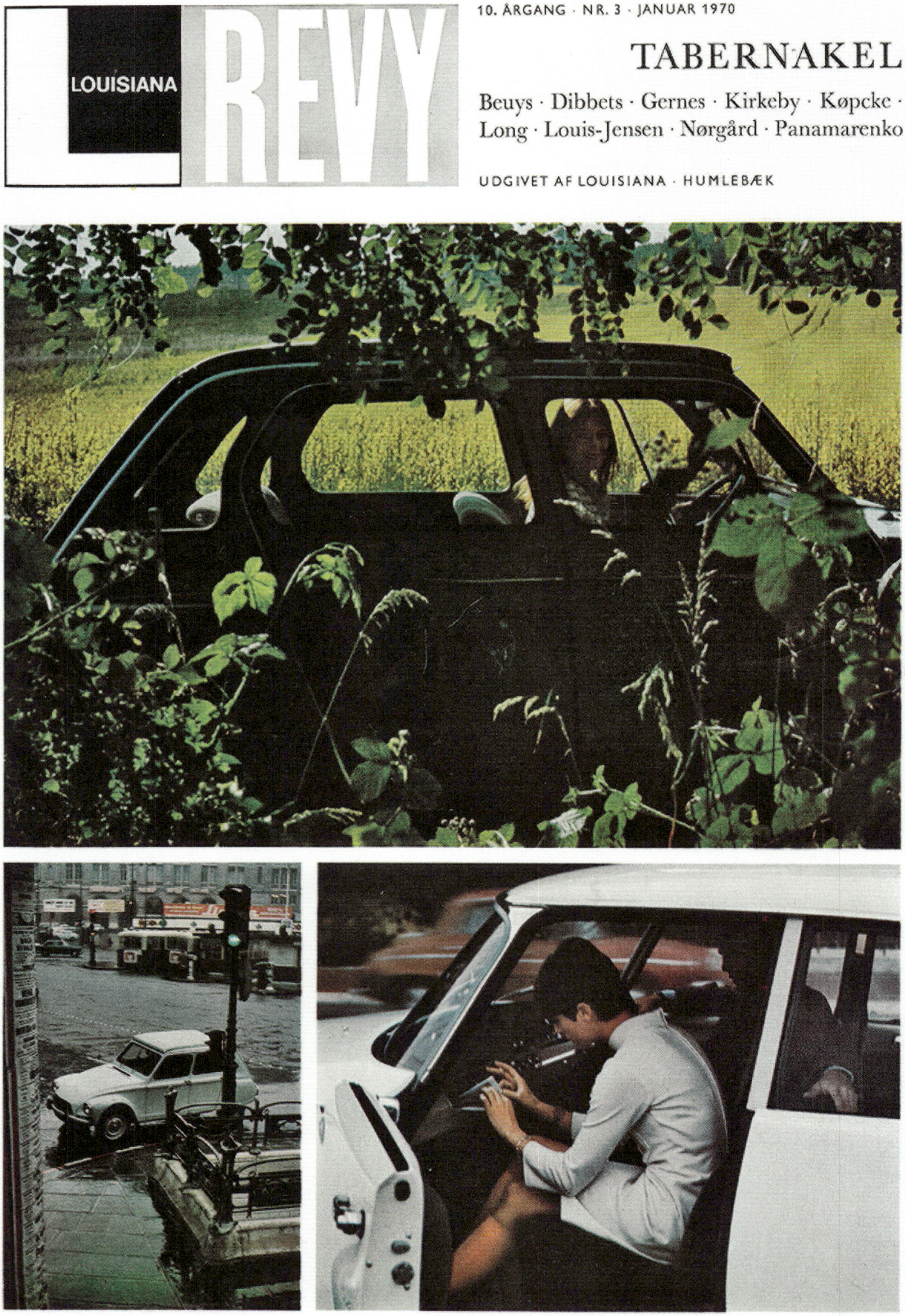

10. ÅRGANG · NR. 3 · JANUAR 1970

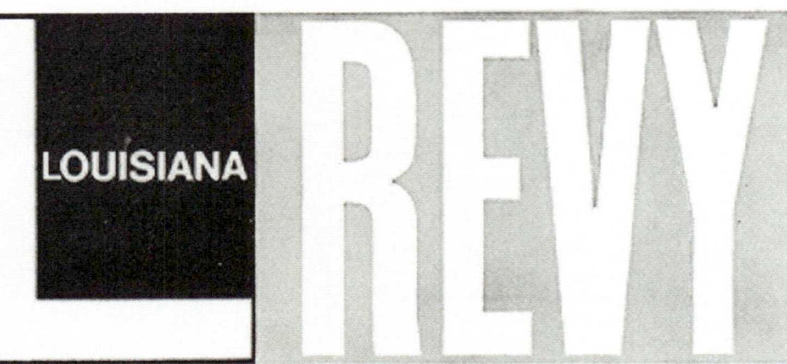

TABERNAKEL

Beuys · Dibbets · Gernes · Kirkeby · Køpcke ·
Long · Louis-Jensen · Nørgård · Panamarenko

UDGIVET AF LOUISIANA · HUMLEBÆK

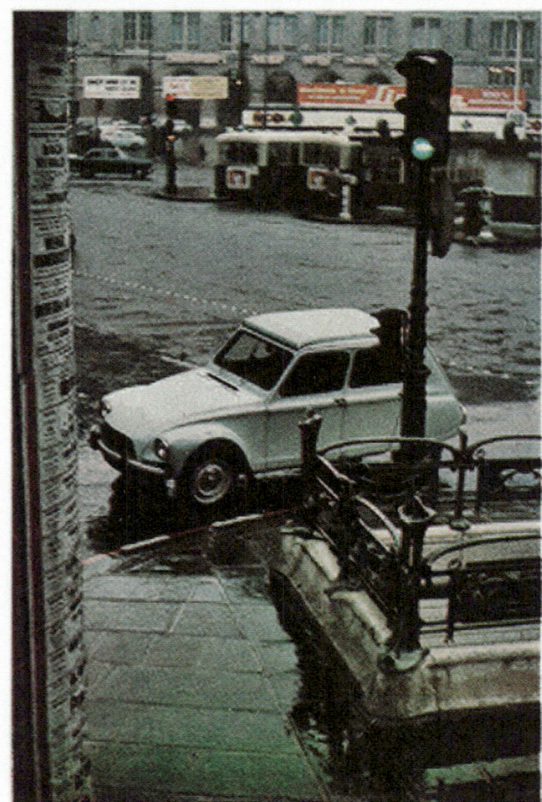

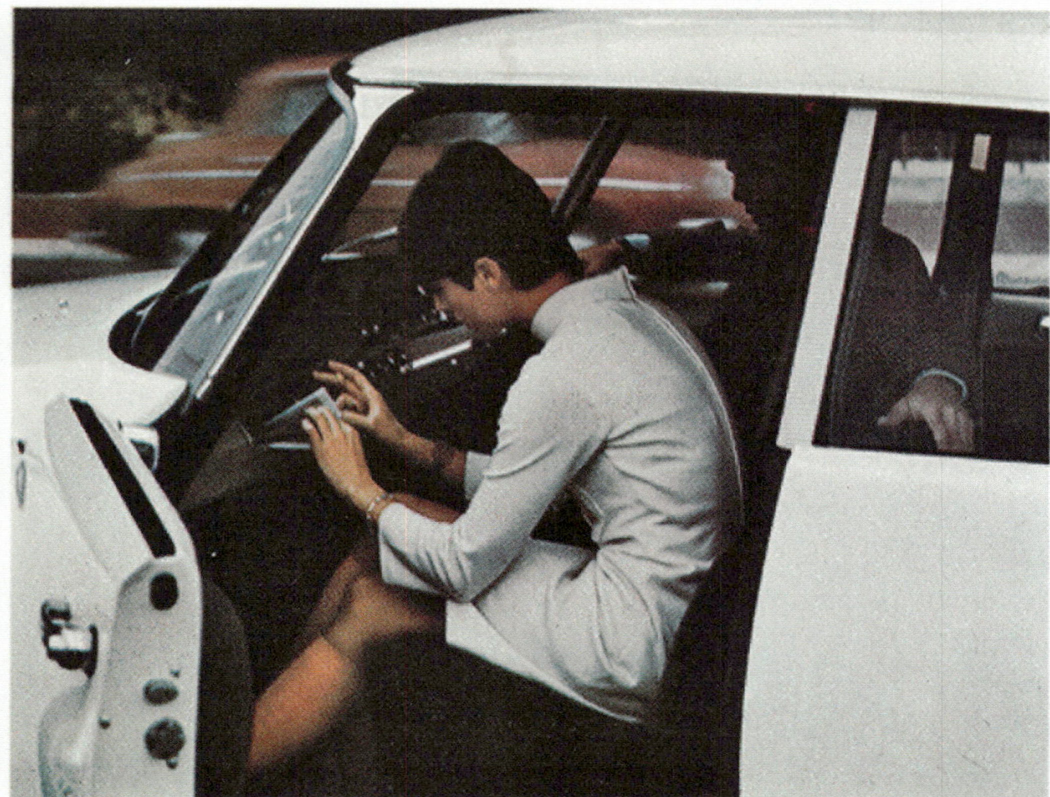

fig. 1

Knud W. Jensen's Louisiana Shock
Tabernakel as the Exhibition That Led Gernes and the Museum to a Crossroads

By Anders Kold

Even today, factory-fresh Citröen cars exhibited in Louisiana's park, complete with professional salespeople, would probably cause some head-scratching among the museum's visitors and clash with the institution's self-image. Yet that is what Poul Gernes wanted to show in 1970, when he was asked to contribute to the museum's big, international *Tabernakel* exhibition. Inside the museum, he wanted machines for coffee, soda and soft-serve ice cream, B&O stereos for sale and a bowling alley. Add to that, an artist-run boat shop and a museum-organized evening school teaching classes in catamaran-building. Tangible aspects of the rapidly expanding Danish welfare state and good Danish design – in the artist's own words, "sponsor art" – but also, of course, an obvious provocation of the museum and its ever lovely location. Gernes had been asked to exhibit with three of his close Danish colleagues – Peter Louis-Jensen, Bjørn Nørgaard and Per Kirkeby – alongside a number of international artists, with the German artist Joseph Beuys as the main attraction. What all four Danish contributors had in common was that they defied the modernist artwork categories, presenting pieces that the museum's founder, Knud W. Jensen, did not consider to be actual works of art.

The first sign that something radically different was going on was the cover of the *Louisiana Revy*, January 1970, with lifestyle ads for Citröen heralding a new mixture of life and art. That the museum saw trouble ahead is evident in the foreword's prediction that the exhibition "will give rise to vigorous discussion and perhaps trigger attacks on Louisiana."[1] Discussion and attacks famously followed Nørgaard's horse slaughter, which kicked up a veritable media frenzy. What the museum did not expect, however, was that the artists themselves would end up attacking the museum and walking out, only a few weeks after the opening, shutting down their contributions to the exhibition. The scandal-embroiled *Tabernakel* exhibition throws a dramatic light on Gernes' and the museum's widely different positions. In the following – step by step and in rapid scene changes – I will try to track the artist's and the museum's paths up to the point where the exhibition became a crossroads for both. Gernes, whose practice in 1970 was simply too radical for the museum, was already going somewhere else with his art, to a place where there was no role for the museum in Humlebæk: he wanted to take his art out of the institution. Meanwhile, *Tabernakel* led Knud W. Jensen to the realization that he now had to take the weight of the museum on his own shoulders.

"BROTHER, I AM SEARCHING"
Trained as a lithographer, Gernes made his debut as a non-figurative painter in 1949 at the juried Charlottenborg Autumn Exhibition in Copenhagen. While most people today associate Gernes with painting, one should keep in mind that his many works with circles and stripes are painted in bicycle enamel on masonite – not exactly a classic technique. Gernes had issues with the modernist tradition and self-understanding, especially when it came to painting. Around the time of his debut and in the years that followed, Gernes never got in with any artists' groups, like the Concrete Linien II. Personal differences may be to blame, of course. We do not know. Gernes, basically, did not want to continue building on the avant-garde tradition,

and his outlook was not academic. To him, the modernist idea of purity in painting was not an expression snugly wrapped up in itself and tradition. His art, when it finally broke away, excelled in methods for bypassing the insider game of painting. As Gernes saw it, an artist's work had to be based on a different set of criteria.

In the 1950s, he must have found himself in a permanent state of crisis: an artist with a legendary capacity for work but essentially strapped for subject matter. At any rate, he was searching, which made his meeting with Troels Andersen, a slightly younger art historian, all the more defining. It was to Andersen that Gernes in 1961, at home in his self-built house in Herlev, declared that his art was "sick." Crucial to his healing, and to what would become a life-long bond between them, was the founding of Den Eksperimenterende Kunstskole (The Experimental Art School), known as Eks-skolen, where their visions of art's social responsibility could be unfolded.[2] There, Gernes met Kirkeby, Nørgaard and Louis-Jensen, the three artists with whom he would be exhibiting at Louisiana almost a decade later. The school was a studio cooperative and learning community with no connection to the academic tradition of the Royal Academy of Fine Arts and with Gernes in charge of the course "Material Experimentation." In the first years of Eks-skolen, instructors and students "accelerated" each other, to use Gernes' term, to a degree that they actually exceeded their individual abilities: collaborative paintings, happenings, materials exercises, exhibitions. Never alone, always together. Out of this, something groundbreaking originated that would later have an impact on the conflict at the *Tabernakel* exhibition.

FROM A BREEZE TO A STORM

In order to retrospectively understand the resistance to Knud W. Jensen's Louisiana and the shit storm that the exhibition unleashed on the museum, we need to go back further, long before *Tabernakel*, to a shock that would be crucial to the museum. It was administered in 1959, when Knud W. Jensen, Louisiana's founder, visited the big *Documenta* exhibition in Kassel and realized the steep challenges his one-year-old museum in Humlebæk was facing. While the museum's buildings, and its programming of concerts, poetry readings and debates, in many ways pointed to the future, the museum's collection at the time exclusively consisted of works of early Danish modernism. His encounter with international contemporary art at *Documenta* led to the stinging realization that the collection was hopelessly behind the times and that the national anchoring hardly jibed with the post-war spirit of modernization. Knud W. Jensen called it his "Documenta shock."[3] This ambition to make up for lost time and bring Louisiana up to speed as a centre of international contemporary art, not least in terms of its own self-image, consumed the museum during the 1960s. The story of *Tabernakel*, which I will here call Knud W. Jensen's *second* shock – his "Louisiana shock" – also includes the fact that it revealed new, far more fundamental fault lines between artists and the institution.

Regarding the affair of Nørgaard's horse slaughter, Knud W. Jensen, at a safe historical remove, wrote: "Such a storm of protests against the artist and Louisiana arose that the affair of the dove in its day was like a mild breeze in comparison."[4] Knud W. Jensen is referring to the institution's first encounter with a negative audience response.

In 1961, the exhibition *Movement in Art* opened in Louisiana's park, featuring the Swiss artist Jean Tinguely's self-destructing *Sketch of the End of the World,* a metres-high pile of scrap and moving components effecting its own wreckage amidst fireworks. The work was a magnificent image of war and destruction – or, in the white dove in a basket atop the sculpture – the possibility of rebirth and peace. The dove failed to be released in time, however, and Tinguely inadvertently caused its demise. Looking at the pictures of Knud W. Jensen beaming in front of the rope cordoning off the audience, we sense that it was moments like these – spectacular and existentially intense – that confirmed to him the necessity of presenting art of the moment. What is also striking is how the event in all respects appears to be cordoned off: artwork and viewers are carefully separated. In his memoirs, *Mit Louisiana-liv* (My Louisiana Life), Knud W. Jensen writes that the event should be considered "art, not reality."[5] Why? Because it took place at a museum.

Even so, in the decade between Tinguely's work, which the press in 1961 made into a story of animal abuse, and the second case of animal abuse, Nørgaard's horse slaughter in 1970, it became increasingly difficult to distinguish all that clearly between art and reality – and, in turn, frame art clearly. In the 1960s, when avant-garde art began to be manifested as what were called "situations," an important new departure was the attempt to erase the cordoning off of the artwork, its autonomy. This aesthetic premise also brings the roles of the museum and the artist into play: Where does the work stop, where does the framework of the institution take over, and which role is intended for the viewer: spectator or participant? The museum's visitors and management may well have asked themselves such questions as they proceeded down the North Wing at the *Tabernakel* exhibition and came to the four Danish artists' custom-made projects.[6]

SUNDRY EXPLORATIONS

Gernes experienced nothing short of a boom during the Eks-skolen years, generated not least by the collective he was now part of. From 1962, he was an uber-materialist pushing Danish printmaking beyond its familiar horizon, making etchings by methodically punching holes in the plate with a hammer and compelling a new pictoriality that also allows an equally valid print to be pulled from the opposite side of the same plate. That is transgressive materiality for you. The entire device clearly illustrates the nature of the new image: economical in form, effectively communicative, devoid of mysticism or hierarchies of high and low materials. Out of this, in part, a new and socially oriented view of art emerges. In direct extension of the school's collaborative work processes, Gernes' art also expresses an acceptance of accident and anonymity as important aspects of a new aesthetics. In 1967, he made a "self-portrait" in the form of a plaster cast of his rear end, fully demonstrating, you might say, that also the artist myth needs to be dethroned in favour of real life. "Mooning" the world is another way to profane the idea of modernist white as being purer or more moral at its core.

As far back as we can trace Gernes' statements about his art, he acknowledged that he was searching[7] but also productively obsessed with the idea of not producing art about, or for, himself or for a narrow cultural bourgeoisie. It is worth bearing in mind on one's way to Humlebæk that

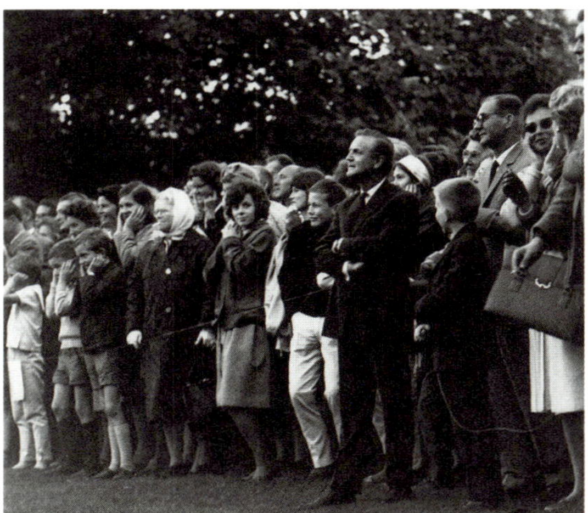

fig. 2

fig. 3

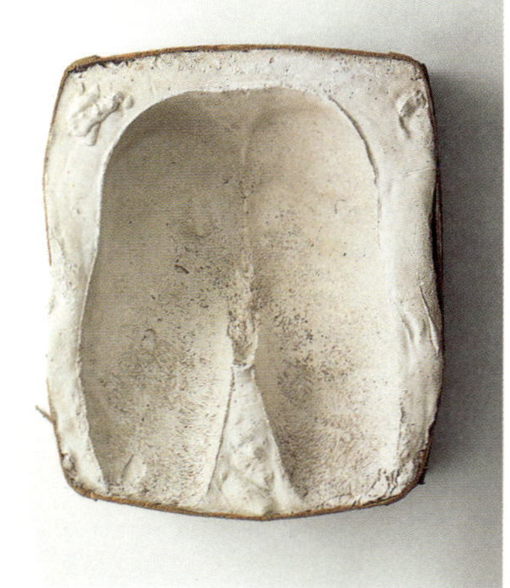

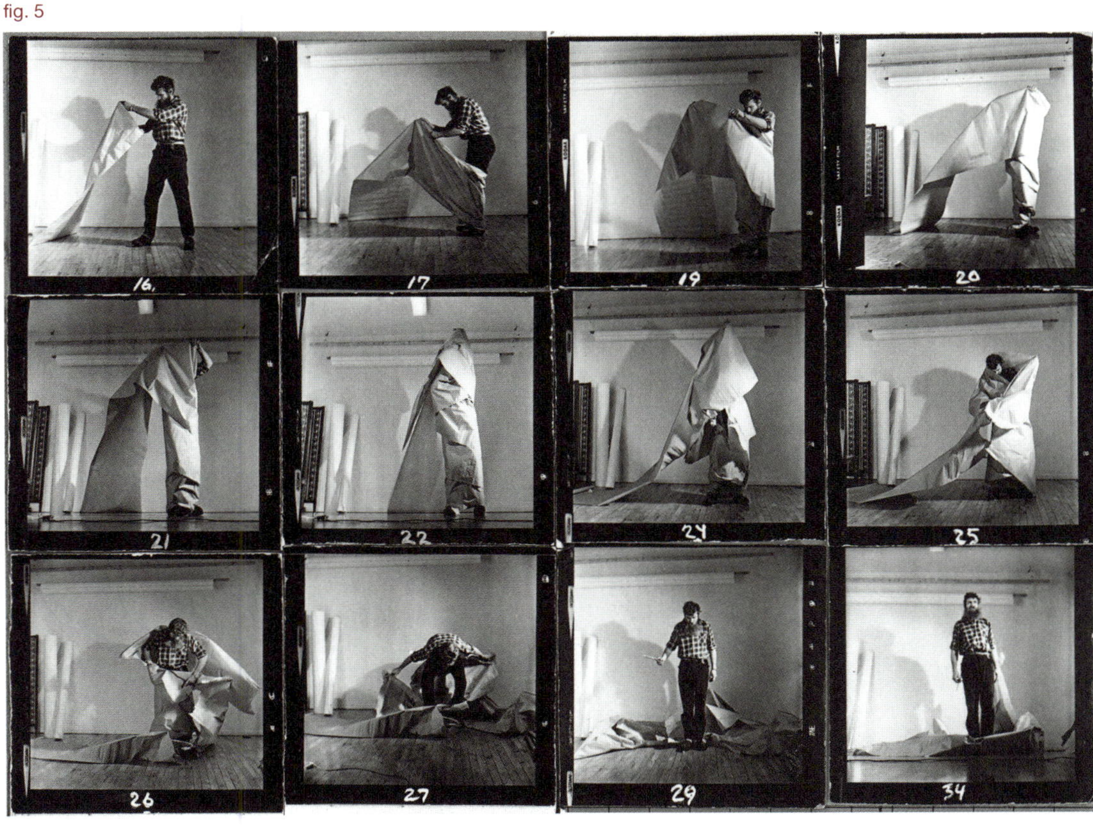

fig. 4

fig. 5

Gernes throughout his life, not without some agony, tried to free art from the private realm – exactly like the hairs we today see stuck in the cast of his rear end: ouch! This inscrutable and deeply funny work productively adds to the portrait of the 1960s by giving us a sense of how, in the Eks-skolen circle, the personal equalled "the impure." Material surfaces, and the idea that everything has a front and a back, are not all that was systematically upended and transformed within the community of the school. The concept of the artist's own figure was also redefined. By being present in various ways as part of their works at *Tabernakel*, the Eks-skolen artists were, by extension, manifesting a desire to reach out and not be cordoned in by the usual authority of the artwork.

SELF-EXPLORATIONS

In 1965-67, just when Gernes' large Systemic series of masonite paintings with stripes, checks and circles were getting off the ground and his pieces were starting to take up substantial space, he effectively turned himself inside out in a small group of works. These works should not be viewed in opposition to the stream of "masonites." On the contrary, they embody ideas that supported and accelerated the radicalness of his contributions to Louisiana a few years later. In three pieces made over a couple of years, Gernes went through a remarkable process of disappearing and reappearing reminiscent of self-explorations or mirror exercises of sorts for artists – as in Freud's "fort-da" exercise,[8] where the child learns to understand itself as an individual separate from both the mirror image and the mother (read: modernism).

Poul's Paper Performance from 1967 is the best known of these pieces. Working from a scripted dramaturgy, Gernes wraps himself in paper from a big roll of brown wrapping paper until he is completely covered, then cuts himself loose with a knife and faces the audience once again.[9] The artist disappears, is gone and returns. This consciousness exercise is also seen in an almost psychedelic series of 16 linocuts from 1966, *Self Portrait (1-16)*,[10] showing the artist gradually growing in size, as we zoom into his eye and emerge out into a greater sphere, where his laughing face with his signature beard finally reappears (see p. 18-21). The last example of Gernes' self-exploration consists of two linocuts, also from 1966. In one, the word "JEG" (I) is repeated all over the sheet, while the other correspondingly repeats the word "MIG" (ME).[11] Two sides of the same coin, but behind the ironic style probably also another note to himself, and the world, that art that narcissistically mirrors only the artist is a cliché. That claim could certainly not be levelled at his "sponsor art" at *Tabernakel*.

It is generally agreed that the time around 1967 marks the end of the intense evolution undergone by Eks-skolen. It was also around this time that painting, as Gernes saw it, stopped generating new results and recognitions.[12] Systems and materials, structures and surfaces, had been explored inside and out. Perhaps the above self-scrutiny provided a sense that a new chapter was beginning.

WANT TO JOIN IN?

1967 was also the year that Gernes started the preliminary stages of his vast decoration of Herlev Hospital. As chairman, he contributed to the anniversary exhibition of Foreningen Ung

Dansk Kunst (The Association of Young Danish Art) at Louisiana. From this point on, his practice changes: works on the wall are, apart from Herlev Hospital, largely replaced by "monuments"[13] – open, that is, anti-authoritarian, models of renewed community. While they may be characterized by familiar historical forms – tower, ship, flag, maypole, bath, pyramid – they are all without exception drained of hierarchal functionality: no kings or captains, no nations, bath attendants or pharaohs! Clearly, Gernes' confrontational attitude to the institution of Louisiana was shaped by a greater social outlook. The change in his art lies less in ramping down the Systemic than in connecting it to societal architecture.

Festival 200 was an international artists' meet at Copenhagen's Charlottenborg in June 1969 and a work-in-progress exhibition that did not focus on a traditional presentation of artworks. Eks-skolen was involved, and Gernes' contributions included a unisex bath and sauna free to use by participating artists and visitors to the show. The spectator was confronted with a sculptural environment, in which the function of the bath was also the content of the work.[14] Of particular interest in relation to Gernes' "sponsor art" at Louisiana six months later was the fact that the plumbing, towels and sauna were provided by the companies Moderne Bad, Thor Vask and Tylö. Apart from the woodwork and a couple of hand-written signs, the work was devoid of any artistic signature. Gernes had left the traditional sphere of the artwork and situated himself in a distinctly social space. Standing there in the shower, was he an artist or a visitor? The action had become the work and, typically of Gernes, the action was an everyday one.

FREEDOM FROM OBJECTS

The run-up to *Tabernakel* cannot be satisfactorily uncovered, though enough information has come to light to illuminate the motivation for the project and why it spun out of control for the museum. In March 1969, Louisiana curator Knud Mühlhausen was in Bern to see *When Attitudes Become Form*. The exhibition was curated by Harald Szeemann, director of Kunsthalle Bern, who the year before had led *Documenta 4* in Kassel. The exhibition was made up entirely of new productions and, as a whole, was critical of Pop and Op art's fascination with images. Front and centre were the artist's actions, not the form and representation of the work: the work is a gesture emancipated from the object. In Szeemann's words, this exploded the triangle of studio, gallery and museum. Returning home, Mühlhausen wrote a memo[15] making clear that the museum was facing a new art form, a mirror of the times, that they could not afford to ignore. Mühlhausen notes that it was hard for him to judge the quality of the art, but doing so was "probably also a criterion that belongs to another age."[16]

At the centre of Louisiana's interest was Joseph Beuys, of whom the museum had declined to do an exhibition a few years before.[17] In the meantime, the Stedelijk Museum Amsterdam had exhibited the German artist, "and then Knud summoned up courage," as Nørgaard puts it.[18] The museum no doubt thought of it as an opportunity to edge in and reactivate the image of Louisiana as the pioneering home of exhibitions like *Movement in Art* and *American Pop Art.* A new curator, Flemming Koefoed, took over, and the archive shows that the museum was in informal contact with the artist through the collector John Hunov.

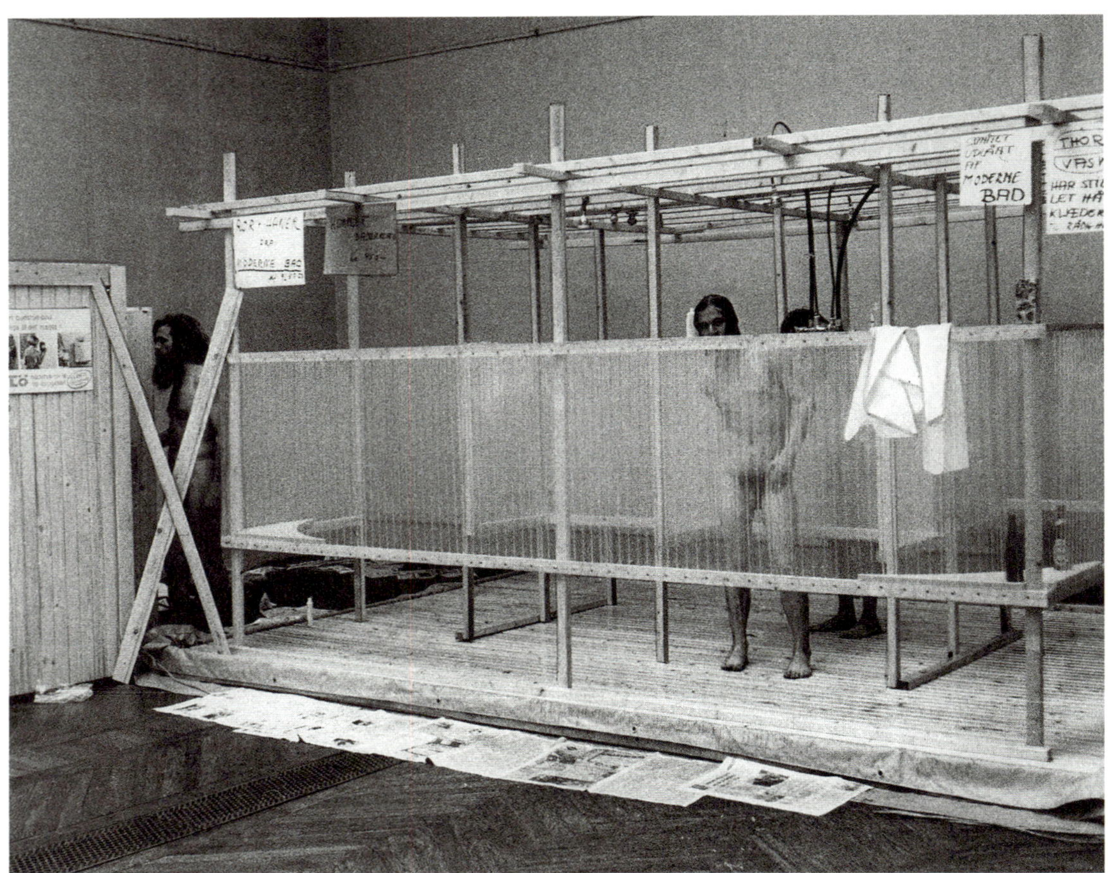

fig. 6

fig. 7

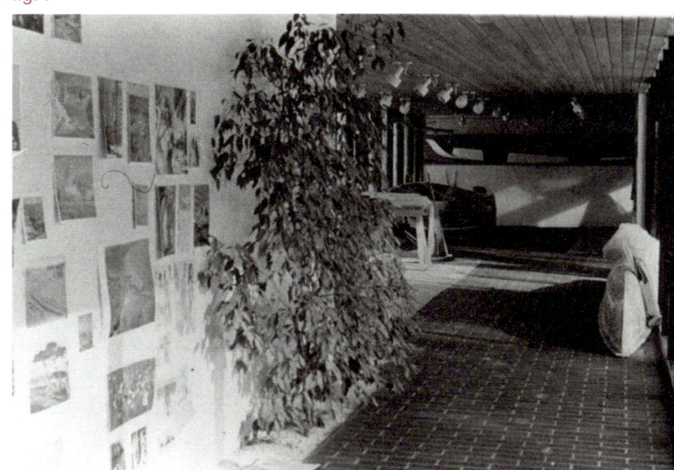

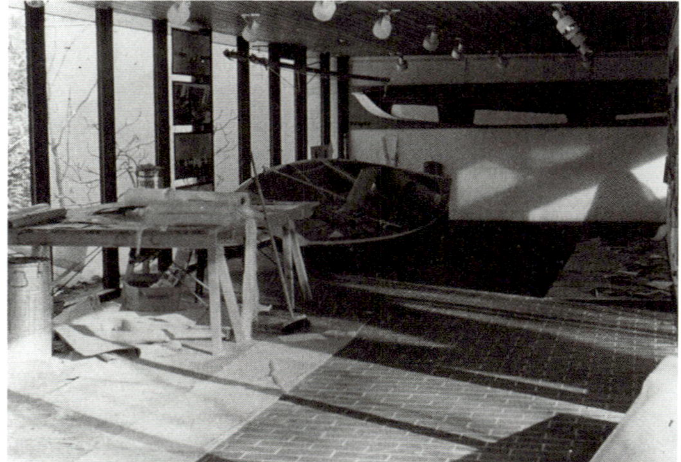

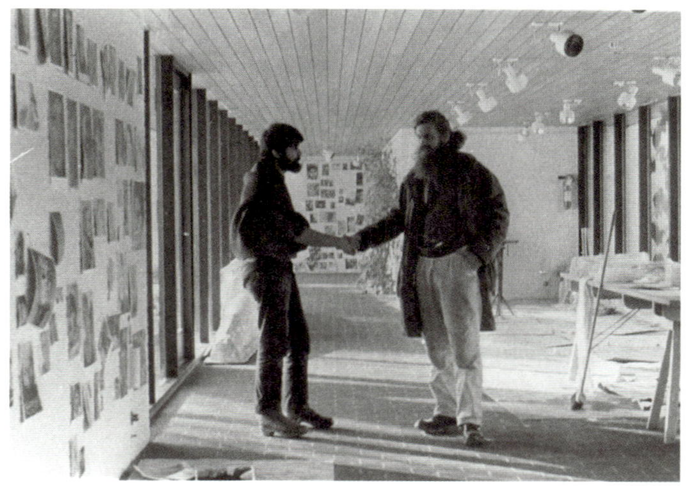

fig. 8

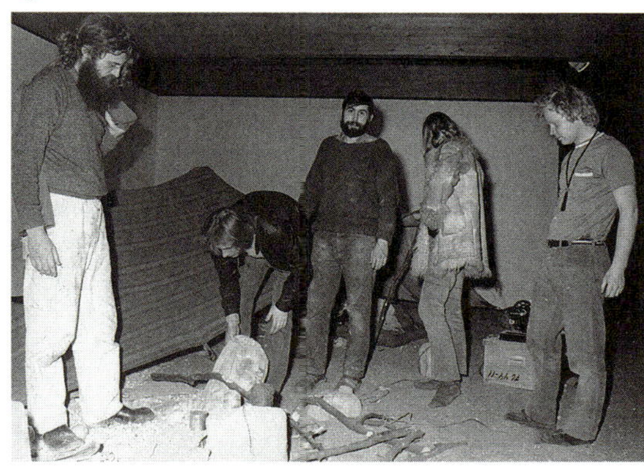

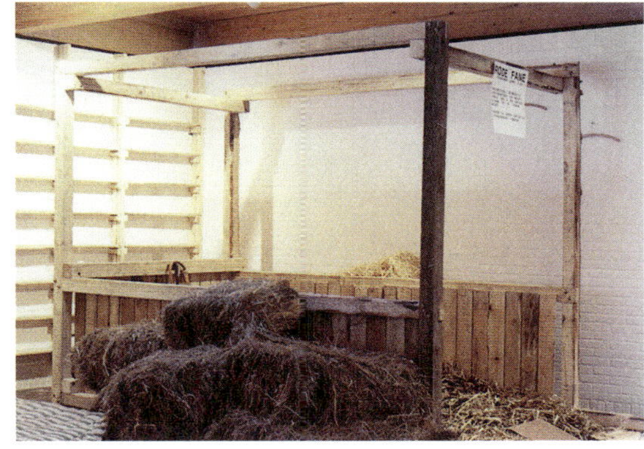

fig. 9

Beuys would be interested in exhibiting "together with some 'young' Danish artists he knows well, has worked in some cases with and finds significant, also in an international context(!) – namely, Per Kirkeby, Bjørn Nørgaard, Paul Gernes, Peter Louis Jensen, Arthur Köpcke(?) and the composer Henning Christiansen (for possible performances)."[19] The museum was perfectly aware that this would be one of the "narrow" exhibitions, but for Knud W. Jensen the primary objective was to get the presentation of Beuys in place. In October, a loan was arranged of approximately 200 works from the major German collector Karl Ströher. Prior to this, it had been decided to supplement Beuys with works by the British artist Richard Long, the Dutch artist Jan Dibbets, the Belgian artist Panamarenko and the Danish-German artist Arthur Köpcke, along with the four Danish artists, Nørgaard, Gernes, Kirkeby and Louis-Jensen. The invitation to the Danish artists reads, "It will be a matter of realizing possible projects, where Louisiana in advance will pay an agreed amount to cover the costs of materials, etc. John Hunov has helped us with the preliminary work and has agreed to continue to serve on the working committee for this exhibition."[20]

In 1970, Louisiana and most other museums were not yet familiar with categories of work that, as our man in Bern reported, were beyond aesthetic judgment. In *Tabernakel*, the museum was confronted with the latest art, as well as works and collaborative forms with which they had no particular experience. Moreover, if we imagine Knud W. Jensen discussing the matter with his closest fellow board members and among friends, it is unlikely that any of these mainly literary people would have been able to convey to him what forms such "possible projects" might take. The museum no doubt assumed that the Danish artists would be suitably impressed at the invitation to show alongside Beuys and that they would certainly also want to be associated with the popular museum in Humlebæk. As far as the latter was concerned, history proved the museum decidedly wrong.

OUT INTO THE MUSEUM
In his presentation at *Tabernakel*, Gernes took a big step away from the traditional artwork, exhibiting products obtained directly through loan agreements with prominent manufacturers of vernacular objects: a working soft-serve ice cream machine, a bowling alley, also free to use, a B&O stereo and TV set for sale, Elvstrøm sailing gear and, finally, the latest Citroën models displayed in the museum gardens. The room also held collages of magazine pictures of everyday living and leisure. The fair-like setting furthermore included a working boat shop building a fibreglass sailboat. Classified ads in the papers announced that, for the run of the exhibition, the cars and stereo could be purchased at the museum from professional salespeople. Everything was anonymous and sourced from the real world. The role of the museum in this context was to house the materials and let the effects of a more open situation do their thing. As avant-garde scholar Tania Ørum writes, "Gernes' contribution can be seen as a protest against the art institution's participation in the commercial art circuit instead of providing socially useful activities. Or, it can be seen as an early example of 'interactive' or 'relational' art, incorporating the audience and blurring the boundaries between the museum and the surrounding world. But there is also an air of resignation about it, as if he despaired of art as

a possible form of communication."[21] There can hardly be any doubt that Gernes by this device cast the museum's refined, modernist architecture in an unaccustomed and harsh light.[22] Personally, he characterized his contribution as "a form of life."[23]

Gernes' contribution makes it clear that the role of art no longer is to put up weird and wonderful pictures on the museum's walls. Instead, it manifests a new kind of presence, demanding engagement far beyond the passive observer role. That also characterizes the other contributions to *Tabernakel*: Louis-Jensen's section invited visitors to cross a spar bridge, a passage that in whole new ways transported the visitor, and her gaze, out into the spaces of the museum. The contents of an artist-run swap shop on Fredensgade in Copenhagen's Nørrebro neighbourhood were also functionalized by Louis-Jensen at the museum. Nørgaard showed a stable, where a horse named Røde Fane (Red Banner) was originally supposed to have been kept for the run of the exhibition. Kirkeby contributed a nomad tent, where tea was brewed and the artist could otherwise communicate with visitors. Communicating and being social – the artists' actions placing them on the same level as the visitors – was key to all the contributions. These were "situations," where everyone, emancipated from what Szeemann shortly before had described as the traditional triangle of studio, gallery and museum, could give themselves over to the work as an invitation, just as the public bath at Charlottenborg had been.

Real life in this way catching up with art and ceasing to be separate from it prompted the museum to make some adjustments – or infringements, as the artists saw it. As Louis-Jensen put it, the artists had been invited into "a bourgeois haven. The museum had been representing the modern, which is also an obligation, and a request is then made of us to do something about the matter. We agreed to a specific political situation."[24] Everything suggests that Knud W. Jensen did not realize the implications of that premise when he agreed to invite the four young Danes. Like Kirkeby, Gernes also imagined that he would be halfway living in his work, an idea the museum rejected. The museum also stepped in to stop visitors from being exposed to the noxious odours of the powerful solvents used in the fibreglass boat-building and moved the shop to an outdoor location.[25] Finally, Knud W. Jensen did not want the new Citroën models in the gardens next to the Moores and Calders. "It was stupid of them to reject Poul's cars, which were like a kind of contemporary Venus de Milo figures," Nørgaard recalls, describing how the artists "sensed that Knud W. Jensen wasn't really ready to commit to the project."[26] Or, as Kirkeby put it, there had "been a conflict between the type of exhibition we have wanted, where there will be some life all the time, unlike a static exhibition, of which Louisiana has made many." By and large, the artists probably had a point regarding key aspects of their critique, although the archived documents only capture the part of the process involving Nørgaard's work and the artists' eventual walkout from the institution.

OUT OF THE MUSEUM
As the *Tabernakel* crisis neared its peak, the museum's director was in Paris to prepare the next exhibition – of Chagall, no less. It is easy to imagine the artists' outrage. The polemic about the horse slaughter may have led them to a cross-

roads, but internally it was just as much the artists' anger at the museum's handling of the planned works and activities that made them withdraw from the exhibition. While Knud W. Jensen was in Paris, the artists changed an agreement he had made with Nørgaard on 3 February to meet about the specimen jars containing the butchered horse remains upon his return. Owing to the frenzied media coverage of the horse slaughter, which was fuelled in no small part by the artist inviting the Ekstra Bladet tabloid to attend, Nørgaard "due to his uncertainty about the present situation [has] wished to postpone the decision about the exhibition of the specimen jars for 8 days."[27] Nonetheless, the following day, 4 February, three artists showed up at the office, demanding that the jars be put up before the agreed date. The museum's general manager, Kirsten Strømstad, then began a dialogue with her boss in Paris and held a meeting with the artists.[28] Knud W. Jensen would not bow to an ultimatum and otherwise believed it *was* likely that the jars would go up.[29] Accusations flew. At the centre of it all stood the 22-year-old Nørgaard surrounded by his older and perhaps also more confrontational "brothers."[30] As notes from the meeting show, Louis-Jensen in no uncertain terms described the postponement of the decision as "outside the agreement and unacceptable [...] Bjørn has been manipulated."[31] Gernes and Louis-Jensen then demanded that the jars be on the shelves by the following Friday. After a 10-minute break, "the three artists return – Bjørn Nørgaard apparently completely brainwashed – and repeat the ultimatum [...] Poul Gernes, Bjørn Nørgaard and Peter Louis-Jensen now launch a strong attack on Louisiana for not wanting to identify with the exhibition [...] That's why the exhibition is a fiasco and that's why they don't want to activate their departments."[32] Or, as Nørgaard put it on Danmarks Radio, in words typical of the time, "They have missed the *situation*."[33]

Their years at Eks-skolen clearly had also trained them in the art of standing together in opposition. It can be noted that the museum and the artists were no longer on the same side publicly during the media storm, as Knud W. Jensen and Tinguely had been. The truth is that Louisiana was simply unable to absorb the critique of its authority as a museum and make the adjustments that these artworks required. As Nørgaard later put it, society and real life, not objects, were now the work. "The artist subsequently becomes politically, ethically and morally dangerous, and then the reaction sets in, especially if you make it public."[34] Since the museum was unwilling to be strong-armed, Knud W. Jensen released Nørgaard from their agreement. Thus, Knud W. Jensen reasoned, no agreements had been broken and he acknowledged the artists' withdrawal from the exhibition.[35] On 7 February, Louisiana received a long list of grievances and a statement saying that the museum had sided with reaction. One of the grievances was that Louisiana had violated their artistic freedom of expression. It should be mentioned that Jensen, only one week before, in a principled defence of art had made the following statement to the press: "Opposing the exhibition of these specimens would be an infringement on the artistic freedom of speech, of which Louisiana also stands as guarantor."[36] Even so, the artists deftly spun their version of the story in the press. Beyond the response to Nørgaard's horse slaughter, critics fell into two camps. The majority basically did not understand why "this" should take place at Louisiana. The minority, represented by the left-wing paper Information, was chagrined and did not see how Louisiana could fail to see what art was up to. The critic and librarian Jane Pedersen, became a leading voise the year after the exhibition, when she published the first real book about the artist Poul Gernes, *Der er dejligt i Danmark* (It is Beautiful in Denmark).

AFTERMATH

In a summary memo, Flemming Koefoed writes, "We agreed to give the artists a free hand." He goes on, "New and experimental art will always aspire to show art in new contexts [...] The yardstick should be whether we find the project to be qualified and relevant in the context in which it is shown."[37] The museum, moreover, did not get the press off its back just because the four artists had walked out. The media game was another new reality for Louisiana. In another memo, headed "A horse pill – new structures in art and exhibitions," which might have been a draft of an essay or op-ed column, Koefoed writes, "Louisiana has not yet responded to last week's smear campaign against the museum and the artist Bjørn Nørgaard, or to the attacks that the four Danish artists' withdrawal from the exhibition Tabernakel has now triggered." Next, concerning the premise of the exhibition, he lucidly writes, "When we made the plans for the exhibition at Louisiana, both sides realized that numerous problems would arise, since an institution with certain established structures was here opening up to people whose declared goal was to break down or radically change those structures [...] In prolonged talks with the artists, Louisiana's management tried to make the exhibition continue in its entirety, which, as we know, failed. There are two possible explanations for the artists' headlong break with Louisiana and their release of a bombastic statement to the press containing so many outright untruths and distortions: 1. a hypersensitivity or suspicion worked up over many years of opposition, or 2. a latent desire to bring about a break."[38]

Everything would suggest that Gernes himself was not the least bit shocked at the turn of events. On the contrary, it merely confirmed his opinion about museums. They were no longer the future for him. As a final reflection of *Tabernakel* in the press, Information in July 1970 reported that the Ministry of Culture, while processing Louisiana's request for increased government support for exhibition activities, had received a telegram from the painter Poul Gernes stating that he wanted a possible grant to be on the condition that the exhibitions show the latest and best and most advanced.[39] At this distance, it is not so hard to tell where the lines were drawn – with Gernes going all in – and why things happened to go the way they did. In a Danish context, *Tabernakel* stands alone as the most spectacular and celebrated example of the change in the art world in the late 1960s – and of plain ideologization and institutional critique. The events left the museum with the undeniably slimmest file in its archive and a feeling of fiasco. As Strømstad notes, Beuys and the other three international artists were to all intents and purposes shut out of the conversation and posterity's awareness of the exhibition.[40] In Knud W. Jensen's mind, *Tabernakel* was subsequently never allowed to play much of a role, either. In a long, strategic memo of August 1973, he mentions an area that the museum had been neglecting, "Exhibitions that the artists build on site,"[41] noting examples from Moderna Museet in Stockholm

fig. 10

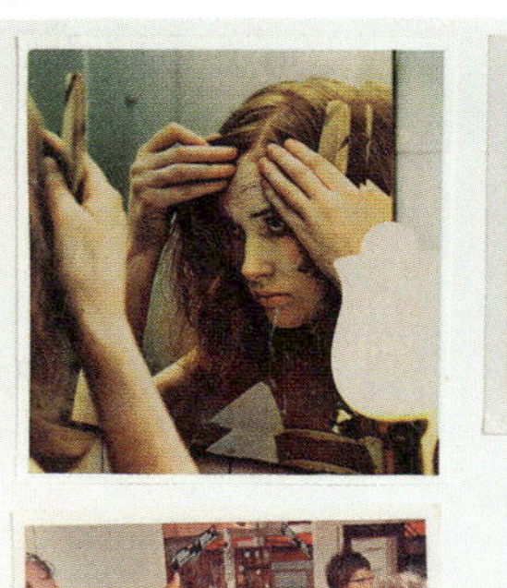
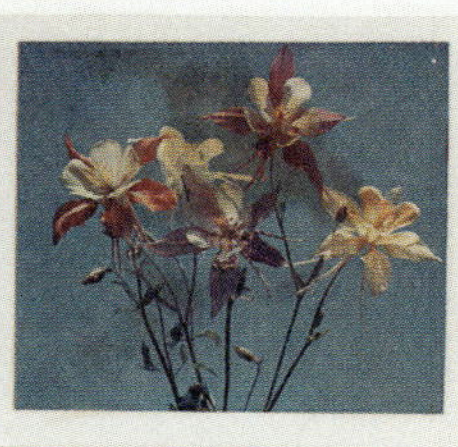
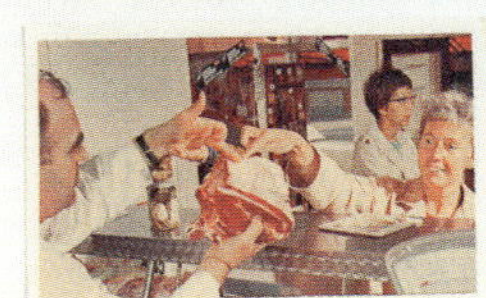
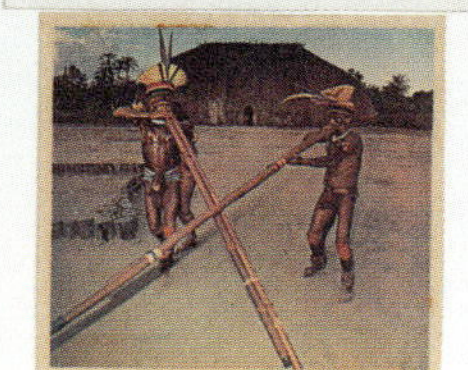
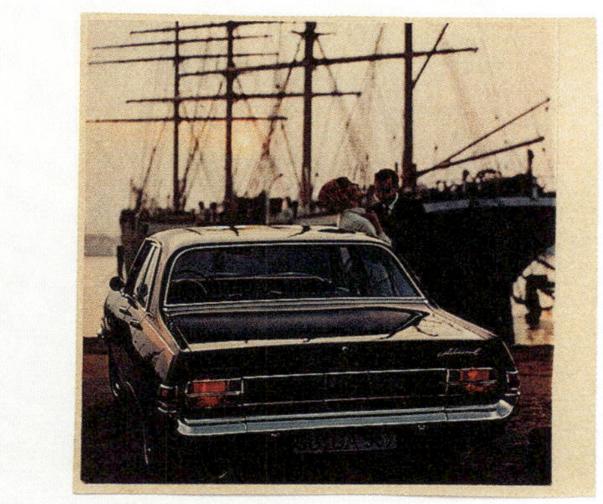
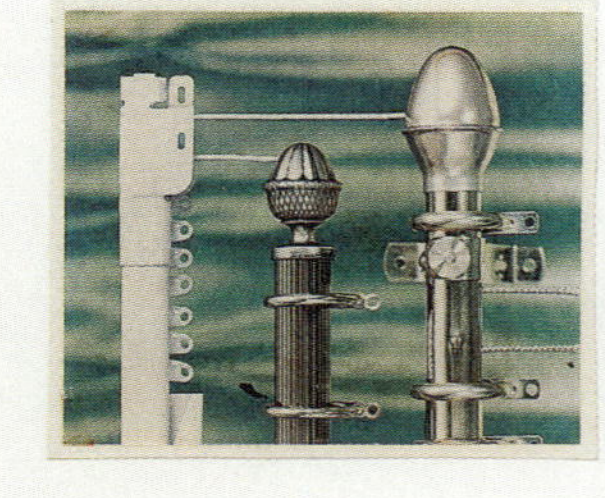
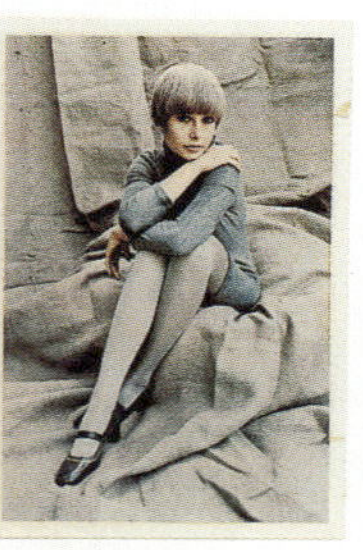

fig. 11

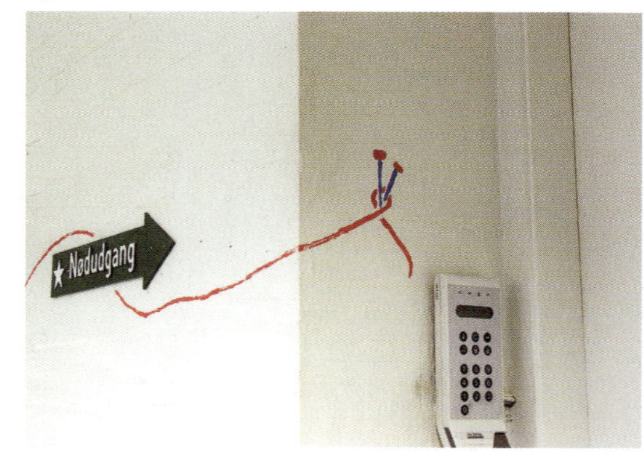

and the Stedelijk Amsterdam. *Tabernakel* is not mentioned at all.

Today, it might seem as if Knud W. Jensen walked into the crisis a bit somnambulistically and ill prepared. In retrospect, the museum was clearly taking a huge risk with *Tabernakel*. The museum, it must be said, was trying to take a timely sounding of an emerging trend but hit the wave at an odd angle and ended up taking a beating from all sides. Knud W. Jensen, consequently, became more resolved in his view of Louisiana's institutional role in Denmark and where he drew his line. He later wrote, "The sudden turn in cultural life at the end of the '60s, as far as Louisiana and myself are concerned, led to an extended pause in seminars and the museum's social engagement."[42] The politicization, including the marginalization of art, did not sit well with the museum's founder. He was undertaking to withdraw the institution from the political battle zone and consolidate the museum in the long run, financially and in terms of content, as a more established entity. The period of battle in a way ended right when the museum itself momentarily became the battlefield.

If, on the occasion of *Tabernakel*, we picture Knud W. Jensen walking down the museum's halls and running into Poul Gernes building a catamaran, the artist's answer to the question of what he was doing might have ended, "I cannot do it alone – want to join in?"[43] Knud W. Jensen was a gracious person, but this man of culture most definitely did not want to get on board. Gernes was searching, and if he was not occupied with one project, he was restlessly looking for a new one. The last time the two of them bumped into each other was probably at Ung Dansk Kunst's anniversary exhibition at Louisiana in 1967. Three years later Gernes did not have the least desire to reach back – traditional objects and the institution were behind him. In his own way, he, too, was looking for a way out. In 1970, he dramatically confessed, "Need a good suggestion for what I should really spend the rest of my life doing."[44] While Knud W. Jensen turned the museum away from the political arena and in the direction of a more traditional art museum, Gernes after 1970 largely dedicated his art to projects that had a social and edifying function.

Anders Kold (f. 1959), MA in Art History from University of Copenhagen. Head of Acquisitions and Curator at Louisiana Museum of Modern Art since 2001, where he has organized exhibitions with among others Louise Bourgeois, David Hockney, Tal R, Jeff Wall, Jorn and Pollock and the present Poul Gernes exhibition.

1   *Louisiana Revy*, Vol. 10, No. 3, January 1970, p. 3.

2   Troels Andersen, *Ude af øje, Erindringer 1940-1973*. Forlaget Vandkunsten, 2014, p. 119ff.

3   Knud W. Jensen, *Mit Louisiana-liv*. Gyldendal, 1985. Cited from the 1993 edition, p. 64.

4   Ibid., p. 217.

5   Lennart Gottlieb, *Skandaler*. Aarhus Kunstmuseum, 1999, p. 73. As Gottlieb sharply notes, Knud W. Jensen, apparently, was not particularly reflective about why Tinguely's work had received its somewhat ominous title, arguing that Tinguely's political engagement and insistent use of "real life" in his expression did not appeal to Jensen's view of the museum's role.

6   Bjørn Nørgaard never got further than furnishing a stable for the horse Røde Fane in an outbuilding at the museum, and the horse was never kept there. Due to further developments in the case, from the slaughter in a field to the controversial and failed presentation at the museum of the horse's anatomical remains in mason jars, his art work largely existed only in the press.

7   "Broder, jeg er søgende." Interview with Gernes by Jens Jørgen Thorsen, in *Aktuelt*, 15 July 1962.

8   In English: peek-a-boo.

9   In its most wrapped-up moments, the performance bears a striking resemblance to Joseph Beuys's *I Like America and America Likes Me* from 1974, where Beuys, wrapped in felt from head to toe, shields himself from a coyote, which he then spends time with in an art gallery. The sole connection is the contemporary interest in draining art of subjectivity.

10   Published in *Hvedekorn* 2, 1966, and in a very limited edition of prints.

11   Lars Morell, *Det grafiske eksperiment. Poul Gernes' tryk 1943-1996*. Thaning & Appel, 2005, p. 41. Citing conversations with Aase Seidler Gernes, Morell writes that she urged her subject-strapped husband to do something with the only thing he thinks about. Judging from the format of the two sheets, the work might very well have been intended for the journal *Hvedekorn*, which Gernes and Per Kirkeby were picture editors of in this period. As an ur-motif of this interest in the (de-) construction of the ego, which was so typical of the time, Robert Morris's epochal 1962 work *Box with the Sound of Its Own Making* could be mentioned.

12   Jane Pedersen, *Der er dejligt i Danmark*. Borgens Forlag, 1971, p. 64 and 90.

13   Ibid., p. 60. There is no reason to believe that the term "monument" did not originate with Gernes himself.

14   According to Troels Andersen, the toilets installed in the immediate vicinity of the bath were not functional. In terms of reading the work as an action, Tania Ørum, in her 2009 book *De eksperimenterende tressere* and in her contribution to the catalogue for the Gernes exhibition at Deichtorhallen, Hamburg, focused on this interpretation of the work.

15   Memo, dated 23 March 1969, and filed in the archive in the folder marked "TABERNAKEL." Mühlhausen, himself an artist, was employed at the museum from 1959-1969.

16   Ibid.

17   Contacts resulting, in part, from Beuys's presence and contributions to the *Tilstande* happening festival, which took place on 14 October 1966, and was organized by Eks-skolen. Two years before, Beuys had performed another work at Charlottenborg.

18   Conversation with the author, 27 January 2016.

19   Memo by Koefoed, 13 August 1969, "TABERNAKEL" folder. Exactly how this exchange of information took place is unclear. What is certain is that John Hunov historically backed these artists and served both as a member of the editorial staff for *Louisiana Revy*, Vol., No. 3 (catalogue), and as a consultant to the exhibition.

20   Invitation from Koefoed to Gernes of 5 September 1969.

21   Tania Ørum, "Det moralske kompas," in *Louisiana Magasin*, No. 44, May 2016, p. 16.

22   Allan de Waal, "Tabernakel arkitektonisk," in *Information*, 28 January 1970. In the article, de Waal, a critic and architect, praises the Danish artists' striking intervention in the museum. On the effect of Gernes' stands selling industrial design, he writes that they are excellent and implicitly (critically) play on "the worst aspects of the house, the Louisiana *style* that, since Bo and Wohlert in Humlebæk, has been a model for no small number of furniture stores and gastronomic motels."

23   "Kunstkronik," radio broadcast on Danmarks Radio, aired 24 February 1970.

24   Ibid.

25   A rather laconic Gernes objects that "we proposed real solutions to the odour issues of the boat-building. It had all been mentioned from the beginning and could be solved." In "Kunstkronik."

26   Conversation with Nørgaard, January 2016.

27   Note of telephone conversation with Knud W. Jensen, February 1970, in the "TABERNAKEL" folder, Louisiana's archive.

28   Handwritten notes from the meeting. Privately owned. Per Kirkeby was not present at the meeting with Kirsten Strømstad and Flemming Koefoed.

29   Conversation between Knud W. Jensen and Kirsten Strømstad, 6 February 1970.

30   Conversations, 28 May 2015 and 6 January 2016, with Kirsten Strømstad, former general manager of Louisiana, who recalls that the atmosphere was hostile and unpleasant. Nørgaard played no part. Gernes, Louis-Jensen and Hunov were the driving forces.

31   See Note 29.

32   Handwritten notes from the meeting. Privately owned.

33   "Kunstkronik," radio broadcast on Danmarks Radio, aired 24 February 1970.

34   Peter Øvig Knudsen, *Hippie II. Den sidste sommer*. Gyldendal, 2012, p. 57.

35   Note of telephone conversation.

36   "Protester mod slagtning af hest," in *Berlingske*, 1 February 1970.

37   Flemming Koefoed, undated memo. Privately owned.

38   Flemming Koefoed, "En hestekur – nye strukturer i kunsten og udstillingslivet." Privately owned.

39   "Maler ønsker støtte betinget af mere avanceret linje," in *Information*, 10 August 1970.

40   Conversation with Kirsten Strømstad, May 2015.

41   Knud W. Jensen, "Generelle betragtninger. Museet: Tempel eller Forum?" In Louisiana's archive.

42   Ibid., p. 156.

43   Jane Pedersen, p. 129.

44   Ibid., p. 34.

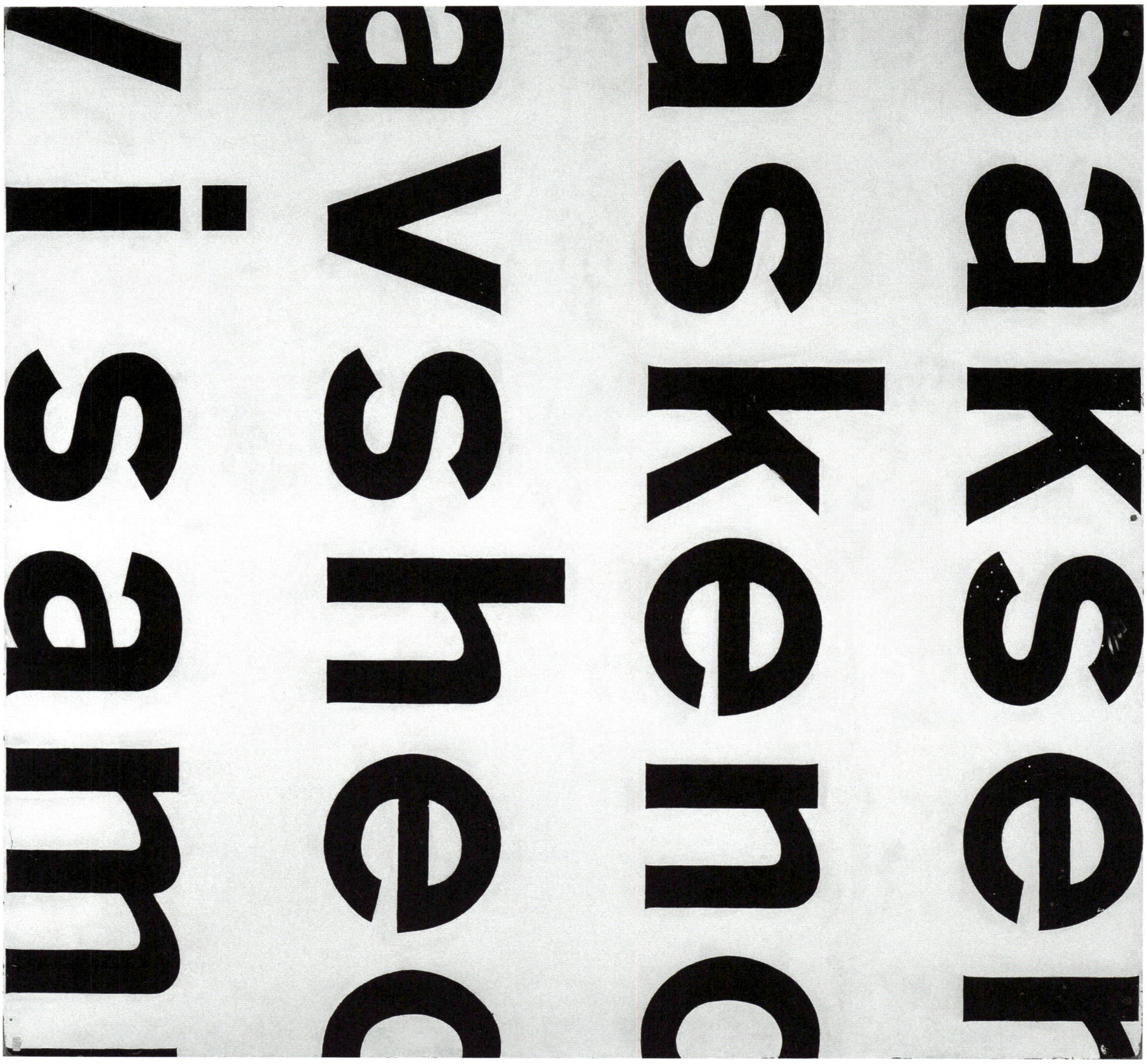

Untitled ("The Scissors"), c. 1962
Black and white acrylic on masonite,
122 × 132 cm

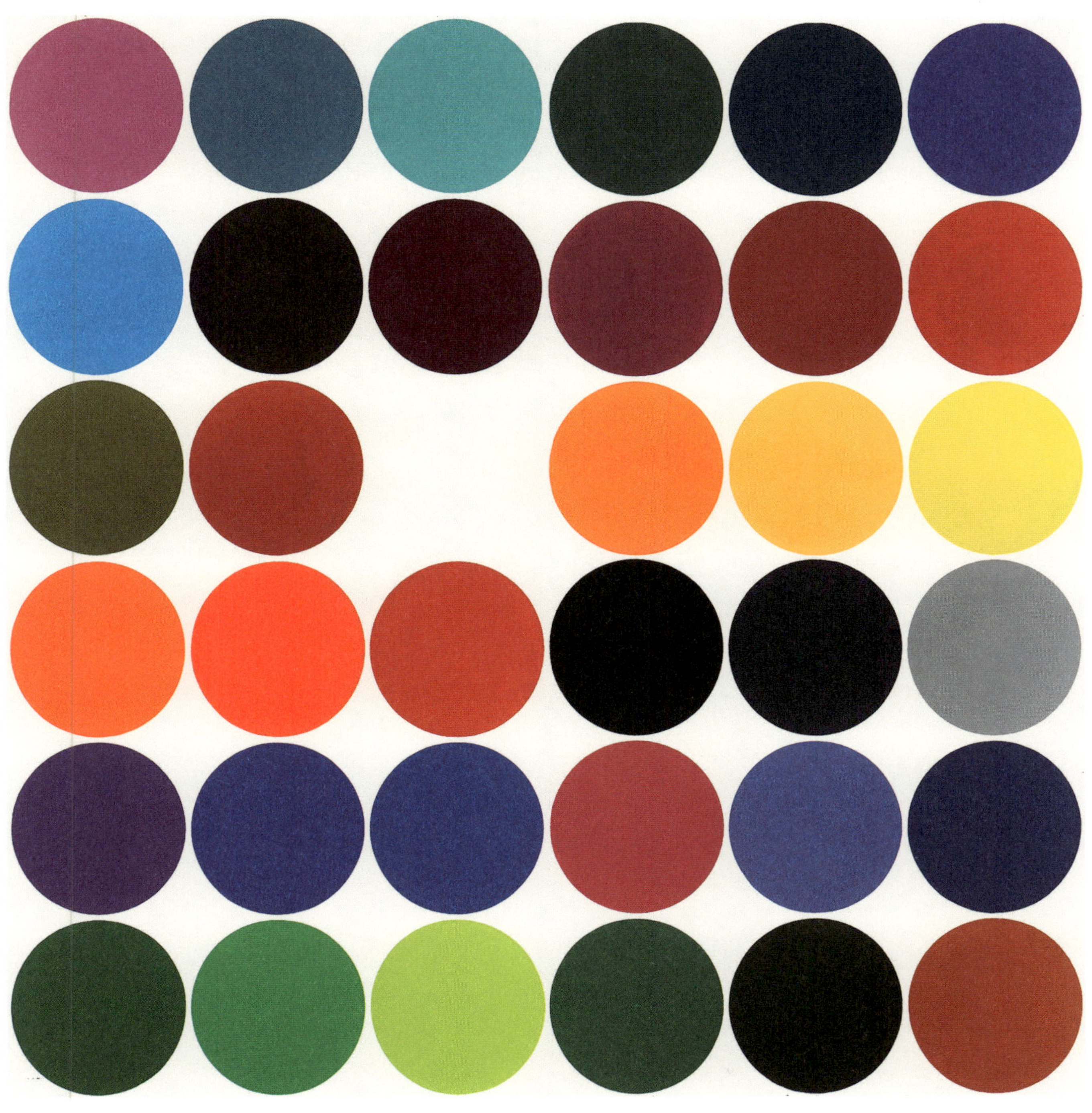

Untitled, 1966-68
Enamel on masonite,
4 parts, total 244 × 244 cm

Untitled (A), 1965
(The Alphabet Series)
Enamel paint on masonite, 160 × 132 cm

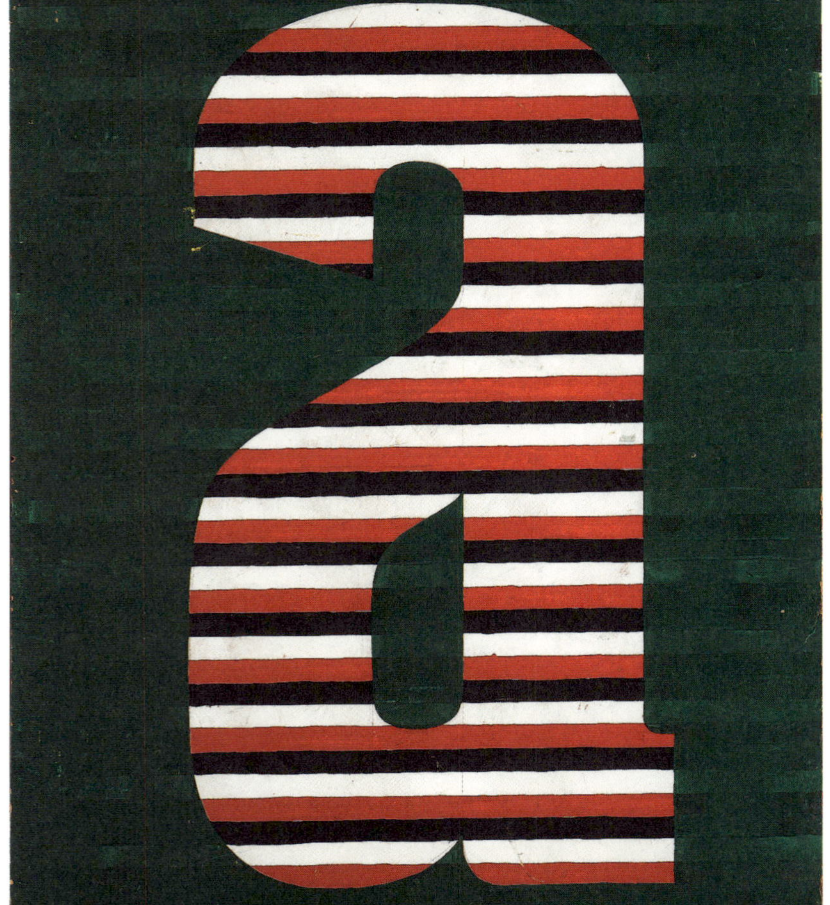

Untitled (F), 1965
(The Alphabet Series)
Enamel paint on masonite, 213 × 122 cm

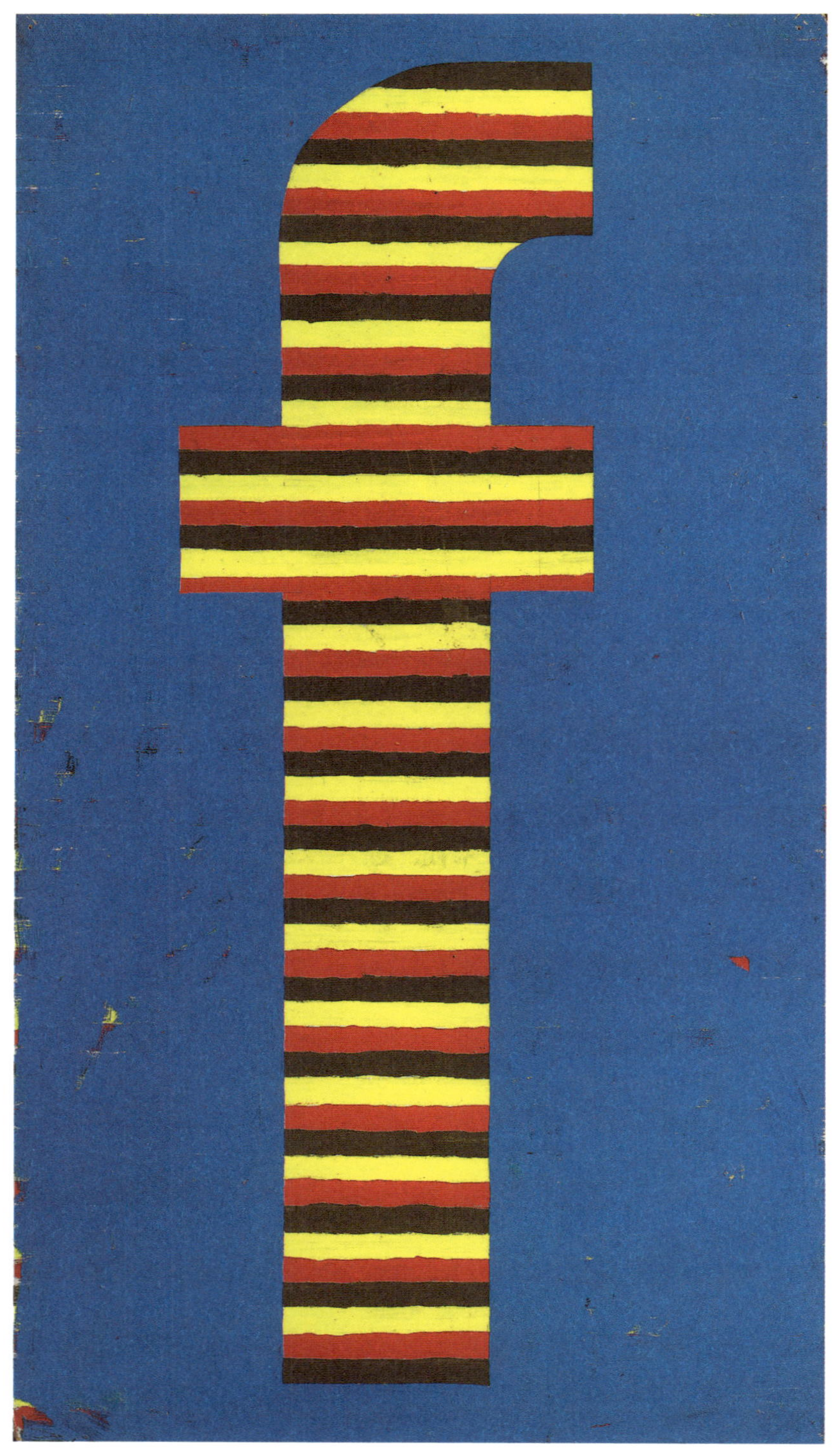

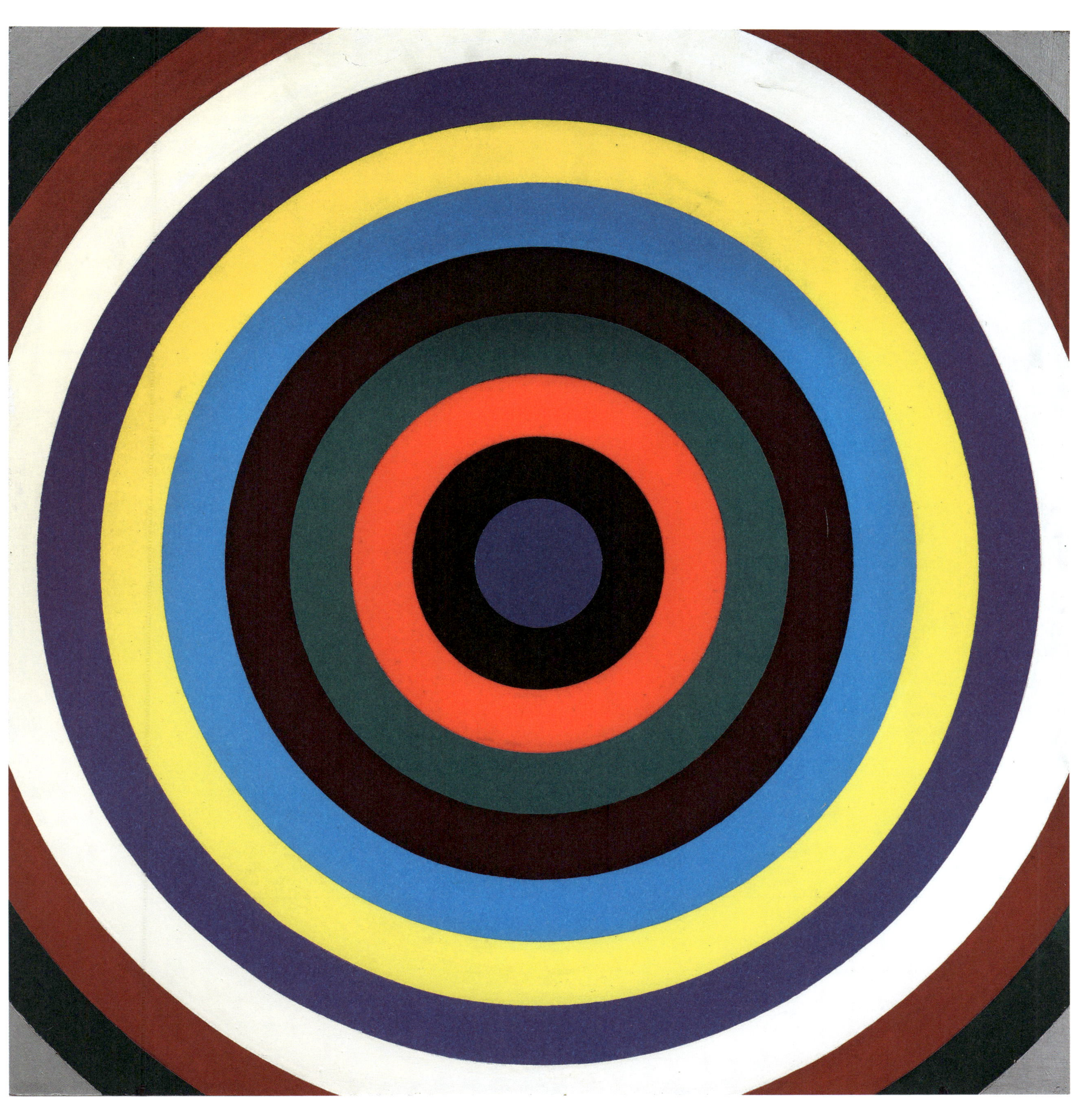

Untitled ("Target"), 1966-68
Enamel on masonite, 122 × 122 cm

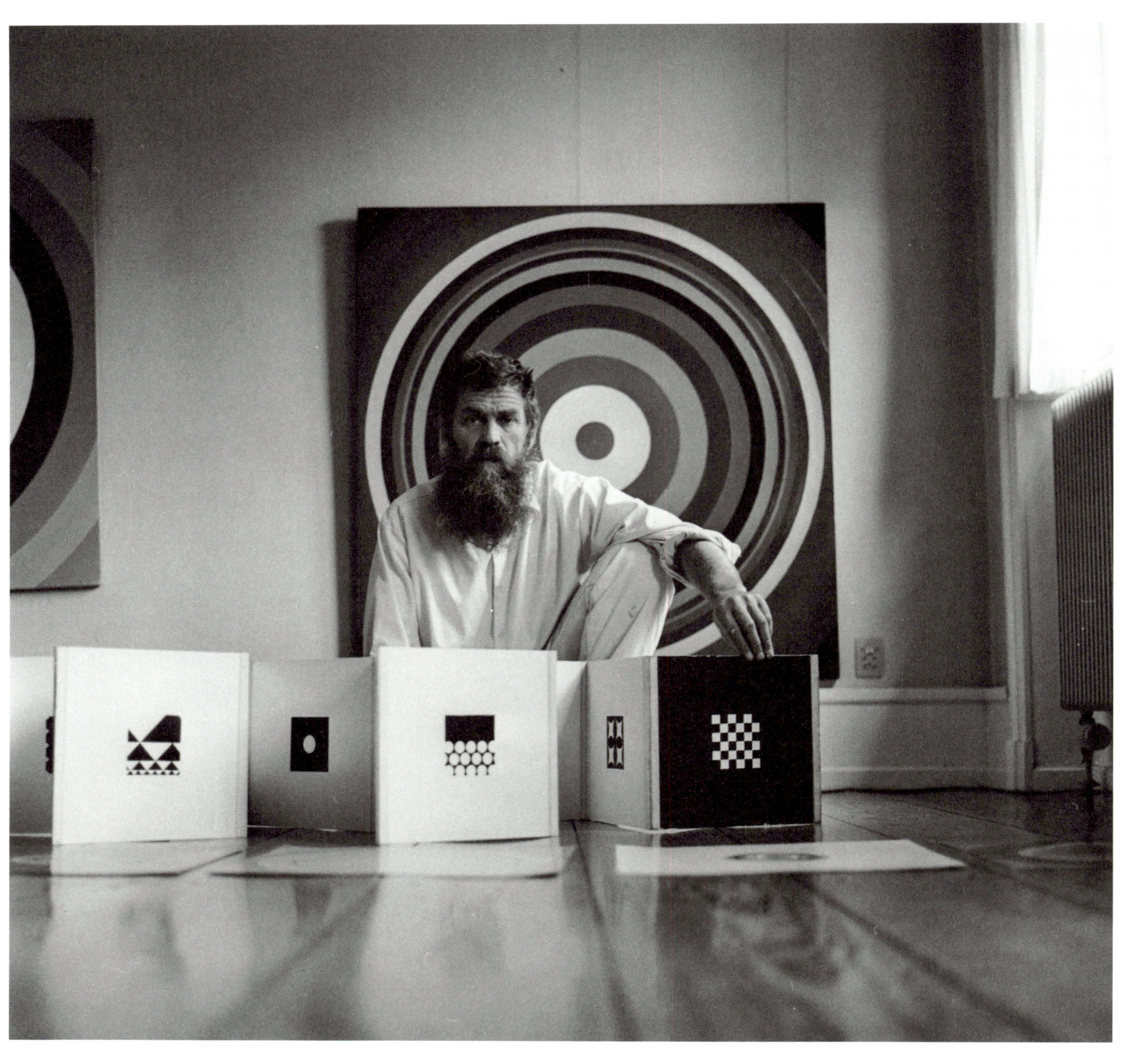

Poul Gernes with Leporello Book, 1968
Linocut on paper, glued on cardboard,
assembled with canvas tape
Unfolded: 28.8 × 1612.6 × 0.3 cm

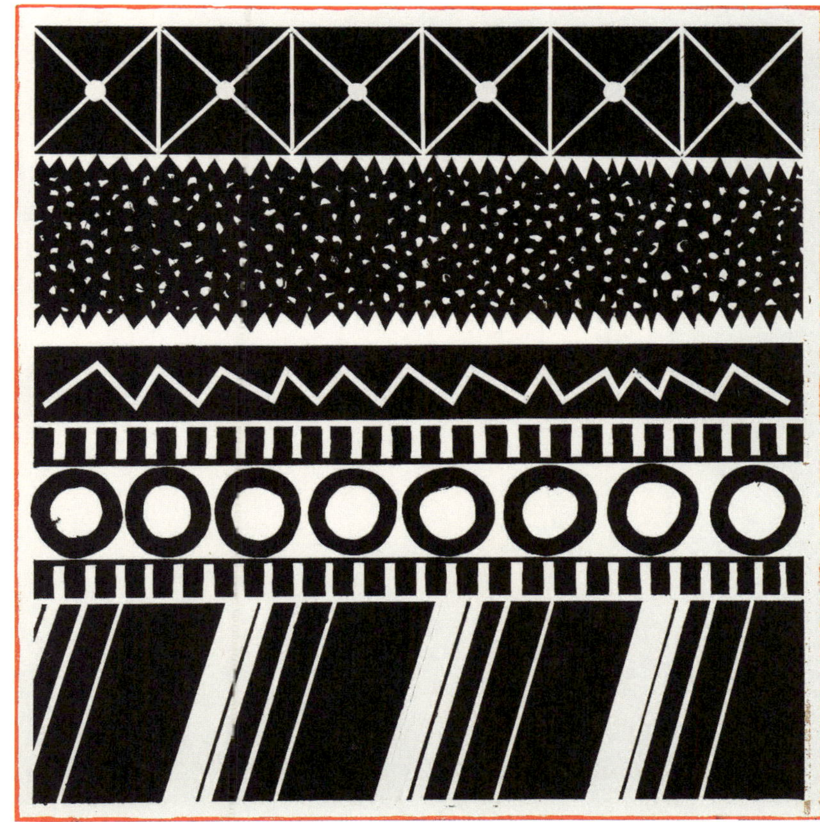
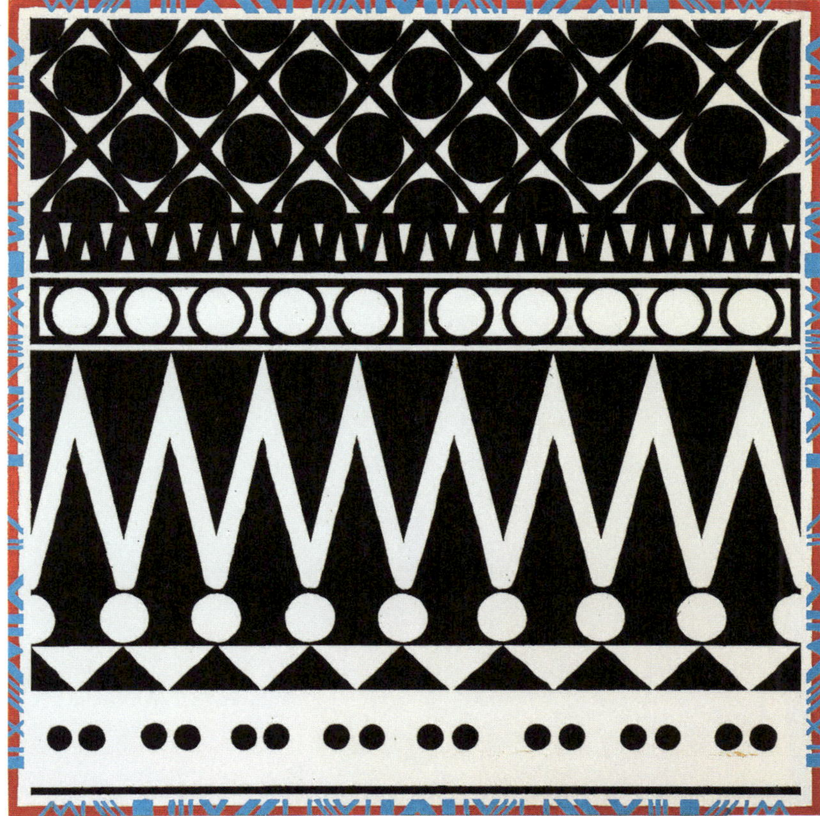
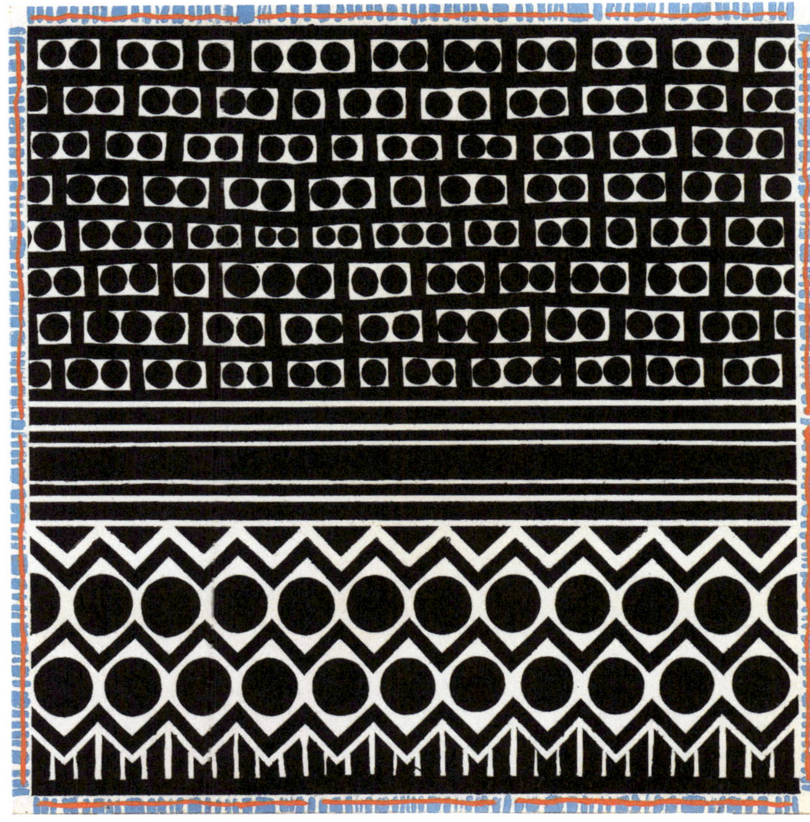
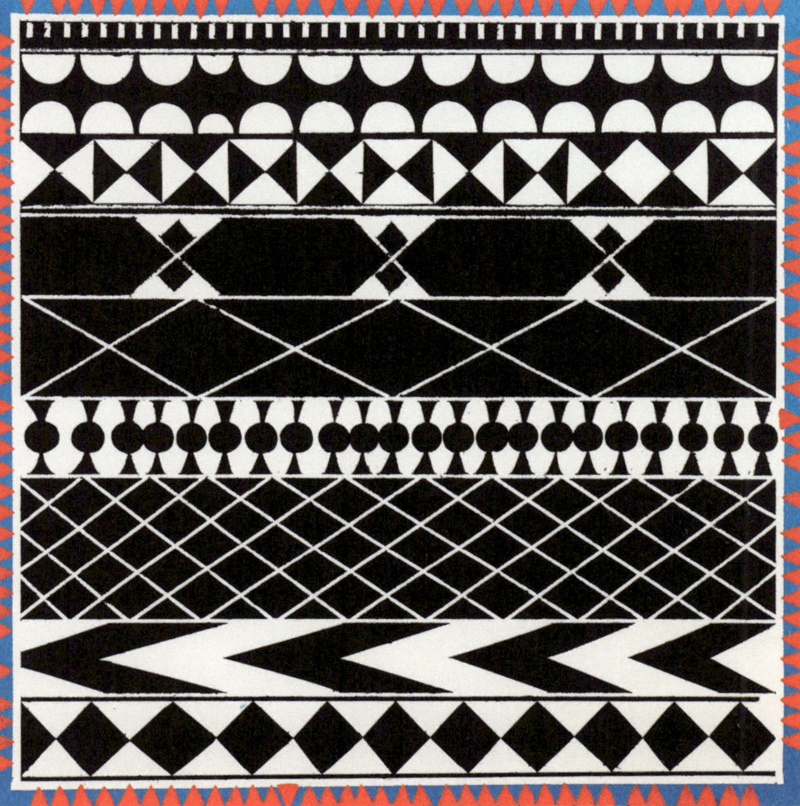

Black-and-White Decoration, 1980
Enamel on masonite, 4 works,
each 122 × 122 cm

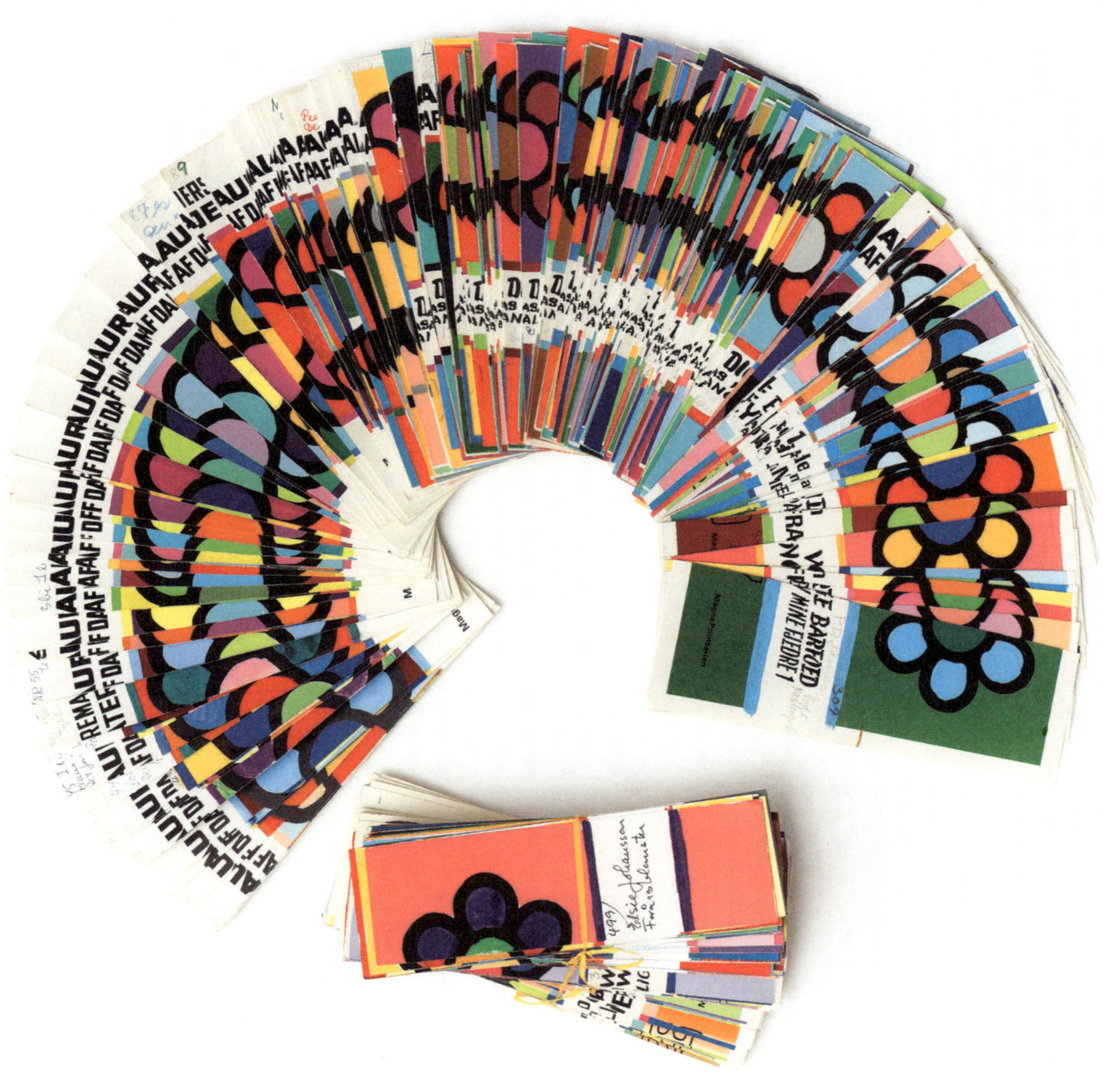

MagnaPrint colour samples, 1971-2003
Colour print on MagnaPrint covers

MagnaPrint books, 1971-2003
Cover for series of books for weak-sighted
384 books, each 22,7 × 15 cm

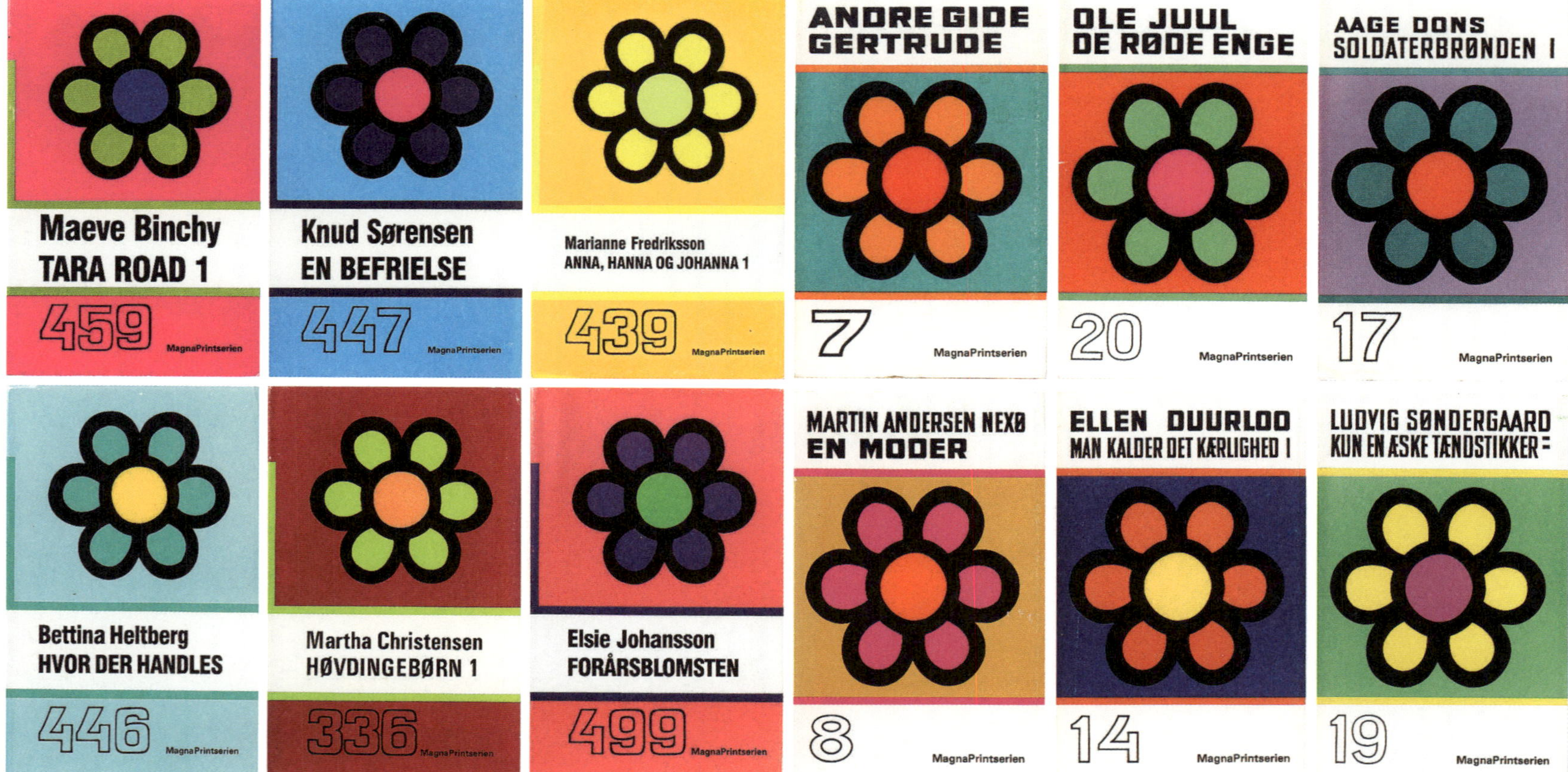

Untitled, 1965
(Series with black and white as
recurring colours)
Enamel paint on masonite
15 works, each 122 × 122 cm

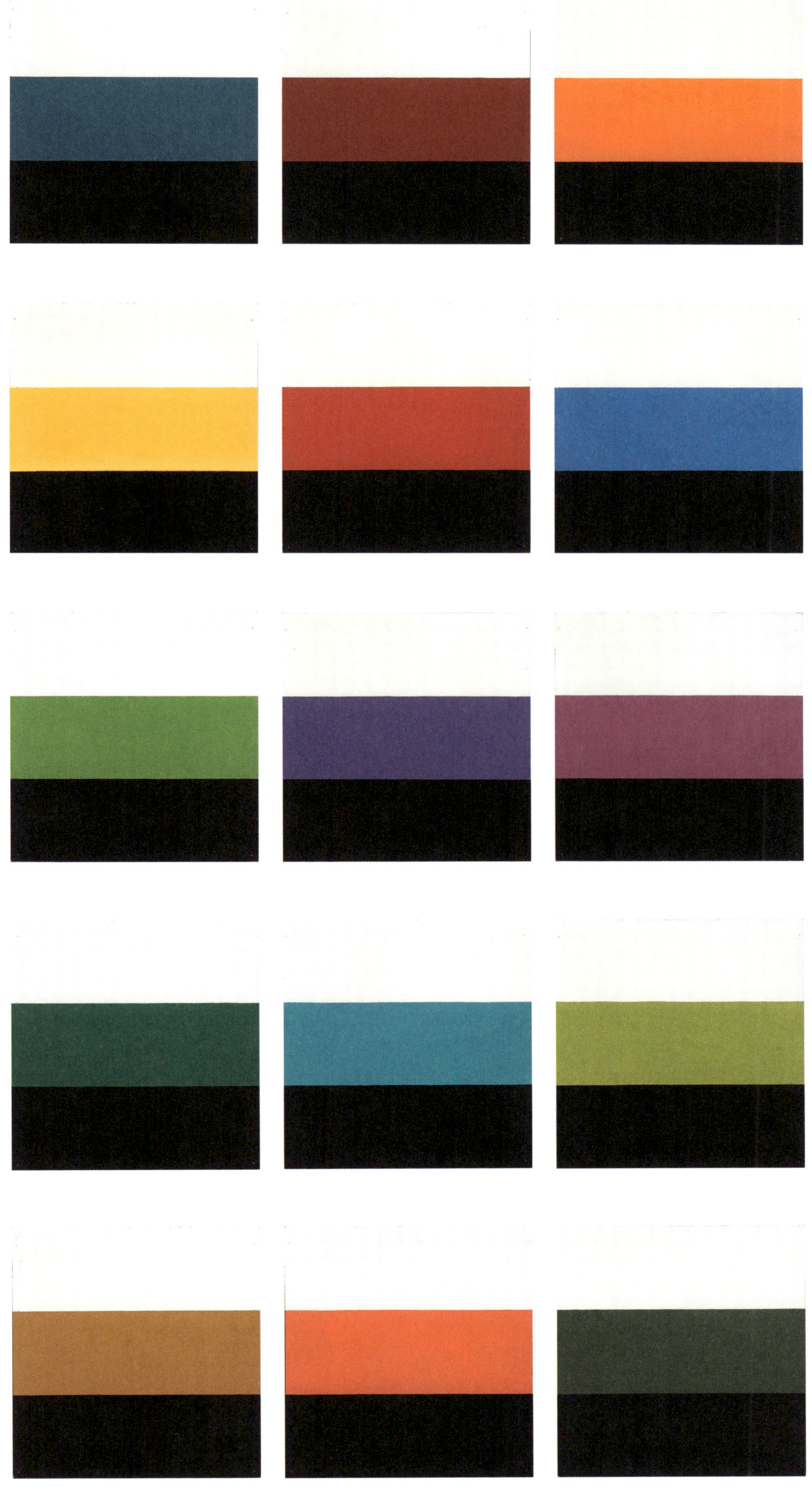

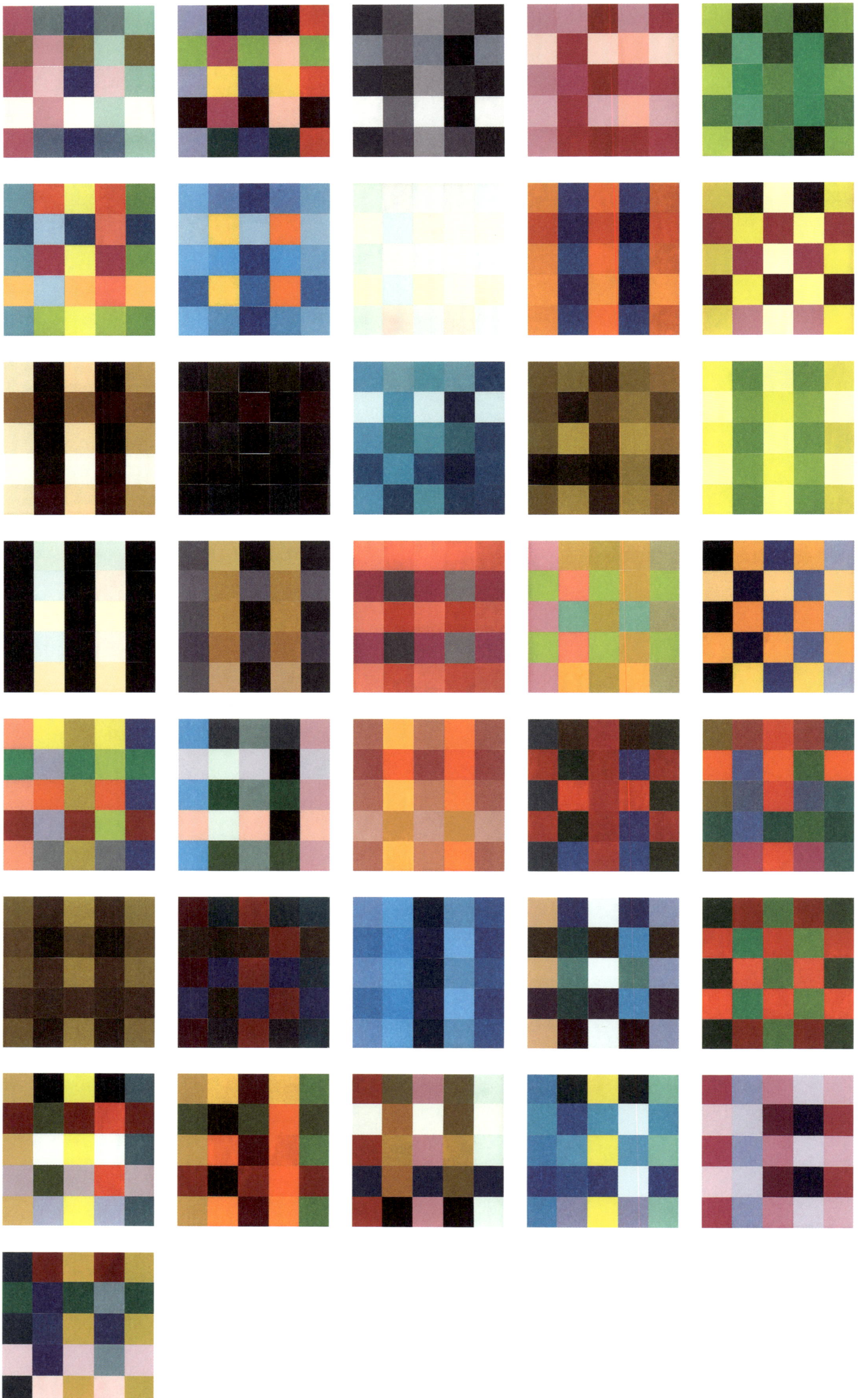

Untitled, 1966-67
Enamel paint on cardboard, collage
Series of 36 works, each 100 × 100 cm

Untitled, 1965-66
("Lottery Stripes")
Enamel on masonite
Series of 8 works,
each 183 × 122 cm

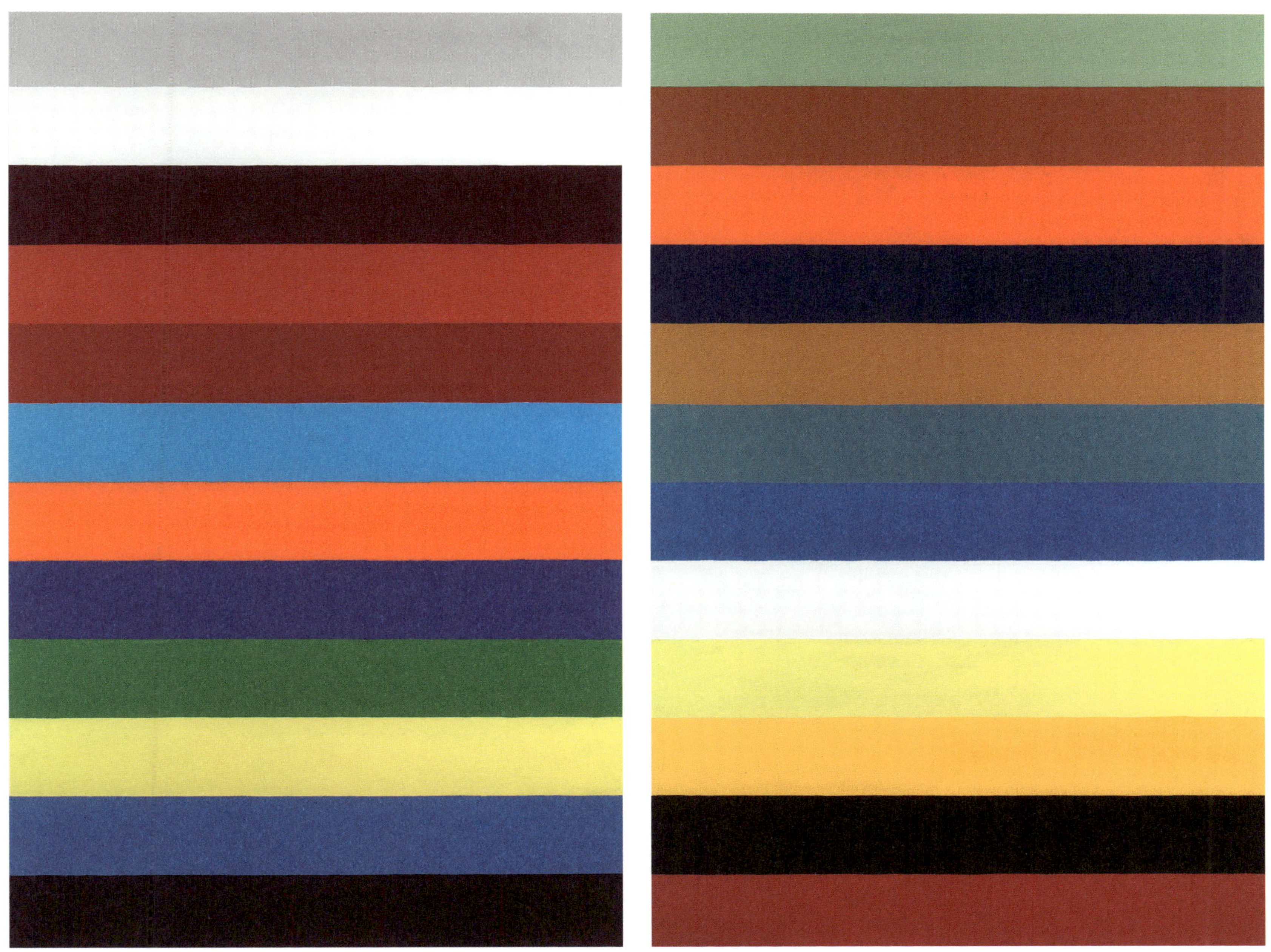

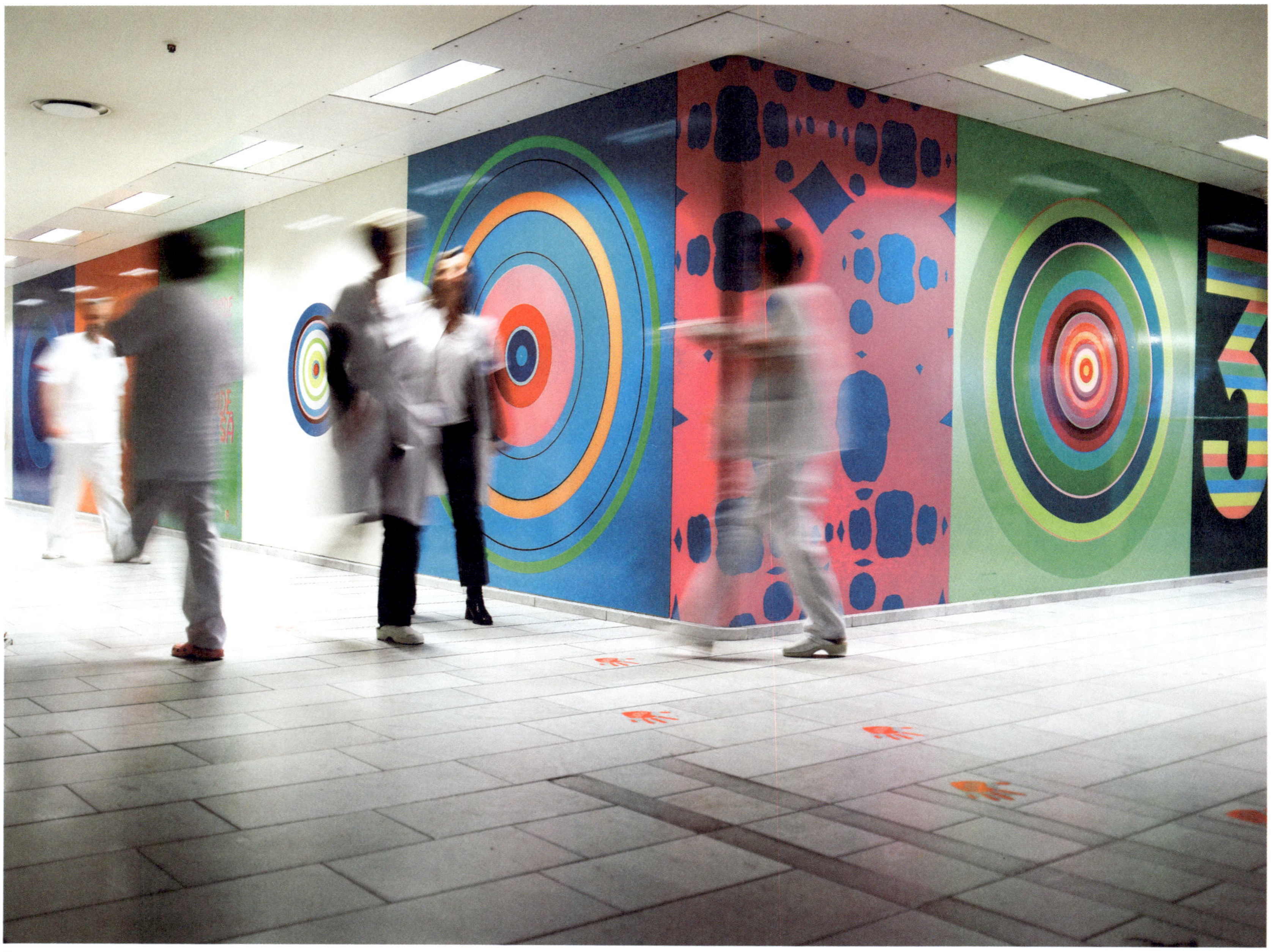

fig. 1

fig. 2

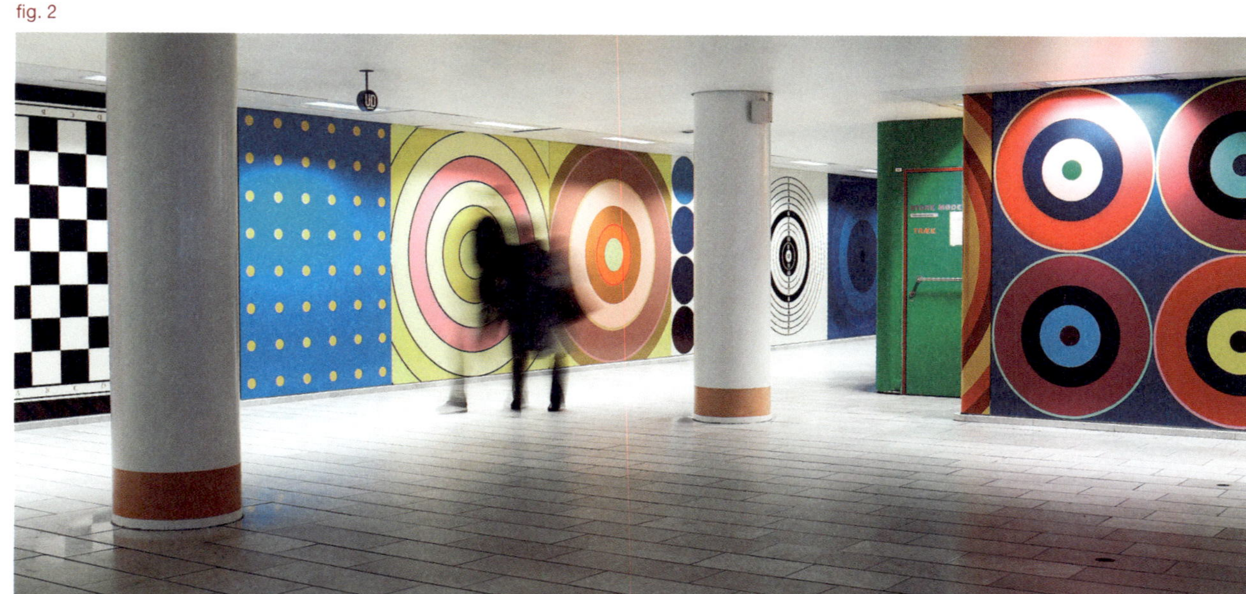

Living Colourlessly Is Downright Unhealthy[1]
Poul Gernes' Decoration of Herlev Hospital

By Lene Bøgh Rønberg

fig.1-2 Poul Gernes' panels in the lobby of Herlev Hospital

"Good Lord, this parrot cage is awful," one patient said. "When I came out of anaesthesia and saw those colours, I thought I'd had a stroke," said another. But there were also positive responses to "The Herlev Department," as the pilot module of the future hospital environment, which was set up and tested by patients and staff at Gentofte Hospital over a three-month period in 1970, was called. "This is more wonderful than the most expensive luxury hotel. The only thing I'm really missing is a bar," one of the more upbeat comments went. Another patient even hoped "it'll be at least a couple of weeks before I get well, because I've never experienced such lovely surroundings."[2] The positive voices were in the majority, obviously, as the trials of the pilot module informed the decision to realize Denmark's biggest art project in public space: Poul Gernes' decoration and colour design of Herlev Hospital which was carried out from 1968 to 1976.

Underlying the project was an expectation that cheerful surroundings would lead to speedier healing. This is evident from an article in the Ekstra Bladet newspaper headed "Artist Fills Hospital with Festive and Cheerful Colours," reporting on a visit to the brightly coloured pilot module. The same attitude is expressed by one of the architects of Herlev Hospital, Jørgen Selchau, who points out that their hope was to possibly shorten hospital stays and "create happiness in both patients and staff."[3] The interest in the impact of the physical setting on parameters such as length of hospital stays and patient stress and well-being has not lessened since those days. This essay aims to show the relevance of the Herlev decoration to the discussions of art in hospitals that have gained new currency because of the many hospital construction projects now underway in Denmark. The method here will be to view Gernes' seminal work and its multifaceted theory through the lens provided by the current discourse on healing architecture.[4]

THE MASTERWORK IN HERLEV
There are several reasons why the total decoration in Herlev can be considered a key work in the artist's production and in Danish hospital decoration in general. Size, of course, plays a role. The decoration is large, vast even, comprising not only the lobby with its more than 50 monumental, square panels employing the artist's minimalist and serial devices of bright, pure colours in stylized circles and dots combined with recognizable subjects like targets, compass roses, letters and flag maps. The lobby was just the beginning, the first stage of the process. The artist next persuaded the architects and the client to let him devise a colour scheme for the entire hospital complex.

The enormity of the project is reflected in its more than 65 kilometres of pink baseboards, 10 kilometres of floral curtain fabric – printed in a variety of colours, of course – and 4,500 doors in over 20 different colours.[5] In other words, we are dealing with Denmark's most extensive work of art and its colour design, which leads from the lobby out into the hospital's far-flung units and up into the inpatient wards. Occupying the floors of the nation's tallest tower, the colours extend into washrooms and storerooms, whose walls, cabinet doors, baseboards, handles, electrical outlets, signs and clocks, to use the artist Erik Steffensen's site-specific phrase, burst out in a full-blown "eruption of polychromy."[6]

The project was also a turning point in Gernes' production, opening the door to a wave of commissions to decorate public spaces. When the Herlev decoration was completed in 1976, after eight years of work, he had several other public commissions waiting for him. Over the course of the '80s and '90s, he and his changing crews of painters carried out around 180 commissions in widely different locations, the overwhelming majority of them public spaces: schools, dormitories and town halls, but also private workplaces and even a secret military complex, Gurrebunkeren, north of Copenhagen, as well as, not surprisingly, more hospitals.[7]

Lastly, it bears mention that the Herlev decoration was the first project to truly express Gernes' original ideas about the social and political potential of art, not least because it operated in public space. His "Eks-skolen brother" Bjørn Nørgaard later underscored that aspect, calling the project "one of our finest sociopolitical works of art today."[8] For Gernes, art was a moral and ethical pursuit, reflected in the notion that art should not be hidden away in galleries but put out there in places where ordinary people come and go and where it could make a difference in everyday life. In that respect, the Herlev project was a "successful attempt at popular monumentality," to borrow another apt phrase from Nørgaard.[9]

THE TECHNOLOGICAL HOSPITAL AND THE HOSPITAL OF THE SENSES

Back in the 1960s and '70s, Gernes' decoration and colour design were carried out for what the authors of *Sansernes Hospital* (The Hospital of the Senses, 2007), Kim Dirckinck-Holmfeld and Lars Heslet, call "the technological hospital." This was a place that focused on innovations in medicine and hospital technology, for example by building vertically to make room in the buildings for as much efficient healing as possible.[10] It was the idea of the hospital as a kind of healing machine, where sick people are put in at one end and healthy people come out at the other end, a system that puts technology, science, efficiency and quantity ahead of human dimensions and an environment in which patients can recognize themselves. What Gernes actually did, however, once he was given the artistic latitude in this new type of hospital, was to decorate and colour it into an entirely different paradigm, "the hospital of the senses."

Today, this new paradigm is best known as "healing architecture," a field of knowledge that focuses on the impact of the physical setting on patients' healing and that in recent years has had a key influence on the discourse on the design of healthcare buildings. Critical to healing architecture is the thesis that the physical setting affects people and that its effect on patients and hospital staff can be measured in terms of stress or well-being.[11] Summarizing decades of Danish and international research in the area, a 2009 Danish report on healing architecture concluded that a number of clinical and health care studies have identified effects of images and colour combinations as a "positive distraction" raising patients' pain tolerance and having a calming effect.[12]

There are obvious similarities between the vision of the healing-architecture paradigm and the thinking behind Gernes' decoration. Based on the avant-garde notion that art and life are inextricably linked, he held that colours affect human well-being and that the qualities of colours should be employed to make places present, humane and uplifting.[13] A panel in the lobby, emblazoned with the familiar verse "Roses are red, violets are blue, sugar is sweet, and so are you," reads like something of a manifesto for that simple and, to Gernes, obvious concept, indicating the relationship between pure, bright colours and human emotions, moods and sensations.

ENTERTAINMENT AND SHOCK

Interviews with Gernes from 1971 by art librarian Jane Pedersen provide a major source of insight into the artist's reflections on the functions that colours could and should have in a hospital.[14] Out of concern for people staying in the hospital, it was important for Gernes to create entertainment, which he believed involved the brightest possible colours and the greatest possible contrasts.[15] Such ideas had a big influence on the artist's consistent work with strong, pure colours and daring combinations of them in contrasts capable of creating unexpected effects in a hospital world that historically had been characterized by the sterility of white and that had no tradition of prioritizing ambient and entertaining surroundings for patients.

Gernes was also aware, however, that powerful colour clashes might produce a shock effect. For him, the shock strategy was a manipulative experience capable of rocking the viewer's mental equilibrium and offering an opportunity to "put something in."[16] He underscored this point in connection with the mixed reactions to the colour environments in the pilot module of the Herlev Wing. By "shock," he means both an actual startle and an experience that more closely corresponds to the encounter with the sublime.[17] As Gernes saw it, by providing a surprise and a sense of being overwhelmed, the work can open up new perspectives and a new form of recognition in the viewer. Accordingly, his reflections tie into a debate about contemporary art in the healthcare sector that has not subsided since the 1970s.

CONTEMPORARY ART IN HOSPITAL SETTINGS: IS IT GOOD FOR THE PATIENT?

In the current debate about healing architecture, two positions are emerging on whether art in hospitals can have a positive effect on patients. One position, which in the following I will call "challenging," is represented by the two art-engaged chief physicians, Ib Hessov and Lars Heslet, who contend that art's inherent power to create experiences, generate reflection and stimulate thought and discussion is essential to patients' well-being.[18] In this is a fundamental belief that art, if it is good art, naturally will contain such challenging qualities and thus have healing potential, whether the art is classic or modern, light or dark, dramatic or muted, abstract or narrative. In hospitals, there is "a wide scope for art, but it should never be innocuous," Hessov says.[19]

The other position I will here call "soothing" because it focuses on art's potential to help improve the condition of patients. It is notably represented by Roger S. Ulrich, an American scholar of healthcare architecture. In studies asking patients what types of picture they would prefer to be surrounded with during their hospital stay, the method of evidence-based design has been used to examine whether images have a positive effect on inpatients.[20] A distinction is

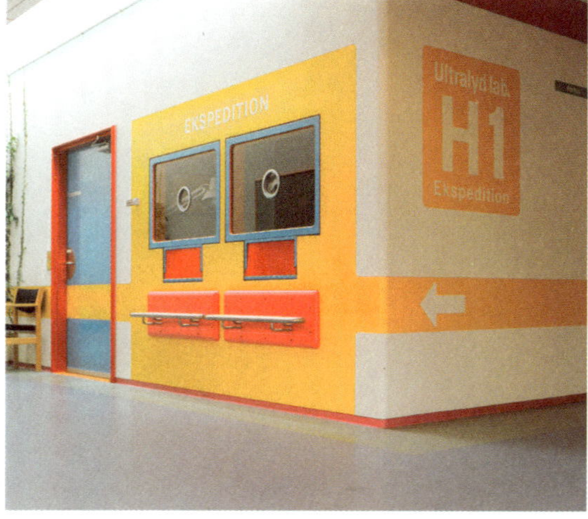

fig. 3

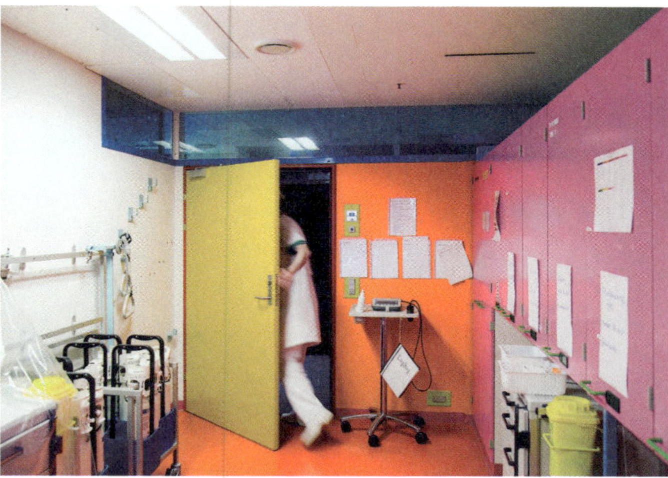

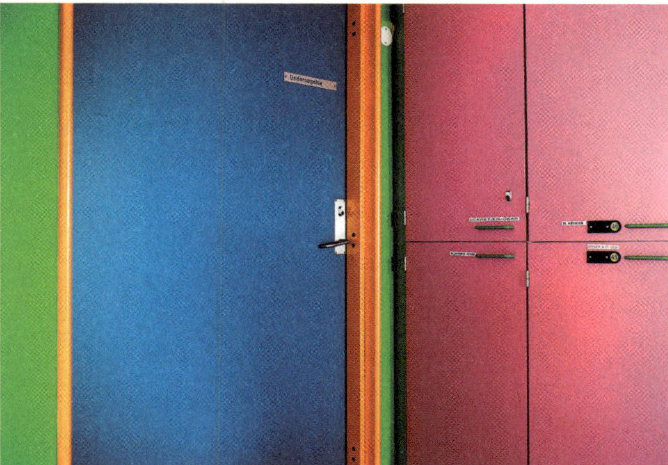

fig. 4

fig. 5

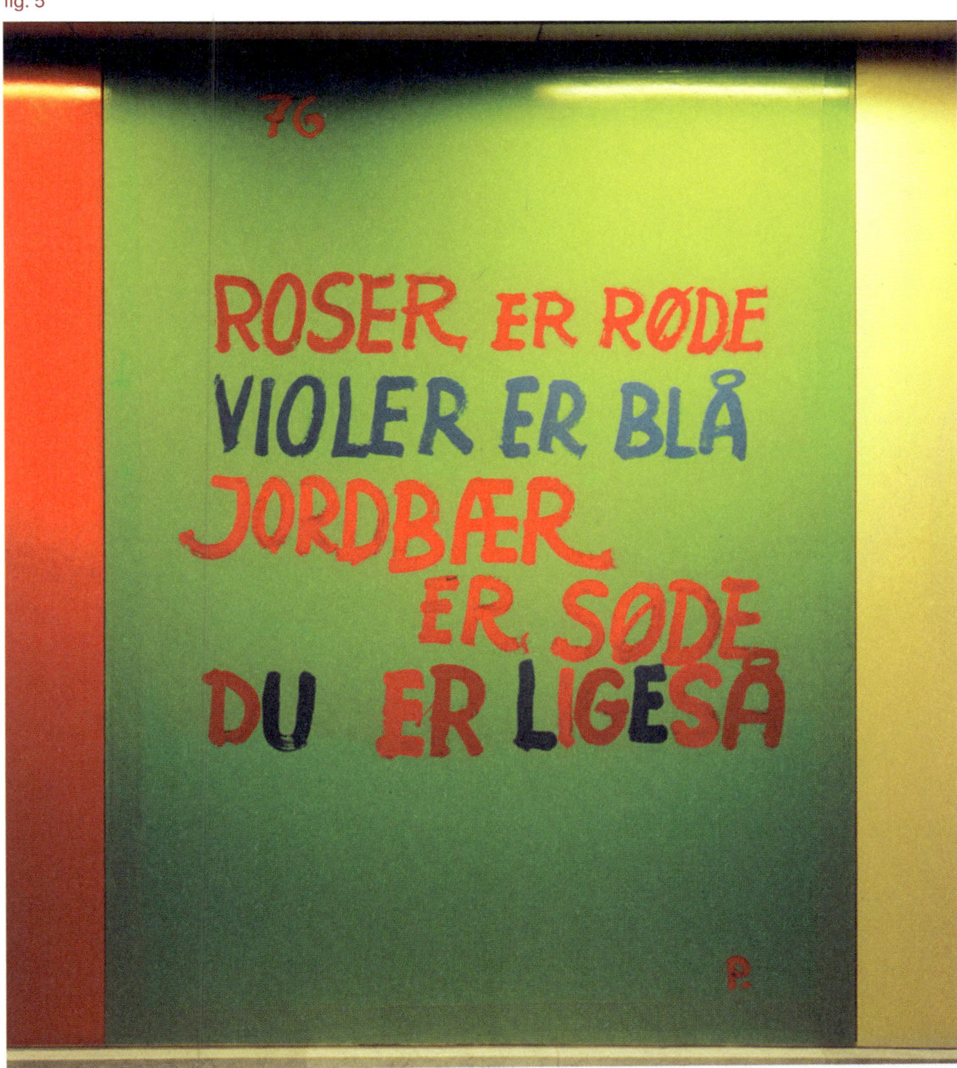

made here between "evidence-based images," the term for the category of images that patients picked as their preferred subject matter, and other forms of visual art. Knowledge gained from these evidence-based studies has resulted in recommendations for landscape and nature subjects, typically what might be called welcoming subjects with open foregrounds and distant views, as well as still-lives of healthy, green plants, rather than abstract pictures or other kinds of subject matter containing an ambiguity that is judged to be unsuitable for delicate, frail patients.[21]

While the challenging position methodologically represents the somewhat laid-back humanistic attitude that you cannot test your way to knowledge of how good art affects the receiver, the soothing position is predicated on evidence-based studies endeavouring to produce measurable documentation and predictable results – that is, knowledge that can relatively seamlessly be inserted into a hospital sector that needs to have the knowledge articulated within its own scientific, evidence-based discourse in order to recognize and incorporate it into its organization.

At the risk of oversimplifying, these two positions, or polar extremes, on the healing potential of art in the healthcare sector can be summarized as follows: one is a position that rests on evidence-based images and has a special focus on art's ability to create a safe and soothing setting for sick and frail patients. It is rooted in an art view that associates images with pleasure and diversion, representing a pre-modern view of art as linked to beauty. The other position, conversely, focuses on "good art," viewing art's power to be challenging as the most important aspect of its healing potential.[22] Behind it can be discerned the contours of a modern art view rooted in the avant-garde tradition that sees art, in part, as shock and transgression.[23]

THE HERLEV DECORATION AND THE POSITIONS OF HEALING ARCHITECTURE

Moving away from the current discourse on the healing potential of art in the hospital sector and roughly 40 years back in time, Gernes' decoration of Herlev Hospital can arguably be seen to embrace both positions. Gernes' concept of entertainment quality seems to fall between the soothing and the challenging, since he oscillated between the poles of comfort and shock. On the one hand, he believed the hospital was a place "that should be pleasant, that should be an experience for the people staying in it," for example by means of uplifting and life-affirming colours. On the other hand, he thought that shock, as elicited by bright colours and stark colour contrasts, could challenge and even provoke the observer or patient to think in new and different ways.[24]

In terms of methods, a lot would indicate that Gernes sides with the position that does not find it relevant to gather evidence from users. This, despite the fact that, before it was decided to implement phase two of the decoration, a step was taken to build an actual pilot module with patient rooms and treatment areas at Gentofte Hospital.[25] As noted in Pedersen's interview, Gernes made two crucial demands of himself when he started on the Herlev decoration. One was to "make the colours pop," a demand that naturally tied into the artist's focus on entertainment quality and his belief that it could be enhanced by bright, contrasting colours. The other condition was that "he had to get it approved."[26] It seems apparent here that the artist was not driven by an interest in evidence. What drove him, more likely, was getting official approval and the ensuing peace to do his work. This motivation is confirmed in Ulrikka Gernes and Peter Michael Hornung's account of the process surrounding the Herlev decoration. As they point out, a lot of people were eagerly waiting for the reactions to the pilot module, but not Gernes. "He knew the answer in advance," they write, and he was never in doubt that colours had both "a preventive and a healing effect."[27]

A COMPLEX PROCESS BEHIND BRIGHT COLOURS

If we look more closely at the cognitive process behind the colour theory underlying Gernes' work on the colour scheme for Herlev Hospital, however, the artist employed a multitude of observations and conceptions that indicate both positions in the current discourse on art's healing potential in the hospital sector. Speaking to Pedersen, the artist articulated a colour theory comprising three factors that together determine what colours best suit a room: 1) the room's dimensions and, possibly, the location of its light aperture, 2) its orientation, and 3) function.[28]

Even so, it is also apparent that Gernes went with his gut first when deciding what colours worked best in the pilot module at Gentofte Hospital. Then, once he could distinguish a pattern in his more intuitively produced systems, he specified his colour theory. This was the case with the often cited factor 2), by which the room's orientation relative to the points of the compass determined the colours of the walls and patient closets. According to Pedersen, this reasoning was only partially supported by architecture critic Steen Ejler Rasmussen's observations that warm colours should face south and cool colours north.[29] The final colour organization shown in the sketch was a development of these ideas, which only emerged after Gernes had analysed the pilot module. The sketch showing the floor plan of the inpatient tower (composed of six separate towers), clarifies the system that Gernes' process resulted in. The walls and patient closets in the rooms of the two north-facing towers were given cool colours, blue and green, while the rooms in the south-facing towers were given warm colours, red and orange. Walls and closets in the tower with east-facing rooms would be yellow, while western-facing rooms would be apricot. The purpose of combining cool and warm colours with the corresponding cool, northern light and warm, southern light was to give the colours the greatest possible intensity, making them look as pure and strong as possible.

Hence, there are arguably elements of the divergent methods of both positions in the colour theory that Gernes developed during his work with the pilot module in Gentofte and that became the key device in his decoration of Herlev Hospital.[30] Indeed, it is this complexity in the underlying method and colour theory, as well as in the art view and expected effect, that makes Gernes' masterwork at Herlev Hospital so interesting and relevant. His decoration embraces and anticipates a substantial part of the expectations and attitudes that are exchanged today concerning the healing potential of contemporary art. Emphasizing either soothing or challenging effects, views of how to qualify art in the hospital sector oscillate between a traditional, humanistic method and a more scientifically oriented method.

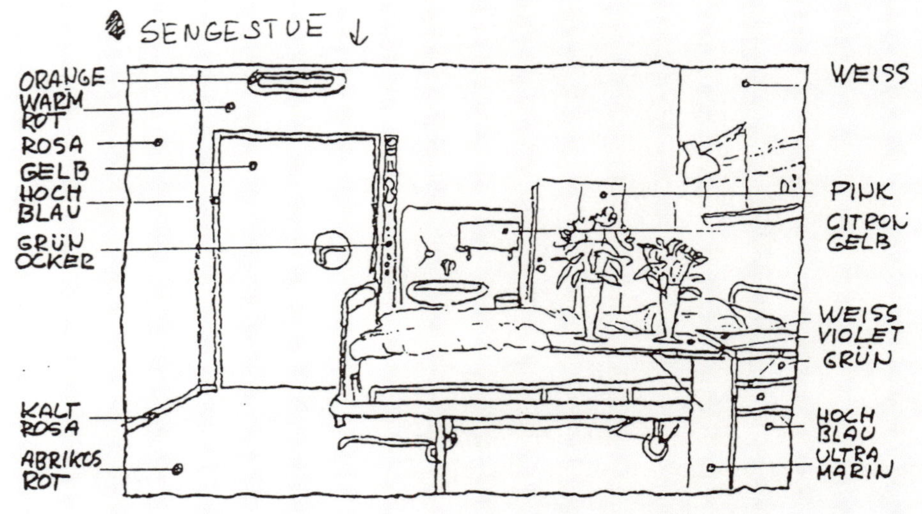

fig. 6

fig. 7

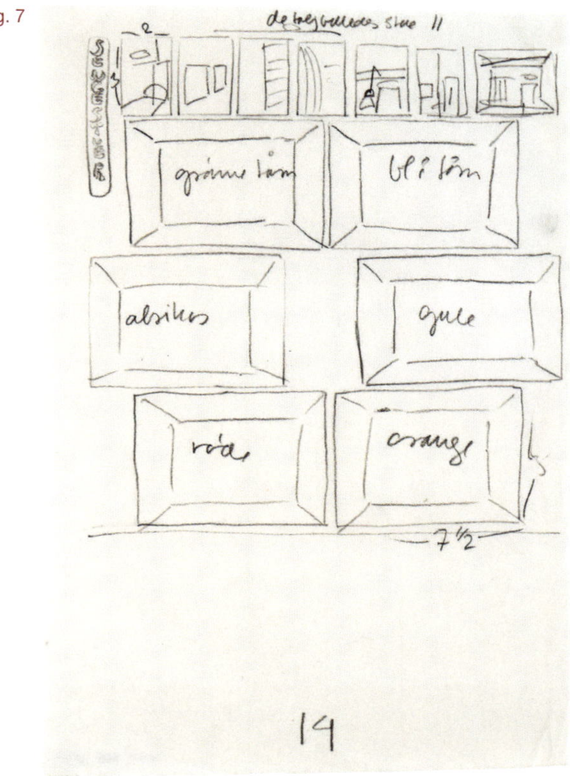

fig. 8

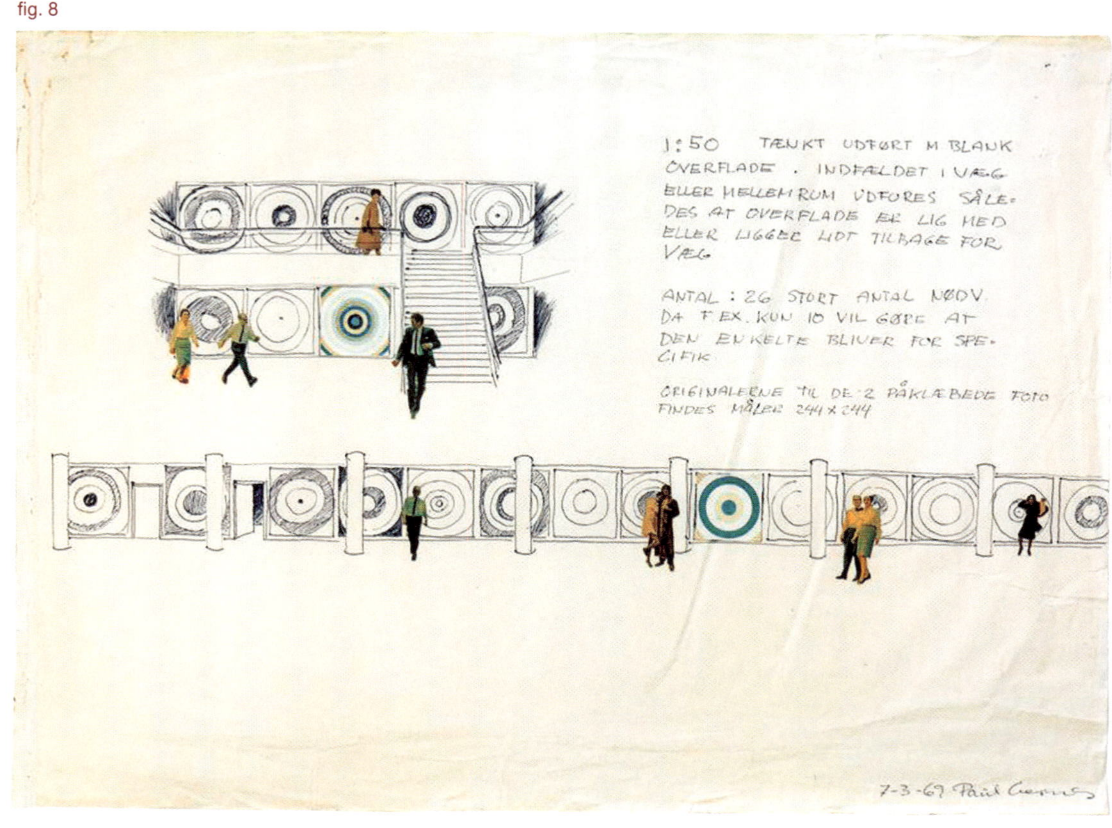

fig. 9

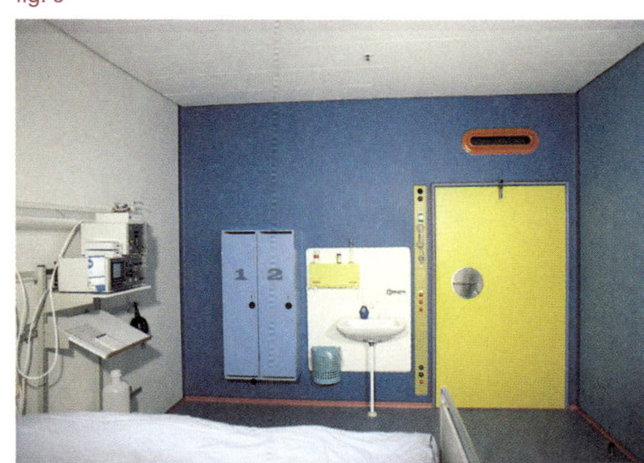

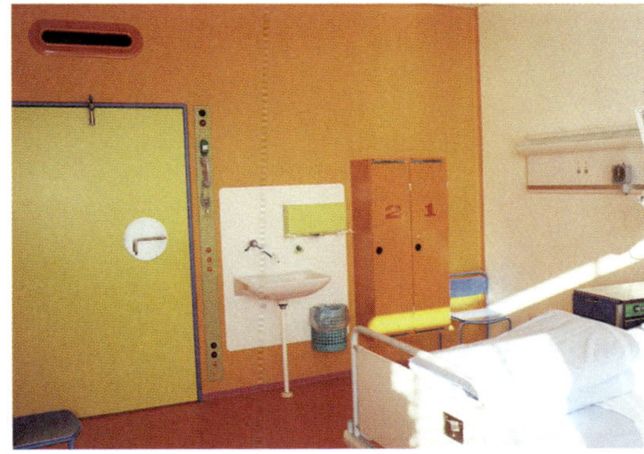

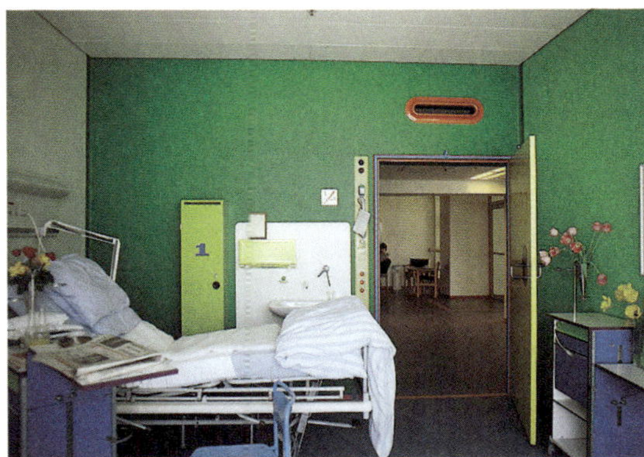

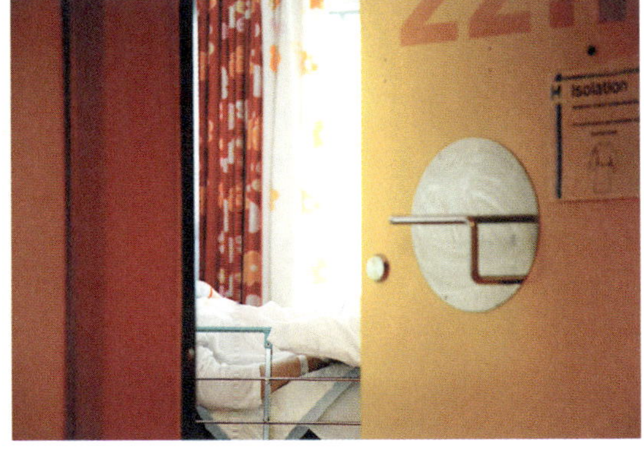

COMFORT AND CHALLENGE IN A BOUNDLESS WORK

Boundless not just in its physical extension but also in its countless colours and bold colour contrasts, Gernes' decoration of Herlev Hospital speaks to the familiar notion that "happy" and "lively" colours can be a seamless strategy for comfort and relief. Moreover, it fulfils expectations that art may be challenging, prompt reflection and stimulate thought – indeed, in certain contexts even startle and jolt the observers, whether it leads them to fear they have had a stroke or engenders an upbeat mood that makes them long for a bar.

Moving from the colour schemes of the tower's inpatient wards and down into the hospital lobby, we are confronted with the same kind of bright, pure colours that Gernes himself and the current discourse of healing architecture find life-affirming. In their simplicity and familiarity, the motifs of the frieze of panels in the lobby (chessboard, compass rose, flag, paper cutting, poetry verse, etc.) can likewise be experienced as welcoming. At the same time, however, the ubiquitous abstract circle motifs clearly provide no easily accessible, atmospheric landscapes to soothingly disappear into. As the text on the preliminary work shows, Gernes weighted the anonymous and impersonal, both in artistic expression and in subject matter, not wanting the individual subject to be too specific. Thus, by ambiguity and an element of the unexpected, challenge has also found a place in the hospital lobby.

In the decades that followed, there are, of course, numerous examples of Danish artists picking up the mantle from Herlev Hospital. Gernes' vast, lavish, sprawling decoration and colour design appear to have been a source of inspiration for a number of powerful and distinct colour schemes and decorations that have broken up the clinical predictability of spaces, creating landmarks and identity in functional hospital buildings.[31] As we move up to the decorations that are currently in the pipeline for Denmark's new super-hospitals, the radical boldness that informed Gernes' efforts is still evident.[32] Not least in how the artist dared – and, just as important, got the opportunity – to get close to patients with his distinct colour scheme for the furniture and walls of inpatient wards. The new projects show a trend towards monumental decorations generally being integrated into arrival areas and common areas, and gradually receding as we move towards the patient areas. In several places, inpatient wards entirely without art are being planned or far more understated art solutions are in play, including plans to give long-term inpatients the opportunity to pick works themselves from the hospitals' existing art collections.[33] Such solutions can create successful opportunities for answering varied and individual needs. Still, moderately sized framed prints are a long way from the explosive shot of vitamins that Gernes' wall and furniture colours were intended to be for patients who have close encounters with them.

Poul Gernes' overarching ambition to humanize the hospital environment by creating a colourful alternative to the technological hospital with its white walls and mechanical equipment in many ways mirrors today's notions that art should contribute to humanizing the hospital sector.[34] In its multifaceted potential to soothe and challenge, in its ambition that healing colours would make a difference to patients up close, Gernes' total decoration in Herlev is a milestone of Danish decoration history. Indeed, the driving force behind the project's enormous colouristic outburst of energy was "the medicine of colours," as Ulrikka S. Gernes and Peter Michael Hornung put it in the title of their 2003 publication about the decoration. It is this motivation, in particular, that gives the decoration the continued power to inspire and nuance debates on the potential of contemporary art within the framework of healing architecture.

Lene Bøgh Rønberg (b. 1965), PhD, Art History, Curator at KØS Museum of Art in Public Spaces. Specializing in art in public space, Rønberg has curated research-based exhibitions on memorials today and contemporary art in churches. She is currently working on a research and exhibition project on contemporary art in hospitals.

1   The title of the article, "Det er direkte usundt at leve farveløst," is a quote by Poul Gernes from an internal report he wrote in 1989 during his professorship at the Royal Danish Academy of Fine Arts. See Camilla Jalving (ed.), *Stedsans. 25 indgange til kunsten derude*. Strandberg Publishing, 2014, p. 125.

2   Povl Sabroe, "Kunstner fylder hospital med festlige og humørfyldte farver," in *Ekstra Bladet*, 18 November 1970.

3   Jørgen Selchau, "Københavns Amtssygehus i Herlev," in *Arkitektur*, No. 5, Vol. 21, 1977, p. 206.

4   I would like to thank two colleagues at the KØS Museum of Art in Public Spaces, director Christine Buhl Andersen and postdoctoral researcher Sabine Dahl Nielsen, for thoroughly reading this essay and for their fruitful comments. For more on the discourse on healing architecture, see p. 42. Key Danish publications in this area of knowledge and research are Anne Katrine Frandsen et al., *Helende arkitektur*. Aalborg University, Dept. of Architecture, Design and Media Technology, Skriftserie No. 29 (2009); Lars Heslet and Kim Dirckinck-Holmfeld (eds.), *Sansernes Hospital* (2007); Ib Hessov, *Kunst giver liv. Om kunst på sygehuse* (2005); and Lars Juel Thiis, "Kunsten i arkitekturen. Om kunst, mursten og den menneskelige dimension," in Jalving, 2014, p. 132ff. The discourse has moreover left a distinct imprint on the art strategies that are currently being devised in connection with the expensive hospital construction projects underway in Denmark. See, e.g., Lars Grambye and Inger Krogh, *Kunststrategi Sygehus Sønderjylland og Psykiatri Aabenraa*. Statens Kunstfond, 2011. The article looks at how several of the above publications, to a remarkable extent and despite the distance in time, make reference to Gernes' decoration of Herlev Hospital. The article thus supplements the literature on the decoration of Herlev Hospital, central contributions to which include the following: Ulrikka S. Gernes and Peter Michael Hornung, *Farvernes medicin. Poul Gernes og Amtssygehuset i Herlev* (2003); Erik Steffensen, *Poul Gernes monografi* (2000); and articles on the decoration in three of the major surveys of art in public space in Denmark that have been published over the last 50 years: Leila Krogh, *Kunst i rummet* (1989); Christine Buhl Andersen and Ulrikke Neergaard, *Det' vores kunst. Statens Kunstfonds projekter i det offentlige rum set med danskernes øjne*. Exhibition catalogue from KØS Museum of Art in Public Spaces (2010); and Camilla Jalving (ed.), *Stedsans. 25 indgange til kunsten derude* (2014). Furthermore should be mentioned architect Sven Felding's *Herlev Hospital som kulturarv. Bevaringsplan*, which was prepared in 2014 in extension of the public debate following the removal of the colour scheme in the renovation of the fourth floor of the inpatient tower. Like the artist's own 1983 colour manual for the hospital, Felding's manual contains crucial knowledge about the principles underlying the artistic colour design of Herlev Hospital.

5   Gernes and Hornung, 2003, p. 31.

6   Steffensen, 2000, p. 152.

7   I am grateful to Ulrikke Neergaard for information about the number. See also Finn Thybo Andersen's upcoming publication documenting Gernes' impressive work in decorations.

8   Bjørn Nørgaard, in Poul Gernes (ed.), *Poul Gernes på Sophienholm*. Exhibition catalogue, 1979, last page, no page numbers.

9   Ibid.

10   Heslet and Dirckinck-Holmfeld, 2007, p. 198, and Part I, p. 13-130.

11   Frandsen et al., 2009, p. 3, 7.

12   Frandsen et al., 2009, p. 3, 7 and 63. It should be noted, however, that the report also points out that, overall, very little scientific documentation exists for the measurable or experienced effects of visual art in the healthcare sector (Frandsen et al., 2009, p. 63), which an ongoing research project at the KØS Museum of Art in Public Spaces intends to remedy.

13   Numerous sources confirm this, variously phrased, see, e.g., the artist's text "Lidt om farve – skole – miljø," in *Gymnasieskolen*, Vol. 73, 1990, p. 34.

14   A large part of the following account of Gernes' reflections on the colours in his decoration of Herlev Hospital is based on art librarian Jane Pedersen's interview book, *Der er dejligt i Danmark*. The book's source materials include tape recordings of her interviews with the artist in spring 1971. He is quoted both directly and indirectly (Jane Pedersen, 1971, p. 7-8), and the extent of the interviewer's interpretation of the source material accordingly varies. I would like to thank Kristian Handberg for information about Jane Pedersen's role during this period and about the publication's importance as a primary source from the period.

15   Pedersen, 1971, p. 110. See also the artist's "Notat om farver, textiler, miljø mm. til brug for Københavns Amtssygehus i Herlev," cited in Gernes and Hornung, 2003, p. 22.

16   Pedersen, 1971, p. 38-39.

17   As when "a sunset can be so captivating that it borders on shock," Jane Pedersen, 1971, p. 39. At this point in the interview, Pedersen directly asks how the artist's overarching thoughts on shock relate to users' mixed, sometimes shocked, reactions to his colour environment at the pilot module in Gentofte, cf. the quoted reactions in the opening of this essay.

18   Heslet and Dirckinck-Holmfeld, 2007, see, e.g., p. 280ff. Ib Hessov, 2005, see, e.g., p. 71-72.

19   Hessov, 2005, p. 71-72. On the theory of "good art," see also Anne-Mette Gravgaard, *Tro, rum, billede. Kunst i kirken. Overvejelser og eksempler*, 2002, p. 28.

20   See Roger Ulrich, "Effects on viewing art on health outcomes," in Susan Frampton et al (ed.), *Putting Patients First. Best Practice in Patient-Centered Care*, 2009, p. 129ff.; Kathy Hathorn and Nanda Upali, *A Guide to Evidence-based Art*. The Center for Health Design, California, 2008; and Karen Frandsen, Tanya Juhl Jensen and Anja Holm Nyland, "Selvvalgt kunst som positiv distraktion på patientstuen," in *Klinisk Sygepleje*, Vol. 28, No. 4, 2014, p. 16-28.

21   For a summary of these positions, see Karsten Andersen, "Samtidskunst på sygehuset – er det godt for patient-en?," http://www.sonovision.dk/kunst-sygehuse.asp. See also Ulrich 2009, p. 133; Hathorn and Upali, 2008, p. 11; and Frandsen, Juhl Jensen and Holm Nyland, 2014, p. 25. I am grateful to Lars Brorson Fich for information about international research on the subject. Obviously, these studies of evidence-based images provide little information about building-integrated contemporary art, since they have so far been conducted mainly using two-dimensional images and, in the case of some of the studies, it has not been documented according to what criteria the works were selected or whether the works in question are actual visual art, see, e.g., Frandsen Juhl Jensen and Holm Nyland, 2014. An ongoing research project at the KØS Museum of Art in Public Spaces is more closely studying this field.

22   Obviously, a number of nuanced positions exist between the two. From the position of good art, it is also argued that art should be considerate of frail patients and not contain too aggressive a message or too graphically depict unpleasant subject matter, see, e.g., Hessov, 2003, p. 72. However, the works' challenge strategy is emphasized more there than in theopposite position. As the objective here is to consider the Gernes decoration in the light of the two divergent positions, stressing the difference between them is a methodological point.

23   See Peter Bürger, *Theory of the Avant-Garde, Theory and History of Literature*, Vol. 4, 1984; and Robert Hughes, *The Shock of the New*, Second Edition, 1991.

24   Pedersen, 1971, p. 110.

25   For a more detailed description of the test module in Gentofte, see Gernes and Hornung, 2003, p. 17ff.

26   Pedersen, 1971, p. 108.

27   Gernes and Hornung, 2003, p. 19.

28   Pedersen, 1971, p. 109.

29   Pedersen, 1971, p. 108-109.

30   Jane Pedersen's interviews include several examples of Gernes' colour theory moving between artistic intuition, systems based on his personal experience, external series that he incorporates and adjusts, and common culturally inherited views reflected in the language, as when he refers to the colour associations linked to expressions like "boudoir red," see Pedersen, 1971, p. 108-113. The partly systematized, partly intuitive colour theory that emerges in the period around the Herlev decoration is, naturally, far too complex to unfold in these limited pages.

31   Among the most important decorations that in exemplary and original ways draw on the heritage of Gernes' effort at Herlev Hospital can be mentioned Michael Mørk's 2009 decoration and colour design of Randers Hospital, which was expanded in 2014, and Bodil Nielsen's 2005 decoration and colour design of the emergency room at Aarhus University Hospital.

32   It should be emphasized that many of the decorations still exist only in sketch form and that an even greater number have not yet seen the light of day, since several of the buildings have yet to be built. For new hospital constructions and their related art projects, see www. godtsygehusbyggeri.dk and the websites of the individual hospital projects.

33   These include a wide variety of images, from original works to framed reproductions. See, e.g., the study of the art collection at Norway's Akerhus University Hospital, in Beathe C. Rønning and Tone Hansen, "Forskyvninger af logistikk og hygge," in Guri Dahl et al. (eds.), *Mer enn du ser. Om kunst og arkitektur i Akershus Universitetssykehus*, 2008, p. 166ff.

34   See Grambye and Krogh, 2011, p. 6, and Juel Thiis, 2014, p. 135, 139.

fig.10   Single-bed unit at Herlev Hospital, colour scheme by Poul Gernes 1968-76 (reconstructed for Louisiana's exhibition)

South-facing patient room with red walls. The wall behind the patient was the only one that was not coloured. According to the artist, it was left white to allow doctors and nurses to read the patient's facial colour against a neutral backdrop

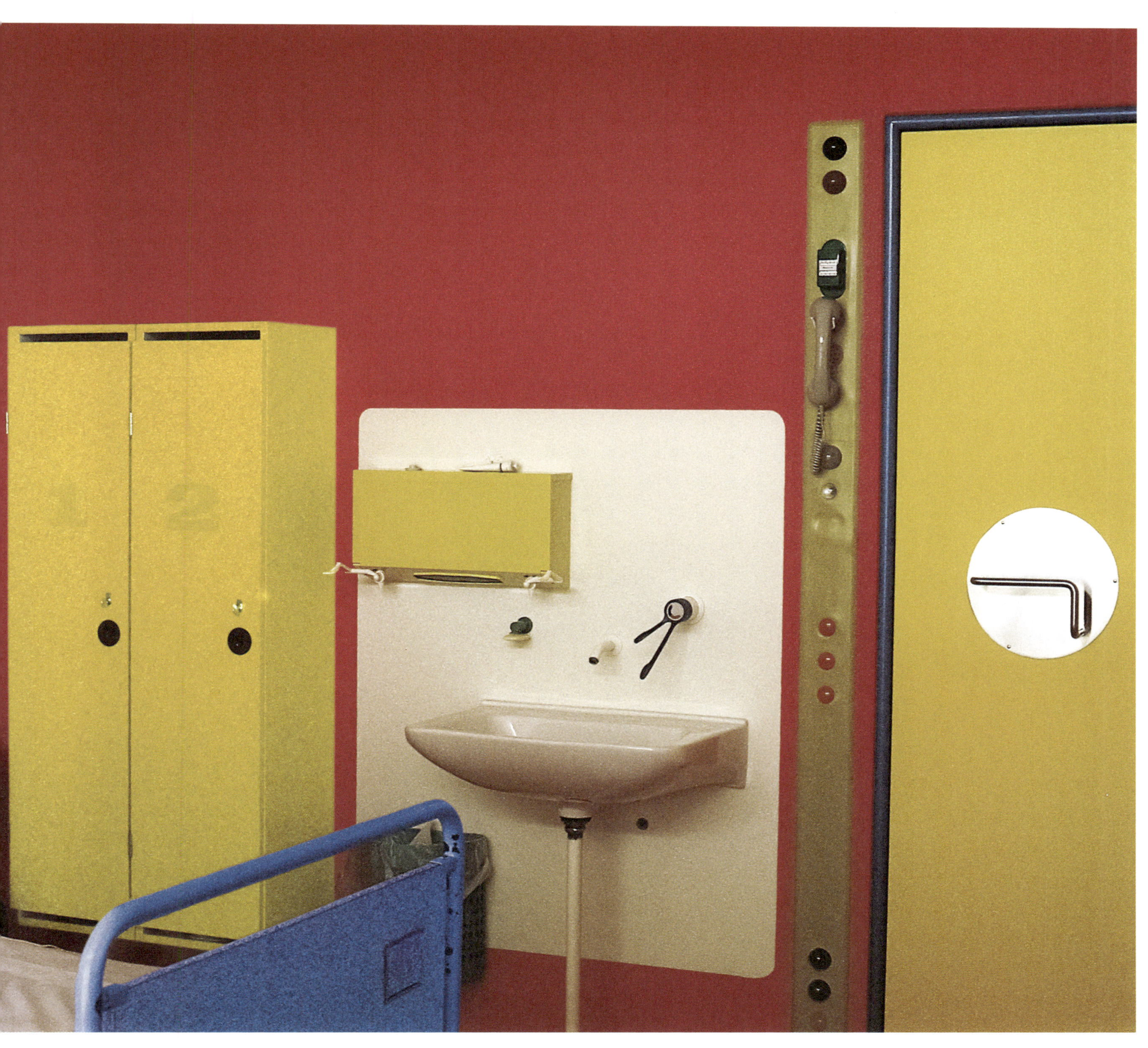

Untitled, 1960
Ink, watercolour on paper, 32 × 48 cm
(detail, see complete work on p. 72)

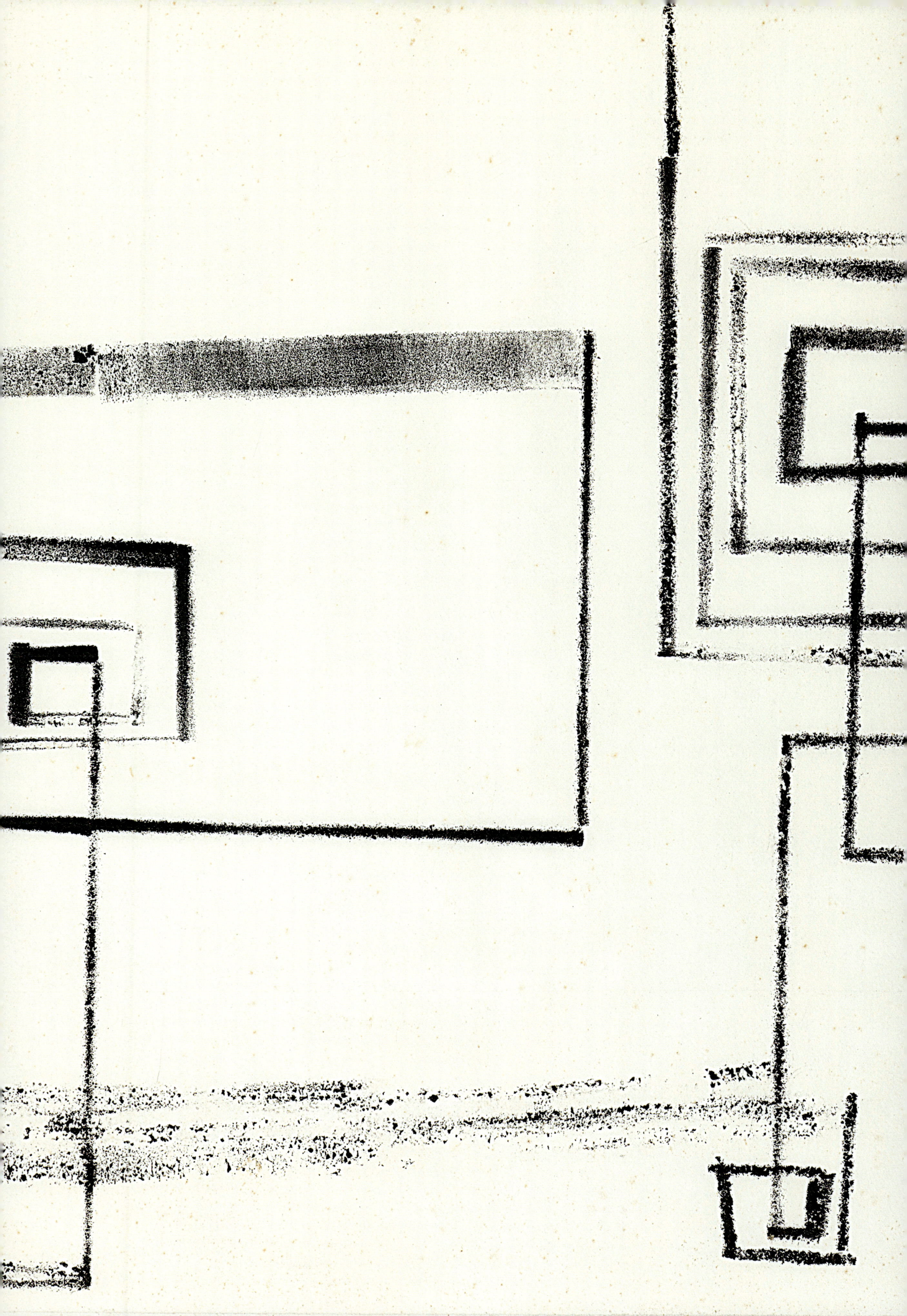

Untitled, (1961)
Oil, collage on newspaper, 56 × 79 cm
(detail, see complete work on p. 77)

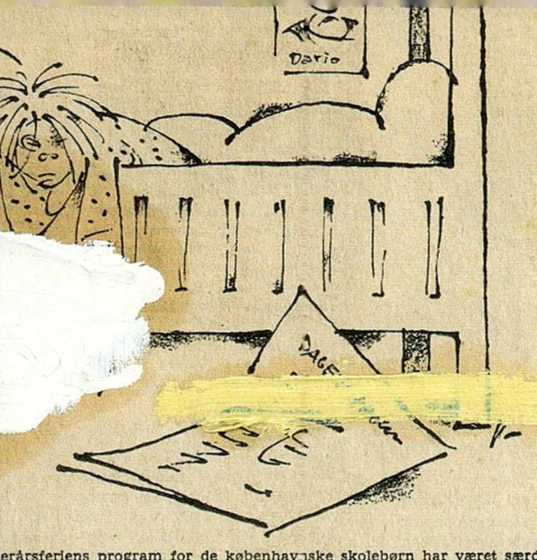

...erårsferiens program for de københavnske skolebørn har været særdeles omfattende.

...nageropvisninger, 3 Ping-film, trykluftsudstillingen, Cirkus Buster, National-... før vi kan komme i skole igen og få hvilet ud ...

på alle
nallerten
kelstien

e trafikbestemmelser

...gade. Farten sættes ikke ned, fordi det er for besværligt at skulle træde maskinen i gang igen med pedalerne. — Vi er klar over, at der er et ... her, og vi har også haft ... under overvejelse, men det ... ordnes administrativt uden ... Det er rigtigt, at dette ... en stor risiko.

Er 30 km for lidt?

I mange ... lande er farten ... for knallerter ... sat til 46 km i timen. Det har ... produktion, der ... kun kan køre 30 km ... vil i ... indvind og op ad den ... tabe så megen fart, at ... lægenommere ved almindelige ... cykler — ude af stand til at føl... normale færdselsrytme. Samtidig ... man skille maskinene helt ad for at konstatere, om de kan køre hurtigere. Kunne kontrollen ikke klares med et simindeligt krav om speedometre på knallerterne. Det ... som så ...

Erhvervsplaner 10 år frem

Tre dages konference med mange emner

Danske Salgslederes Fællesråd, bag hvilket der står en omfattende kreds af kendte folk fra alle grene af erhvervslivet, arrangerer inden længe en tre dages konference, som har til formål at give impulser til erhvervsplanlægnnig en halv snes år frem i tiden.

— Der er et stort behov for viden, som kan danne grundlag for fremtids-bedømmelser, sagde fællesrådets formand, dir. *Asger M. Hirschspru...* i går, og vi vil prøve at imødekom... dette behov. Planerne om Eu...

Kra... dagen før

Konfe... som finder sted i ... den 15., 16. og 17. no... ...er at ville samle næsten ... erhvervsfolk, direktører, ... produktionschefer — man ... dre folk hvem tidens afsæt... ...mål er af største betyd... E... ikke danske eksperter ...butionsforsk..., markedsanalyser, teknisk produktion, ...ende- og personalepolitik, ...ætter og mange andre emner ... ...

Som optakt til konferencen vil udenrigsminister *Jens O...* fællesrådets frokostmøde d... vember opridse nogle hovedlinjer markedsdannelserne.

Den jævne mands "udskejelse"

...ellands-Posten (S) om afgifts-... ...øjelserne:

De... konkrete indhold af regering... ...slag kan naturligvis diskut... ...s. På den nye finansminister be-skyl... nu, ligesom hans forgænger af ... elig partifarve, for at v... ...lide tofindsom" — men spørgs-... et ... ...deobjekter angår, ville blive ... hilst ... bifald.

Re... ...tidligere bleget ha...

Undergravet

... omtale af porto-forhøjel-... ...kritiserer *Roskilde Tidende* ...n service, postvæsenet ... ...avisleverne:

Vi ... ...rer os ved at tro, at trafik-mini... ...n synes, at denne service er tilfre... ...llende endsige berettiget til forh... ...

I ... ...d, hvor mange blade kæm-per ... ...hård kamp, og hvor mange har ... ...t bukke under, vil trafik-mini... ...s forslag derfor yderligere ...grav... ...ansk presses eksistensmulig...

Venstremand frygter for høj kornpris

Venstres formand i hovedsta-den, cand. jur. *Niels Westerby,* udtaler i et interview i *Hus-mandshjemmet* frygt for, at korn-prisen ved De Seks skal blive for høj:

Vi må huske, at det nuværende Fællesmarked — med det i dag gæl-dende prisniveau — er nær ved at være selvforsynende med fødevarer. Vi har interesse i, at forbruget — og dermed vore salgsmuligheder — kan stige. Derfor må Danmark ar-bejde for, at basisprisen for korn i Fællesmarkedet ikke bliver højere, end at forbrugsudvidelse og dermed afsætningsforøgelse for vore for-ædlede produkter bliver mulige. Vi må heller ikke glemme det europæiske prisniveaus betydning for konkurrenceevne *uden for* ...

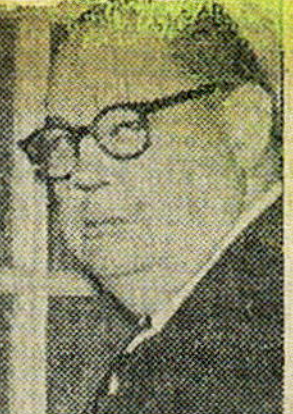

Trafikminister Kai Lindberg

... må endelig ikke genere det brede forbrug, men avisportoen og den del af portoen, som vedrører for-retningsmæssige forsendelser, sæt-tes op. Mere tåbeligt kunne det ikke være.

n landbrugsreform er nødvendig

Af SVEND BERGSØE

...rationalisering, der foregår inden for landbruget... ...gen fra håndværk til industri, siger fabrik... ...skelligere for de små brug at svare e... ...s gennemføres, fordi dansk landbrug e... ...er for vi på landet, og fordi ... brug for arbejdskraft.

På... ...uropæiske tionspriserne. ...at ikke blive ... pital, arbejdskra... af m... ...erne. Smørret bliver frit skal kunne b... dumpe... ...re, Irland og Ar-det særsyn, at d... gen... ...oducere æg. Det hele ved at producere s... ...lendighed. Med en mi-det virkelig rigtigt? ...ntning klarer gårdene ...

Vi kan ikke levere fl... ...nsigten i sin tid, England, end markedet ... ...de mange snk vi leveret fær... ...ulle "gå på a fjor. På månede ...os herremanden 85 øre pr. kg s... ...pet.

Det giver en... ...60.000. ...lioner kroner s... ...narkedet ... ...tes eller så... ...en i det ble-...aner... ...ed... Også har ... ...lande il...satssub-...a af korn til pri-...

ROCK HUDSON med SANDRA ...
...a hans eget produktionsselsk...
RIVIERAEN

...rækken af Hollywood-stjernerne, der ... ...eres egen herre og ... ...ere de film, d... ...drollen i, som H... HUDSON nu opt... ...film "Come Sept...ber", i aft... premie... på Palad... Teatr... under tit... VI MØ-DES ... RIVIERAEN

Gyldendal

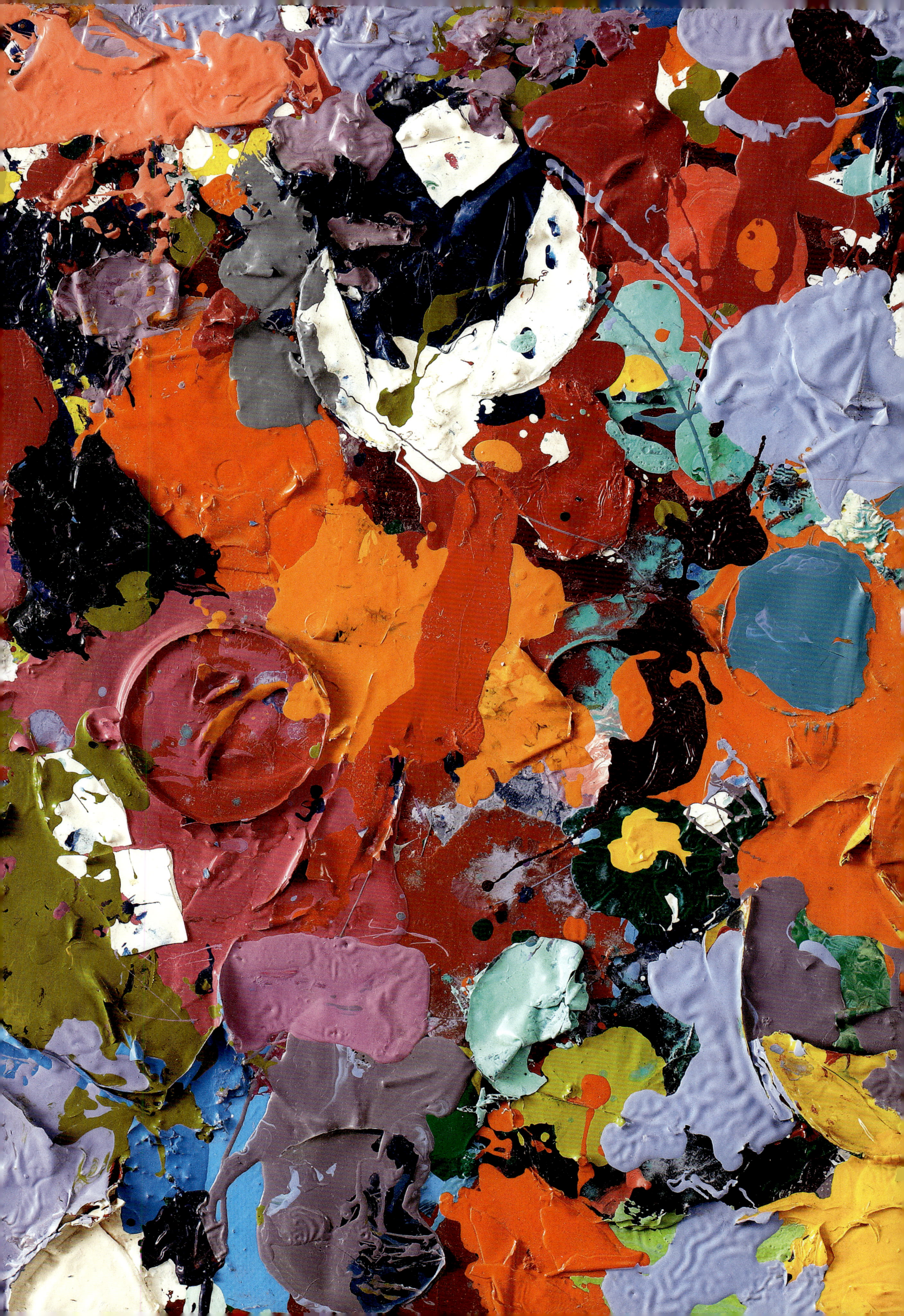

Untitled, 1966-67
Enamel paint on cardboard, collage
Series of 36 works, each 100 × 100 cm
(detail, see complete work on p. 38)

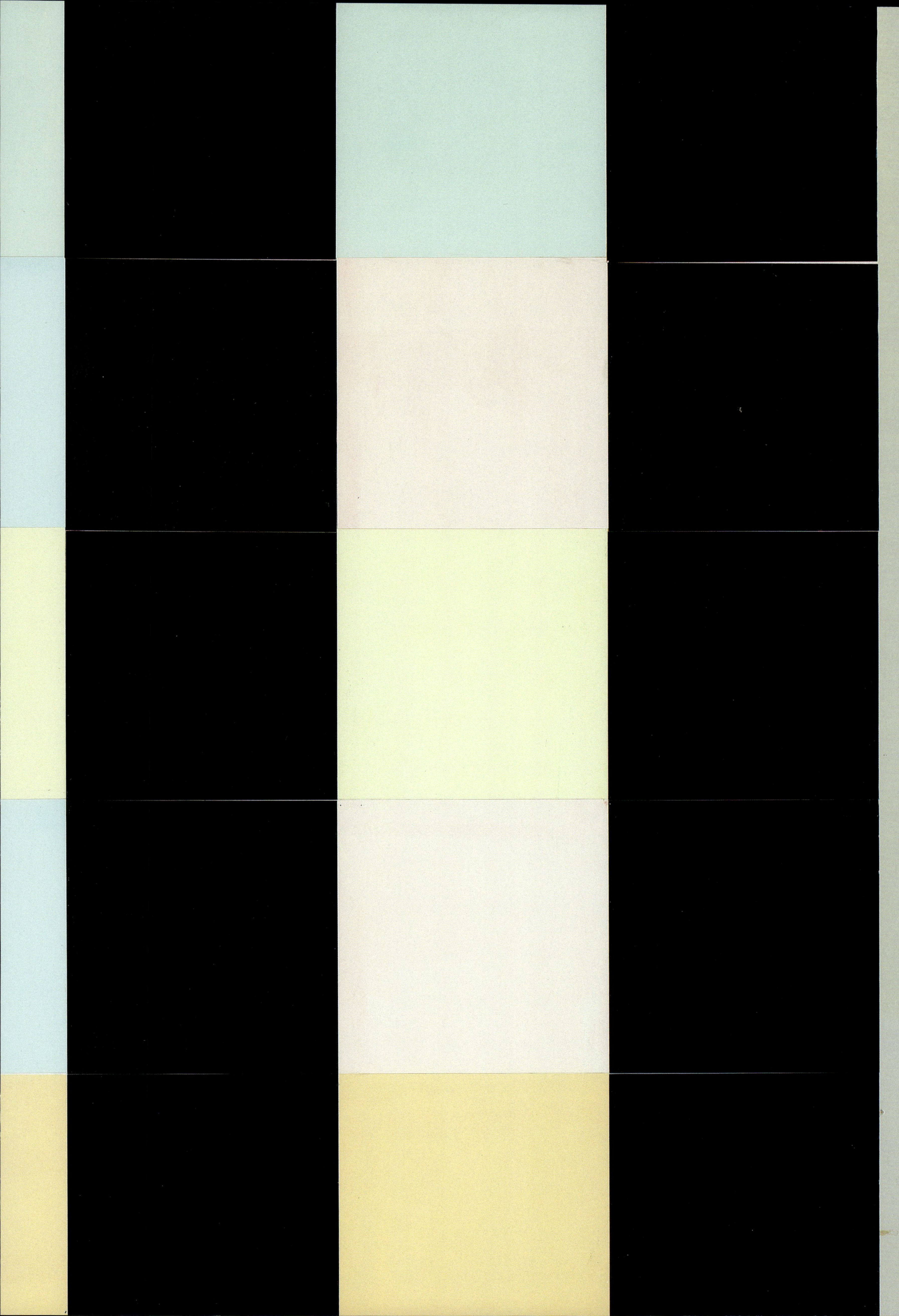

Untitled, 1962
Enamel paint on wood (Bedpost),
90 × 130 × 9 cm
(detail, see complete work on p. 79)

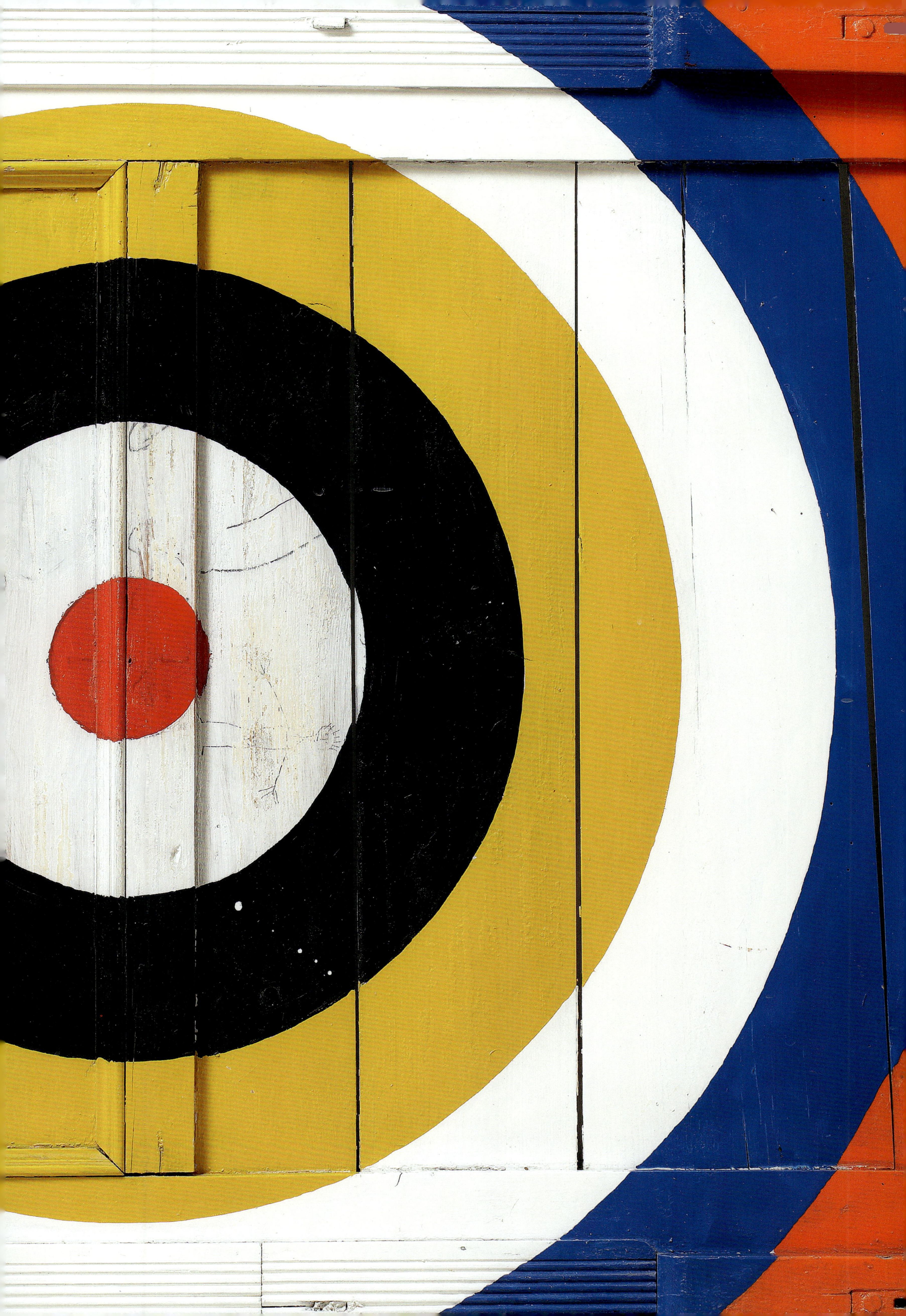

Untitled (Z), 1965
(The Alphabet Series)
Enamel paint and hair on masonite,
160 × 130 cm
(detail, see complete work on p. 12)

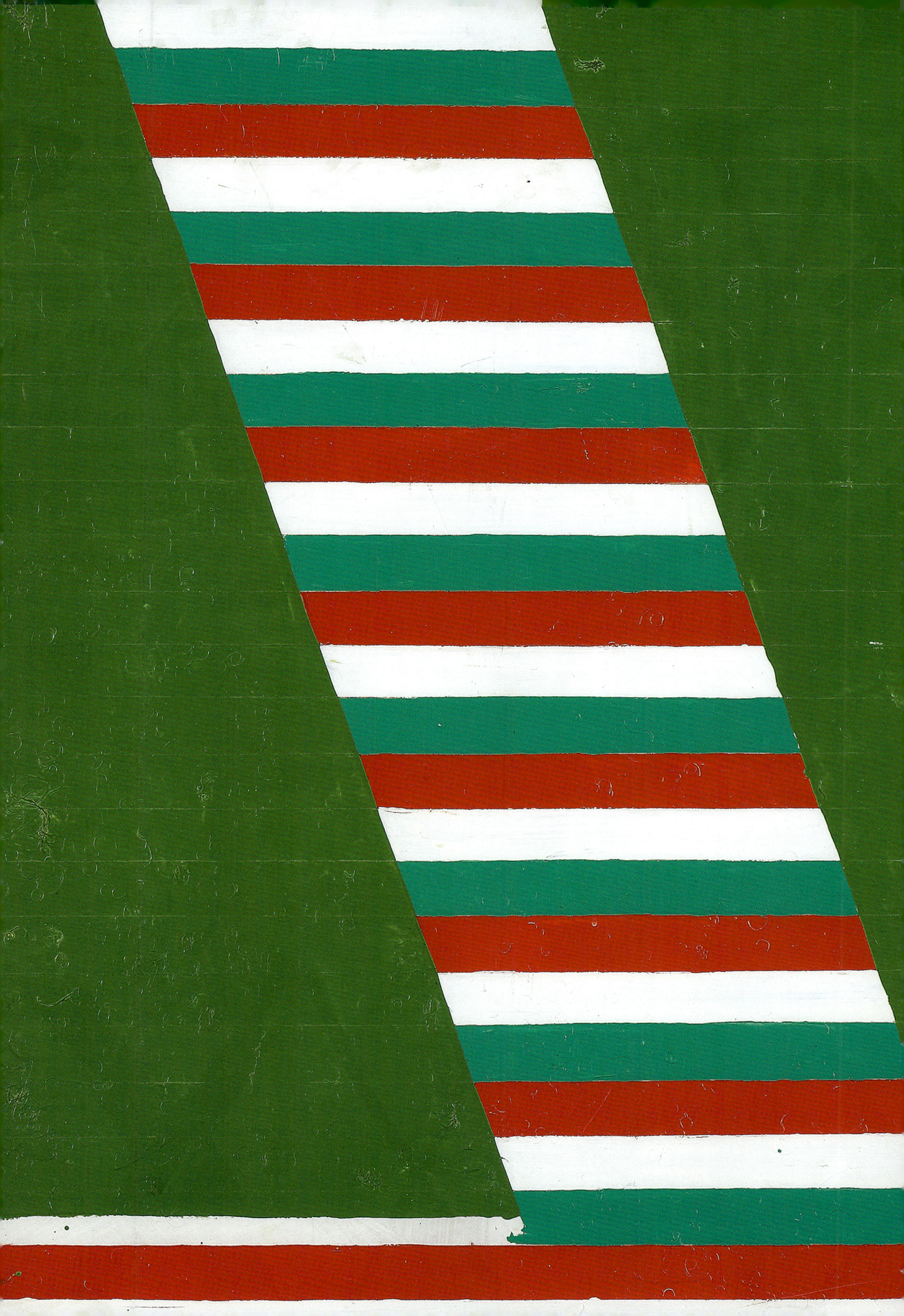

Untitled ("Ass"), 1967
Plaster and cardboard, 57 × 47 × 24 cm
(detail, see complete work on p. 24)

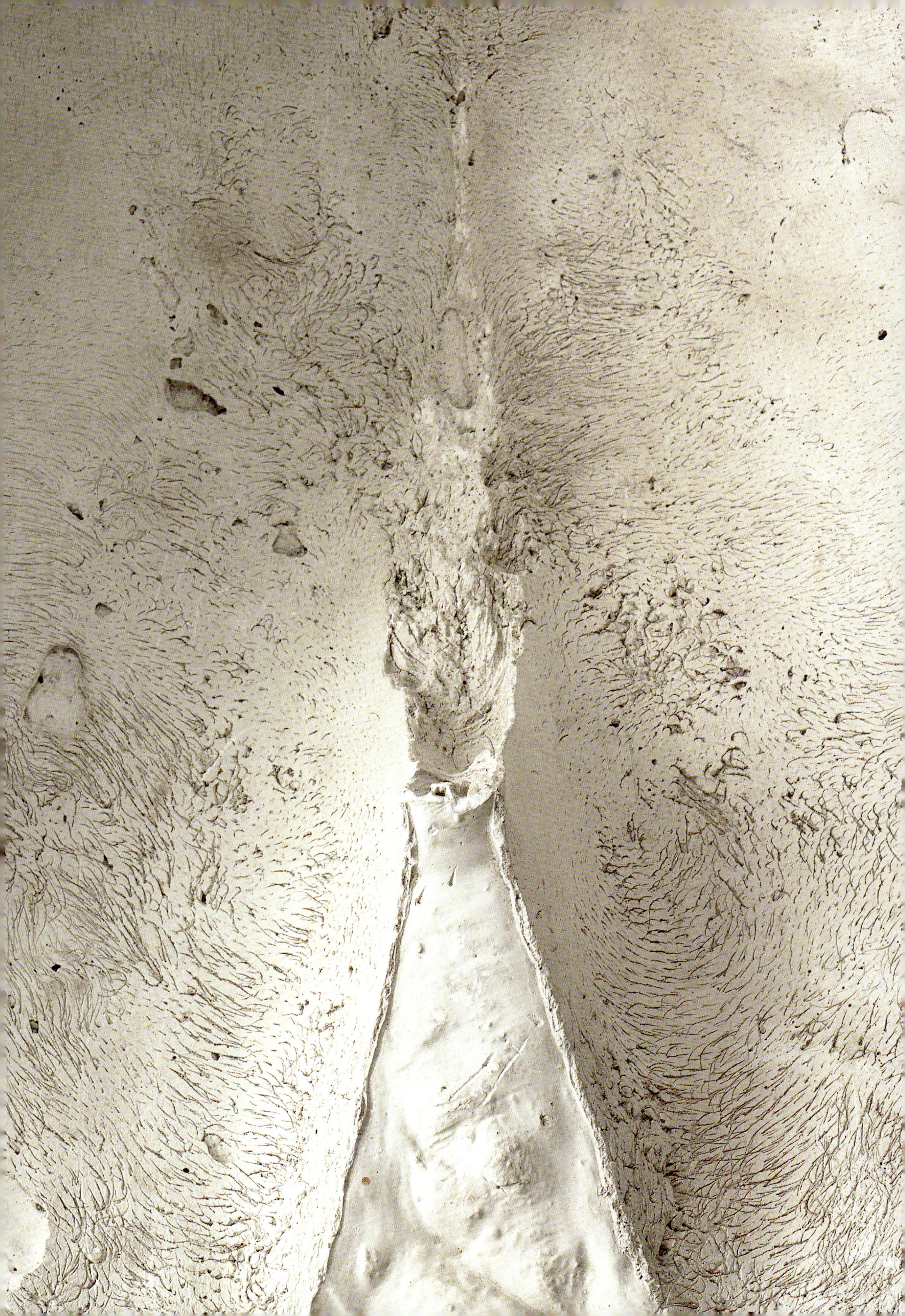

Art as a Collective
Poul Gernes as the Architect of the 1960s Fusion of Art and Life

By Kristian Handberg

fig.1-2 Eks-skolen's printing experiments on Kgs. Nytorv, Copenhagen, September 1962

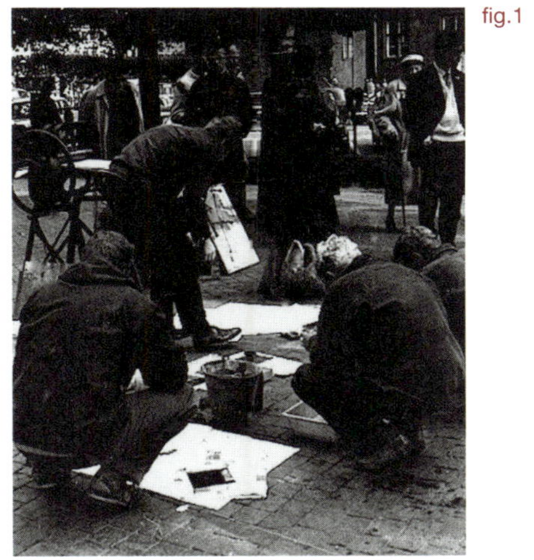

fig.1

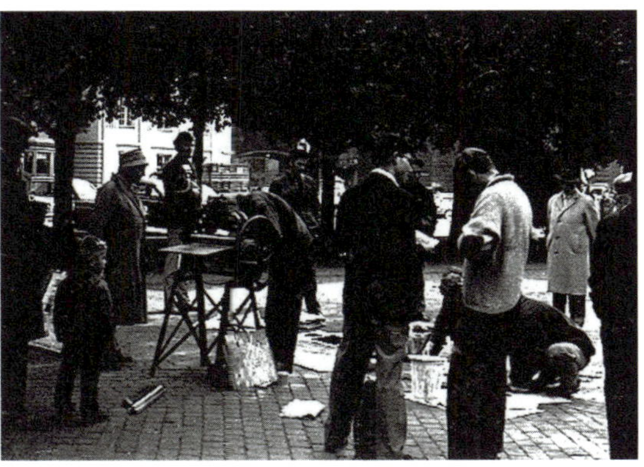

fig.2

"Social responsibility" was the central demand when Poul Gernes, with the art historian Troels Andersen, took the initiative to found The Experimental Art School, also called Eks-skolen, in 1961.[1] With this initiative Poul Gernes assumed a crucial role in the art explosion of the 1960s in Denmark, and in fact it was only with Eks-skolen that Gernes himself acknowledged a status for himself as an artist and became a recognized part of the art environment. Afterwards it became his ambition to create a new aesthetics that involved everyday life in art – in short, art as a way of life. This article takes its point of departure in the collectivity that surrounded Eks-skolen's art scene in the 1960s – the decade that the avant-garde researcher Tania Ørum has characterized as an "avant-garde period that breaks down old forms, experiments with new models and leaves behind a wake of indignation, nostalgia and influence."[2] The following will also shed light on Gernes' various experiments with uniting art and life: from do-it-yourself graphics of industrial primitiveness through collages that filled the whole space with segments of reality, to his well-known colourful decorations of the buildings of the welfare society. When we add to this the development of Danish art's most important artist-run school, a wealth of experiments with exhibition forms and even the building of communal family houses, we get an idea of the range of the work of the master-builder of experimental art, Poul Gernes.

EKS-SKOLEN UNDERSTOOD AS A SCENE

The residents of central Copenhagen quickly saw something of Eks-skolen: in September 1962 a new term began with a sensational event on the public square Kgs. Nytorv. Just opposite the Royal Danish Academy of Fine Arts, Eks-skolen had set up graphic equipment such as acid baths and a so-called "shoemaker press" under the open sky.[3] There, Gernes and others from Eks-skolen instructed passers-by in the making of graphic artworks – so much for the Academy's official training! In the 1950s Gernes had designed lamps and chairs and painted tightly composed pictures inspired by the movement Linien II's geometrical style. Now he wanted to teach people how simple and down-to-earth art could be. In his own artistic practice this came to expression for example in graphic works created with hammer blows, tyre tracks and imprints of both front and back covers. Gernes announced a new art, a new artist-role and a new culture around the idea "Out with useless connoisseur art and in with a collectively practiced and experimentally lived folk art in industrial society" – precisely at the historical moment when for the first time more people in Denmark were employed in industry than in agriculture.[4] As the artist Richard Winther, who was involved in the school in its early years, put it: "Graphics fits industrial society like a glove. It is multi-art made on a machine."[5]

Like much else in Gernes' own career, Eks-skolen started with an address to the public: *Who wants to join in?* [6] All applicants were admitted to the ambitious art school – although in a modest economic and physical framework – where the starting point was artistic experiments conducted jointly by teachers and students and a collectively-based structure inspired by the Bauhaus school.[7] Much has been said about this project,[8] which quickly assumed the form of a working collective or an artist group more than a school, with Gernes, Peter Louis-Jensen, Per Kirkeby, John Davidsen, Stig Brøgger and Bjørn Nørgaard as some of the central members. What took place at the school and made it into a major scene in the experimental boom of the 1960s was a wide range of performative and material experiments. Eks-skolen wanted to break with the academic tradition, with the traditional concept of the work, and the subjective artist "through the use of game rules, randomness, collective works and manifestations, unsigned or anonymous art, ready-mades etc."[9] In the cultivation of forms of practice such as new graphics, environments and happenings, and interpretations of art currents like Pop, minimalism and conceptual art, Eks-skolen was inspired not least by the American scene. It seems reasonable to draw parallels with an alternative academy like Black Mountain College (1933-1957) or with Andy Warhol's lively studio The Factory (1962-1984) – just two examples of artistic environments which like Eks-skolen sought a fusion of art and life and a new distribution of roles between artist and public.

A poster for (S)Ex-skolen from 1963 made of cuttings from erotic magazines shows with all possible clarity that this is not a school of visual art in the traditional sense. Rather, it is relevant to regard it as a *scene*. In cultural studies the scene concept is used to characterize a partic-ular rallying-point for social and cultural activity which is tightly embedded in the life of the city. A scene is further characterized by mutability and is known only to an "in-crowd" – unlike established institutions. Another characteristic is that it is not played out in just one cultural field but overlaps with others.[10] This also applies to Eks-skolen, which despite the starting point in visual art was an acknowledged part of other milieux and branches of the arts, and in the course of the 1960s authors, composers, architects and critics also became part of the circle. But they not only operated within "culture"; they also included broader social developments. In particular the ideas of the time about the communal and the collective were central to Eks-skolen, and as a result they aspired to an anonymized artist-role.[11] This can be seen clearly from a portrait of five artists from 1964, in which they stage this idea by holding their hands in front of their eyes. They engaged in collective work production and joint exhibitions in which it was not stated who the originator of the individual work was. One example of this is Gernes', Kirkeby's and Louis-Jensen's joint work *Trækvogn 13* (Handcart 13) from 1963, where each had painted a three-panelled picture and they were assembled into one – with no indi-vidual artists' signatures, only the joint "Handcart 13". They sent this in to the Artists' Autumn Exhibition, but it was rejected.

The art was in other words closely related to the sociality that surrounded the project. The art librarian Jane Pedersen writes in the book *Der er dejligt i Danmark* (It is Beautiful in Denmark)[12] from 1971: "Poul Gernes had the experience of the school that the people who came together there were able to 'accelerate' one another. Something was happening";[13] a collective dynamic which is also expressed in the subtitle of Louisiana's exhi-bition, which is a quote from Gernes: *I cannot do it alone – want to join in?*[14] Gernes' addressing of the members of the school as "brother" is famous, as is his persistent effort to create a collective spirit, supported by his monumental appearance with his long beard and paint-stained working clothing. In 1962, in the newspaper Aktuelt, one could read an interview with Gernes about Eks-skolen beneath the dramatic heading "Brother, I am seeking." In this he said to Jens Jørgen Thorsen that a "brotherhood" had to take the place of individualism, and that the purpose of the school was that the artist should be able to "mend a broken morality," just as a joiner exists to "mend a broken chair leg."[15]

The distinction between teacher and pupil was gradually blurred, and in retrospect Gernes has said that he would have liked to see it totally eliminated.[16] Despite this, the Eks-skolen artist Frank Rubin replied as follows when asked who was in charge of Eks-skolen: "The first impression – which I also think is correct – was that it was Poul Gernes. He was a personality of eminence; he didn't say so much, you only discovered him along the way, he listened, and then he got some-thing going without influencing you."[17] A look at the history of the school suggests that there was no laid-back cozy collectivism in the artistic life of Eks-skolen. A number of teachers like Richard Winther and Roger S. Pring had to leave the school after heated discussions of the artistic line and even physical encounters. It is a far cry from the original, inclusive idea that everyone, even older amateur painters, was to be admitted, to the hard core that quickly came to constitute the school. Diplomatically, Troels Andersen described the school's ambitious and sometimes harsh milieu as typified by "fracture lines that were sharp, but also productive"[18] – something that Gernes, despite his taciturn guru-like behaviour, absolutely did not shun.

AN ART DEVELOPED IN REALITY

If the collective was one axis in the activities of Eks-skolen and Gernes, another was experiments with the materials and form of the work. Per Kirkeby has afterwards spoken of the "material breakthrough that The Experimental Art School stood for,"[19] which involved "a kind of graphics that was not developed in the acid bath, but in 'reality', in materiality."[20] Gernes was in charge of Eks-skolen's "material experiments": an innova-tive rethinking of artistic processes that had the character of both works and pedagogical exer-cises. Often works were made collectively and presented at joint exhibitions – in keeping with this collective ideal Gernes had no solo exhibitions in the Eks-skole years.

At one of Eks-skolen's first joint exhibitions at Galleri Gl. Strand in 1963 they showed a collage that spread out over the whole space, loosely inspired by a living-room interior. There were furniture and other objects on the floor and on the wall there was a large, joint assemblage of small works, everyday objects and things like playing-cards and bicycle wheels – obviously a result of the object-gathering trips to the garbage dump on which Gernes often drove the group. On the windows Gernes also pasted up small things from the surroundings, as shown by a photo from the hanging. They made use of the whole space in the chaotic staging of the prosaic materiality of the surroundings – a form which in the latest American art was called *assemblage*. Troels An-dersen singles out the Museum of Modern Art's exhibition *The Art of the Assemblage* in 1961, known from the accompanying catalogue by the exhibition's curator William C. Seitz, as an import-ant inspiration for Eks-skolen and its attempts to home in on "what was happening."[21] This is anoth-er example of Eks-skolen's focus on the American

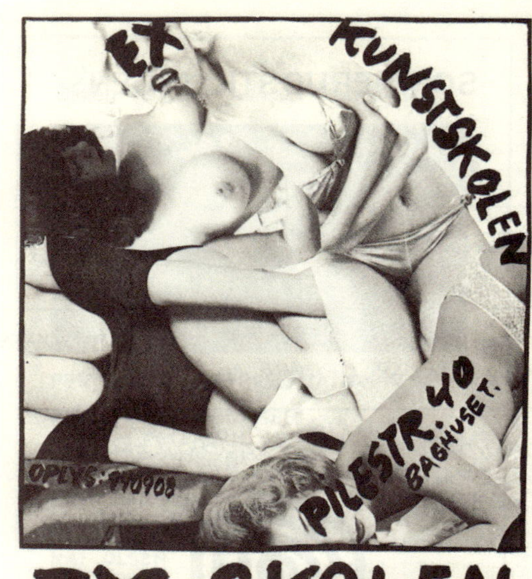

fig.3

fig.4

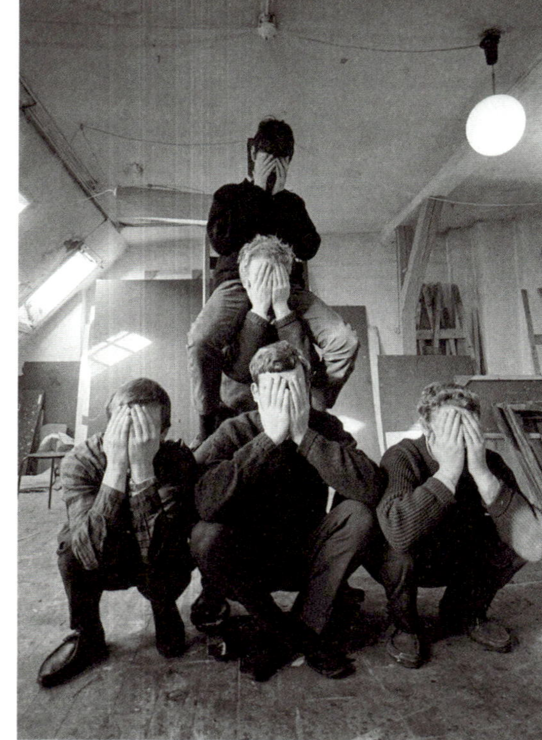

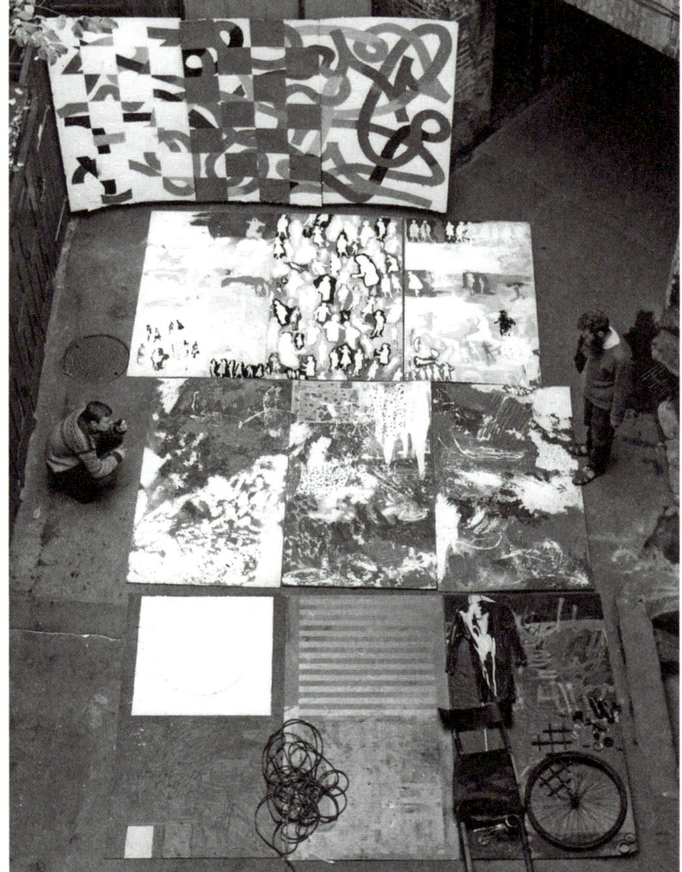

fig.5

fig.6

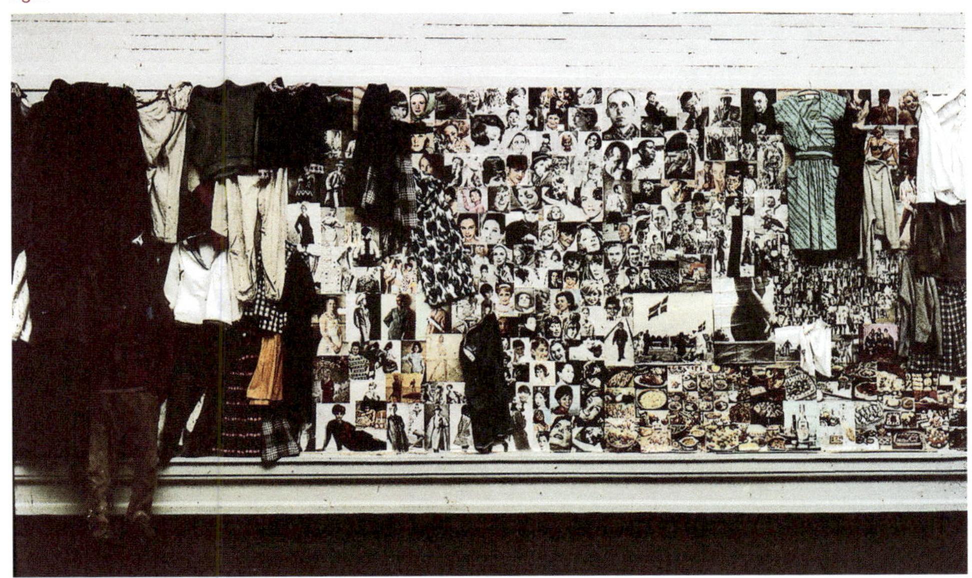

fig.7

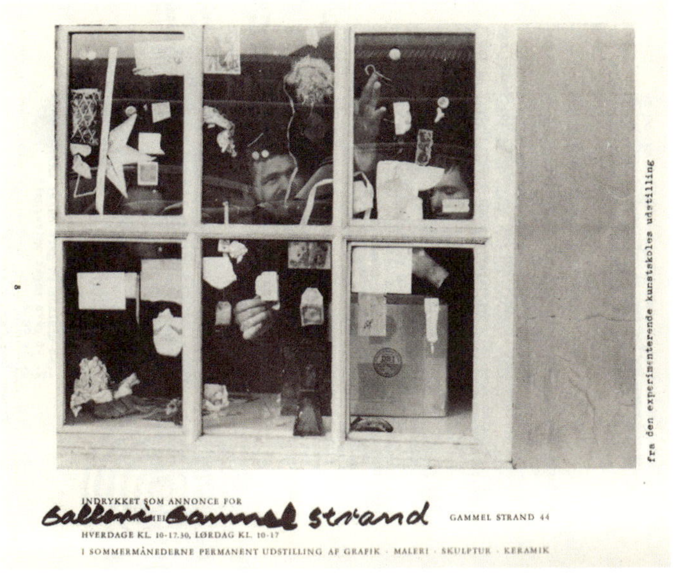

scene and their redefinitions of art and life through concrete objects taken from daily life into art. At one point the ambition was to get the American assemblage artist Robert Rauschenberg to come to Eks-skolen[22] – Rauschenberg, who in 1959 said of his practice: "Painting relates to both art and life. Neither can be made. I try to act in that gap between the two."[23]

Gernes' work also unfolded in such a gap between art and life – from the early material experiments through Eks-skolen's Pop-art-like thematic exhibitions *The Car Exhibition* and *The People Exhibition* at the Copenhagen Public Library in 1965 to the intention to sell new Citröen models at the Louisiana Museum in the *Tabernacle* exhibition in 1970, which can be seen as an even more radical effort to bring together art and life. A striking expression of the more social-commentary-like impulse in Gernes' work, compared with the pure abstraction for which he was otherwise known, could be seen at the Young Danish Art exhibition at Den Frie Udstillingsbygning in 1965, where Gernes had created a large assemblage of cut-out images, mainly faces from the media flow of the time, along with various items of clothing and even a mannequin-like figure in trousers and sweater out on the floor, which can be seen as a self-portrait.[24] This accumulation seems both easily readable and cryptic. Is it a critical image of surface and consumer culture or a celebration of humanity and its variegated everyday life?

WHAT'S HAPPENING, BABY?
Happenings were a radically new art form in the 1960s which concretely embodied fusions of art and life and brought art into interaction with the public – a controversial attraction and a major arena in the notorious culture gap, already testified to by the Danish Language Council's registration of the word in Danish as early as 1963.[25] The concept has been attributed to the American artist Allan Kaprow, who also developed the form *environments*: sculptural collages that involved the public as participants in the work. Eks-skolen's artists created many happenings, and Gernes was an easily recognizable participant in several. For example he appeared as a bearded heraldic savage along with Finn Thybo Andersen in a performance of the Danish national coat of arms in 1967, as part of a show with a number of tableaux. The bringing together of the small recognizable fragments in a more abstract totality can be seen as a performative assemblage – as if the large collages were being dramatized.

However, environments are a more central form in Gernes' work, in which he could set the scene in a simple yet monumental way, as he did with the striped decoration of Eks-skolen's premises at Store Kongensgade 101 for the performance festival *States* with Joseph Beuys as a participant in 1966. On decoration paper – a typically cheap, everyday material – horizontal coloured stripes of magenta, lemon yellow, ultramarine, chrome yellow, orange, pale green and vermilion, each of about 35 cm, ran through the locality (see p. 68). "The disjointed storage room was linked together and crucially restructured,"[26] according to Troels Andersen – incidentally in contrast to Beuys' mystical performances and highly subjective mythology.

Once more the traditional work types were to be broken down and the role of the artist was to be redefined more socially. This was expressed in Eks-skolen's "manifesto" in the first issue of the periodical ta' with a checquered minimalist cover by Gernes from 1967, in which the author Hans-Jørgen Nielsen's text "WHAT'S HAPPENING, BABY?" proclaimed "depersonalization, anonymity, mechanics, material-promoting game rules, formal templates, flatness, monotony, co-ordination instead of super- and sub-ordination" as an artistic expression of the transformed "self- and world-understanding" of a new age.[27] Despite these radical experiments with the form and materials of the work and the role of the artist behind it, Gernes' and Eks-skolen's activities remained up to the mid-1960s within the art scene and had a consistently apolitical rhetoric. However, this changed towards the end of the decade, when the transformation of life took a new turn with many examples of "transitions from aesthetic to political radicalism,"[28] movements from artistic collectivities to social experiments. In varying degrees the artists of the 1960s were involved in the manifestations of the youth revolution, ranging from confrontational activism to playful utopias. An example of this linkage can be seen in the underground magazine Hætsjj, which appeared from 1968 until 1970 as an anarchistic illustrated magazine for the counterculture with close links to experimental art. For a period Bjørn Nørgaard was responsible for editing it; some of those from the scene around Eks-skolen contributed content, and events connected with the art scene were announced – from the "Giant stroboscopic midsummer flip-out" in the Art Academy Council basement through a call to conquer the Artists' Autumn Exhibition in 1968 to *Festival 200* the following year, Charlottenborg's bicentenary, which was put in the hands of the younger experimental artists from Eks-skolen and their collaborators from Joseph Beuys' class at the Academy of Art in Düsseldorf. There Gernes built a bathhouse with showers and a sauna set up as communal public baths at Charlottenborg, as described in a spread in Hætsjj. This environment had been set up in the middle of the exhibition space with boards and plastic sheets and handwritten notices stating that the pipes and taps had been lent out by the dealer Moderne Bad. The work thus also showed how the suppliers of the consumer society were engaged in the direct, consistent involvement of everyday life in art with an accent on the collective, as people undressed and bathed in the full public eye – an iconic work for the cult of sociality in the late 1960s and, as staged togetherness, a precursor of what later became "relational aesthetics."[29] Instead of the artist creating a happening for a gaping audience, everyone there could take a bath at Charlottenborg and participate in the work on an equal – bare – footing.

ARCHITECTURE AS AN OPENING-UP OF ART

Gernes took no part in the activist or youth-cultural contexts like the younger Eks-skolen artists, but he did demonstrate a consistent engagement in experimental dwelling forms and architecture. This engagement in the design of life-frameworks can be seen as a way of fusing art and life – as an opening for inward-looking and internally conceived visual art. That the interest caught on in the Danish art milieu is expressed in the ambitious periodical Arkitektur+Billedkunst (A+B) (1969-1970), which symbolically replaced the earlier Billedkunst (1966-68). In this Gernes at one point had an image and quotation column "Finger on the pulse," which commented on current matters as yet another example of Gernes' far-reaching *orientation towards the surrounding world*; a term foregrounded in Jane Pedersen's biography.[30]

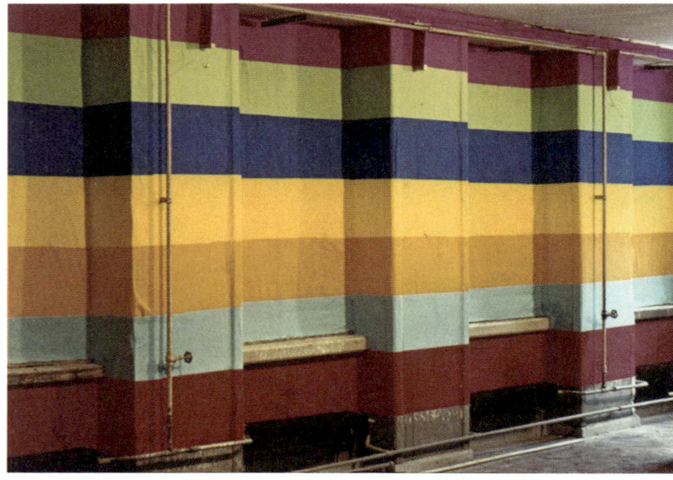

fig.8

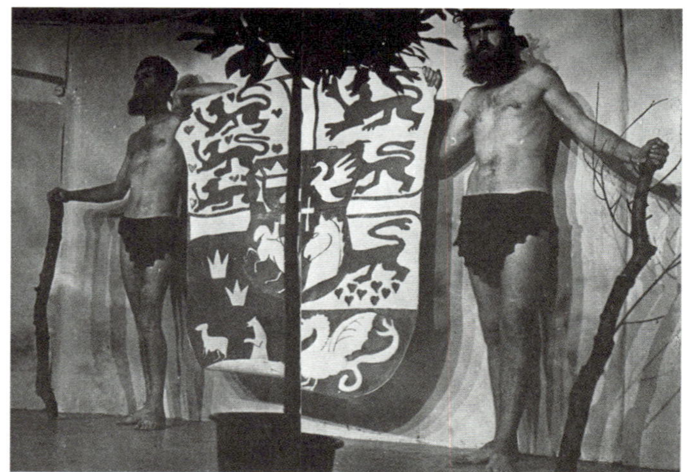

fig.9

fig.10

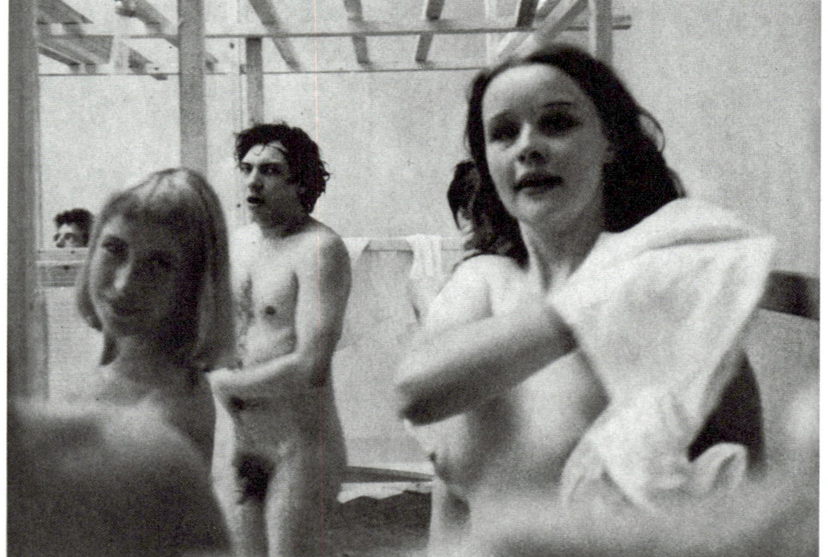

Gernes' interest was particularly focused on combining self-organized construction work with collective life in extended families as a substitute for the nuclear family. As early as the 1950s he had built his own house in Herlev as both a family home and studio, and he took this interest with him into the Eks-skolen scene by starting up a working group in 1967 around living conditions and urban planning. From this came several articles, including some in Billedkunst, and a whole issue of Hvedekorn on "Extended families" in 1968. In this issue Gernes, who was the regular editor of the periodical's graphic contributions, left out the art and instead prioritized the current social theme by inviting a number of authors, artists and collectivists to write contributions about living together.

An even more consistent project was to build up an extended-family home from the foundations in 1968-1969: with Gernes' technical and crafts-manship assistance the living collective Elverhøjen in Herlev was built. In a report in Ekstra Bladet it was described as a self-built "luxury commune": there were collective luxuries such as a library, a washing machine and a sauna alongside the more Spartan rooms for the private sphere.[31] For Gernes, however, the luxury commune was not "social" enough, so against the background of ads in *Information* calling for interested parties he started a new living experiment in Humlebæk on more radical collective principles. One of the ads, for example, said, "*There is too little security,* warmth, solidarity, love. We feel that it is necessary to try. Want to join in? Box number 824 Storfamilie to Information."[32] Life was to follow collective decisions and a shared diurnal rhythm, influenced not least by the boat-building and fishing at the coast that contributed to the household economy.[33] The collective project only lasted, however, until 1971, and the next year Gernes started up a social project for recovering drug addicts, involving among other things the refurbishing and decoration of local authority holiday camps – with the firm Hjælp (Help).[34] The work there resembled the decoration commis-sions to which Gernes devoted most of his career after the Eks-skolen years with their beginning and climax in Herlev Hospital, executed in 1968-1976. There his detailed work with colours, expressing a theory of colour composition and the healing power of colour, could form a higher unity with the ideal of the social and the collective – he involved fellow collectivists, students and his own family in the painting work. Gernes' commitment to collectivities thus continued after the Eks-skolen collaboration ceased around 1970. And as yet another radical reorientation it was not enough for Gernes to create small experimental enclaves; instead he wanted to decorate the buildings of society where people were and had to live their lives – town halls, schools, halls of residence, the Palads Cinema and even the top-secret govern-ment bunker in Gurre in northern Zealand. To this we can add the proposals he submitted to various architectural competitions and other visions that were never realized, including his thoughts on colouring a whole town – Helsinge;[35] consistent interpretations of social responsibility, not as breaking out *of*, but as seeking integration *with* the institutions of the welfare state.

ART AS A WAY OF LIFE

In the catalogue of his exhibition in the Danish Pavilion at the Venice Biennale in 1988, Poul Gernes formulated his view of art under the heading ART AS A WAY OF LIFE. He distanced himself in the text from a purely aesthetic artistic practice and from an unworldly cultivation of theory – instead Gernes' art was to be a "great, good, social, human act of love, which current contemporary art for example has no possibility of living up to";[36] a vision which expressed the inadequacy of established art in precisely such an exclusive setting as the Biennale, and the demand for "social responsibility" that he had already sought to meet by founding Eks-skolen in 1961. A similar ambition was expressed at the beginning of the 1960s, when policy-makers and writers had held a series of meetings at the Louisiana Museum about the potential of culture to inspire modern society. On this occasion the Danish Prime Minister Viggo Kampmann said: "If only the culturally interested would abandon their critical stance and begin to advise us in a loving and understanding way, much would be gained. They may of course refrain, but then they must realize that society will be governed anyway."[37] That the country's Prime Minister assigned art such an important role in society says a lot about the spirit of the age: the statement embraces both the decade's eruption of experiments and the incorporation by the cultural policy of the welfare state of art into society. There almost seems to have been a consistent understanding that life had to be particularly malleable and open to reinterpretation and redefinition in the period. As this article has attempted to show, in the artistic life of the 1960s Gernes was a leading figure as one of the principal stage-managers of the most influential avant-garde groupings, and took it in several directions on his stubborn journey from experimental art school to intensely coloured decorations. But he also broke with the picture, and refused to be pigeonholed, either artistically, culturally or ideologically. Perhaps for that very reason he is still able to "accelerate" us and make things happen.

Kristian Handberg (b. 1980), postdoc at Louisiana and Department of Arts and Cultural Studies, The University of Copenhagen. PhD with the dissertation *There's no time like the past: Retro between memory and materiality in contemporary culture* (2014) and carries out research in the arts of the postwar era as part of the Louisiana Research project Multiple Modernities.

1   Said to Troels Andersen during the first discussions of an art school in 1961. Troels Andersen, *Ude af øje. Erindringer* 1940-1973. Forlaget Vandkunsten, 2014, p. 119.

2   Tania Ørum, *De eksperimenterende tressere – kunst i en opbrudstid*. Gyldendal, 2009, p. 16.

3   Lars Morell, *Broderskabet. Den eksperimenterende Kunstskole 1961-1969*. Thaning og Appel, 2009, p. 70.

4   http://danmarkshistorien.dk/historiske-perioder/kold-krig-og-velfaerdsstat-1945-1973/hoejkonjunkturen-1958-73/

5   Morell, 2009, pp. 17-18.

6   Press releases were sent out which led to coverage in the national newspapers *Politiken* and *Aktuelt*, and invitations went out to all unaccepted applicants to the Artists' Autumn Exhibition. The school was presented as among other things "a free organization which, in modest material conditions, can perhaps lay a basis for an existing art" and was to strengthen the artist in "not being superfluous in society". Troels Andersen in *Eksperiment, Kunst, Skole, Ex-skolen 1961-1969*, Museum Jorn Silkeborg, 2010, p. 34.

7   Ørum, 2009, pp. 92-93.

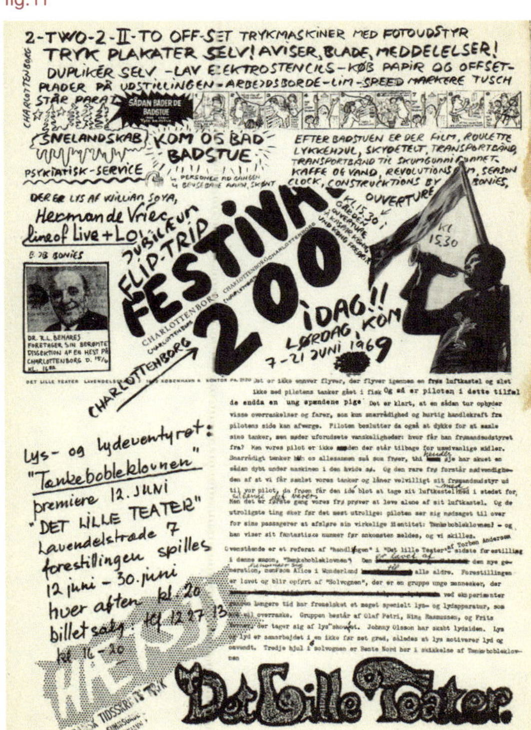

fig.11

8   In recent years the history and importance of Eks-skolen have been treated in detail in Tania Ørum, *De eksperimenterende tressere* (2009); Lars Morell, *Broderskabet. Den Eksperimenterende Kunstskole 1961*-1969 (2009); Peter Øvig Knudsen, *Hippie I-II* (2011-12); and in the exhibition and catalogue *Eksperiment, Kunst, Skole, Ex-skolen 1961-1969*, Museum Jorn Silkeborg (2010).

9   Ørum, 2009, p. 23.

10   Such cultural 'scenes' have been described for example in "Cities/Scenes" in Janine Marchessault and Will Straw (eds.), *Public*, no. 22/23, 2002.

11   "The collective and anonymous ways of working that Gernes introduces are to be of great importance to the participants. On the one hand they evoke a team spirit or even a brotherhood [....] On the other they help to keep personal ambitions down". Ørum, 2009, p. 95.

12   The book is an experimental artist book with the declared aim of "expanding the autonomy concept of the New Criticism, of seeing art not only in relation to art but also as a correlative of social and existential conditions", written by the art librarian Jane Pedersen and "built up over [Poul Gernes'] own statements and views tape-recorded in the spring of 1971", and is therefore to be viewed as a central source close to Gernes.

13   Jane Pedersen *Der er dejligt i Danmark*. Borgens Forlag, 1971, p. 54.

14   Pedersen, 1971, p. 129.

15   Jens Jørgen Thorsen, "Broder, jeg er søgende" in *Aktuelt*, 15 July 1962.

16   Ørum, 2009, p. 96.

17   *Alternativ dansk grafik i tresserne*. Kastrupgaard-samlingen, 1978, p. 42.

18   Meeting with med T.A. in February 2016.

19   *Alternativ dansk grafik i tresserne*. 1978, p. 68.

20   Ibid., p. 76.

21   Troels Andersen, "Notater om ex-skolen i 60'erne" in *Ex-skolen Eksperiment Kunst Skole*. Exhibition catalogue, Museum Jorn Silkeborg, 2010, p. 20.

22   Ibid., p. 38..

23   In the catalogue of the exhibition *Sixteen Americans* at the Museum of Modern Art, New York, 1959.

24   Ørum, 2009, p. 133.

25   The Danish Language Council's list of new words in the Danish language: http://dsn.dk/noid?q=happening

26   Troels Andersen, *Eksempler og motiver*. Borgen, 1988, p. 178.

27   Hans-Jørgen Nielsen, "What's happening, baby?" in *ta'* 1, 1967, p. 3.

28   Ørum, 2009, p. 25.

29   The concept of sociality-promoting art was created and described around the turn of the millennium by the French curator Nicolas Bourriaud in *Relational Aesthetics* (2002).

30   A longish chapter about the artist's ideas on society and working life has this title in Jane Pedersen's book.

31   Lizzie Bundgaard, "Byggede selv luksus-kollektiv for 135.000 kr." in *Ekstra Bladet*, 19 March 1969 pp. 8-9.

32   Pedersen, 1971, p. 26.

33   Ørum, 2009, p. 706.

34   The collective, which was called 'Knastager' with reference to the famous collective Kløvedal, and the work with 'Hjælp' are described by Birgit Pontoppidan in the article "Om et af de mange kollektiver" in *Billedet som kampmiddel. Kvindebilleder mellem 1968 og 1977*. Informations Forlag, 1977.

35   Spoken of as an unrealizable project by Gernes in conversation with Erik A. Frandsen in the film *Rum* (Steen Møller Rasmussen, 1994).

36   *Poul Gernes: Colour and Space*. Exhibition catalogue, Danish Pavilion, Venice Biennale, 1988, p. 78 ("ART AS A WAY OF LIFE – is a great good, social, human act of love, which contemporary art, for instance, does not really have any chance to live up to").

37   In an interview for *Information* 1960. Quoted here from Anne-Marie Mai (ed.), *Kættere, kællinger, kontormænd og andre kunstnere. Forfatterroller i den danske velfærdsstat*. Syddansk Universitetsforlag 2013, p. 12.

fig. 12 Poul Gernes' contribution in Hvedekorn about extended families,1968

fig. 12

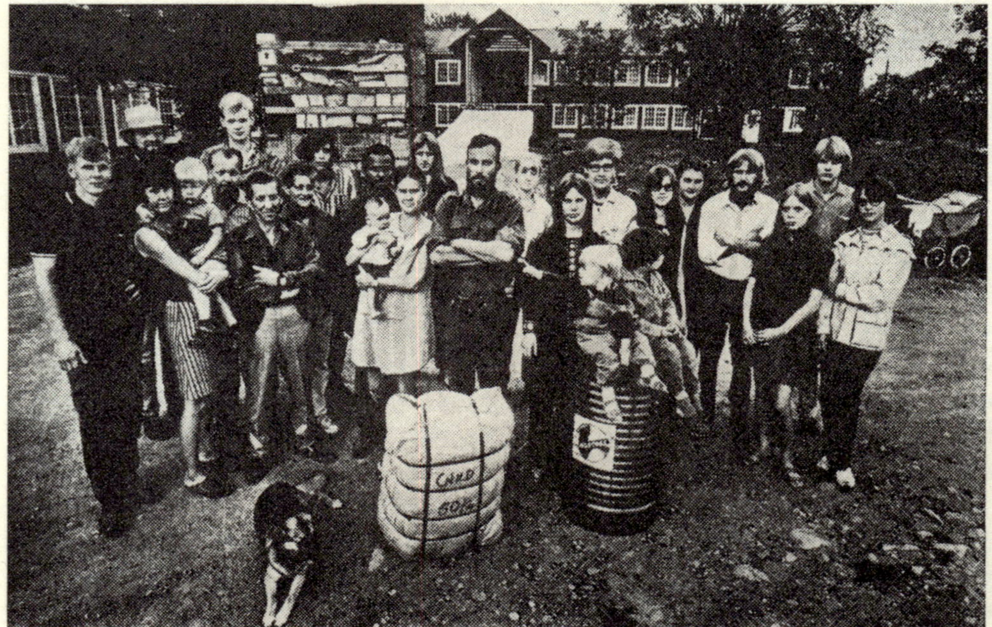

STORFAMILIEN

Til læserne: forklaringen på at Hvedekorns grafiske afdeling har givet plads for indslag om »Storfamilien« er meget enkel, nemlig, jeg fandt at det var rigtigere end at lave et nummer med grafik.

Til bidragyderne: det viste sig at emnet gav en større mængde stof end det var muligt at bringe, hvorfor en udvælgelse blev nødvendig, dette kunne have været gjort på flere forskellige måder, f. ex. kunne det være rimeligt at foretrække de saglige, de lyriske eller jeg kunne have udeladt de uforståelige indlæg eller de der omhandler kollektiver, men jeg har fundet det rigtigst og også interessantest at tage noget af alle slags med, selv er jeg i alt fald meget glad for det samlede resultat, derfor tak.

Paul Gernes.

181

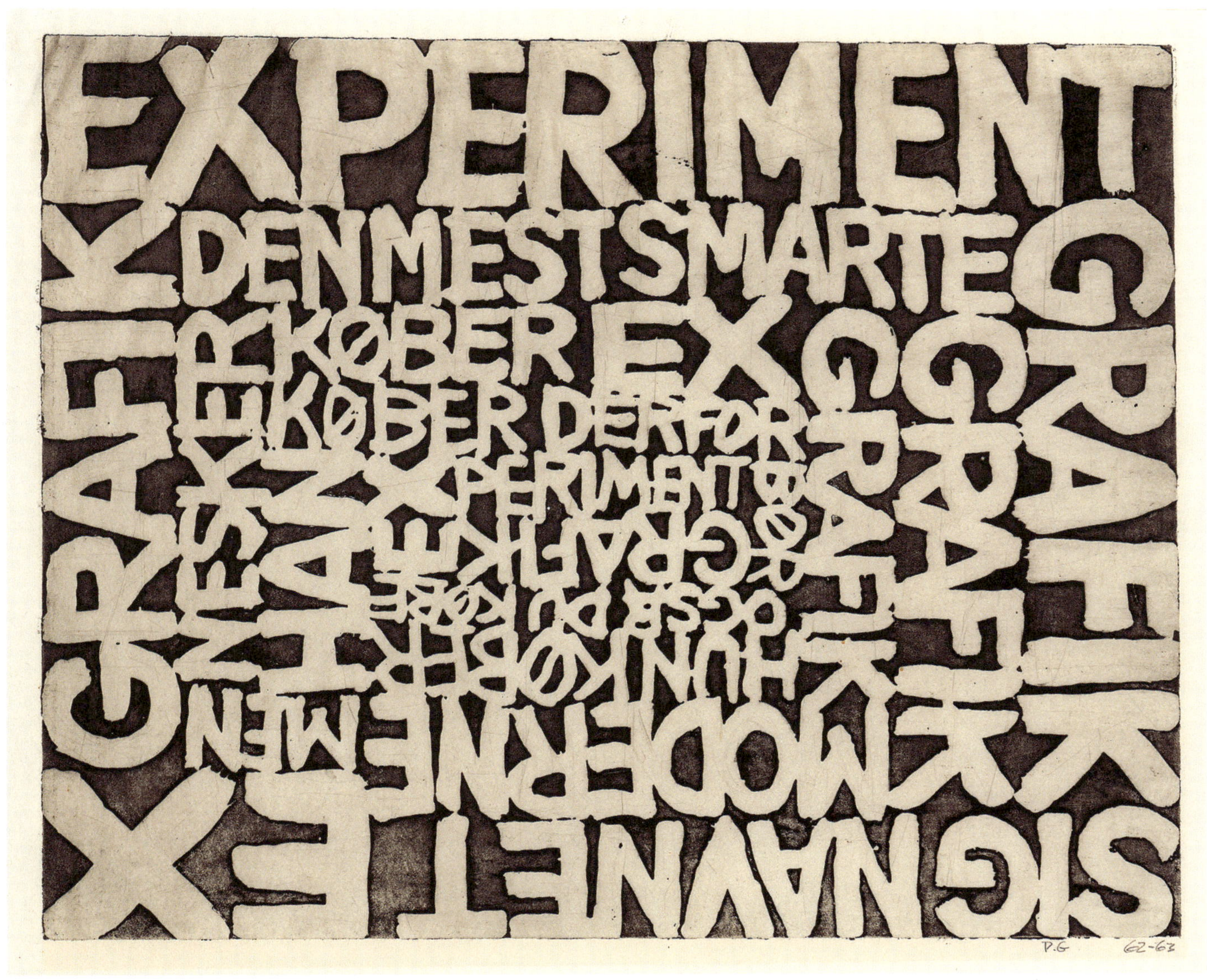

Untitled ("Experiment"), 1962-63
Etching, 42 × 54 cm

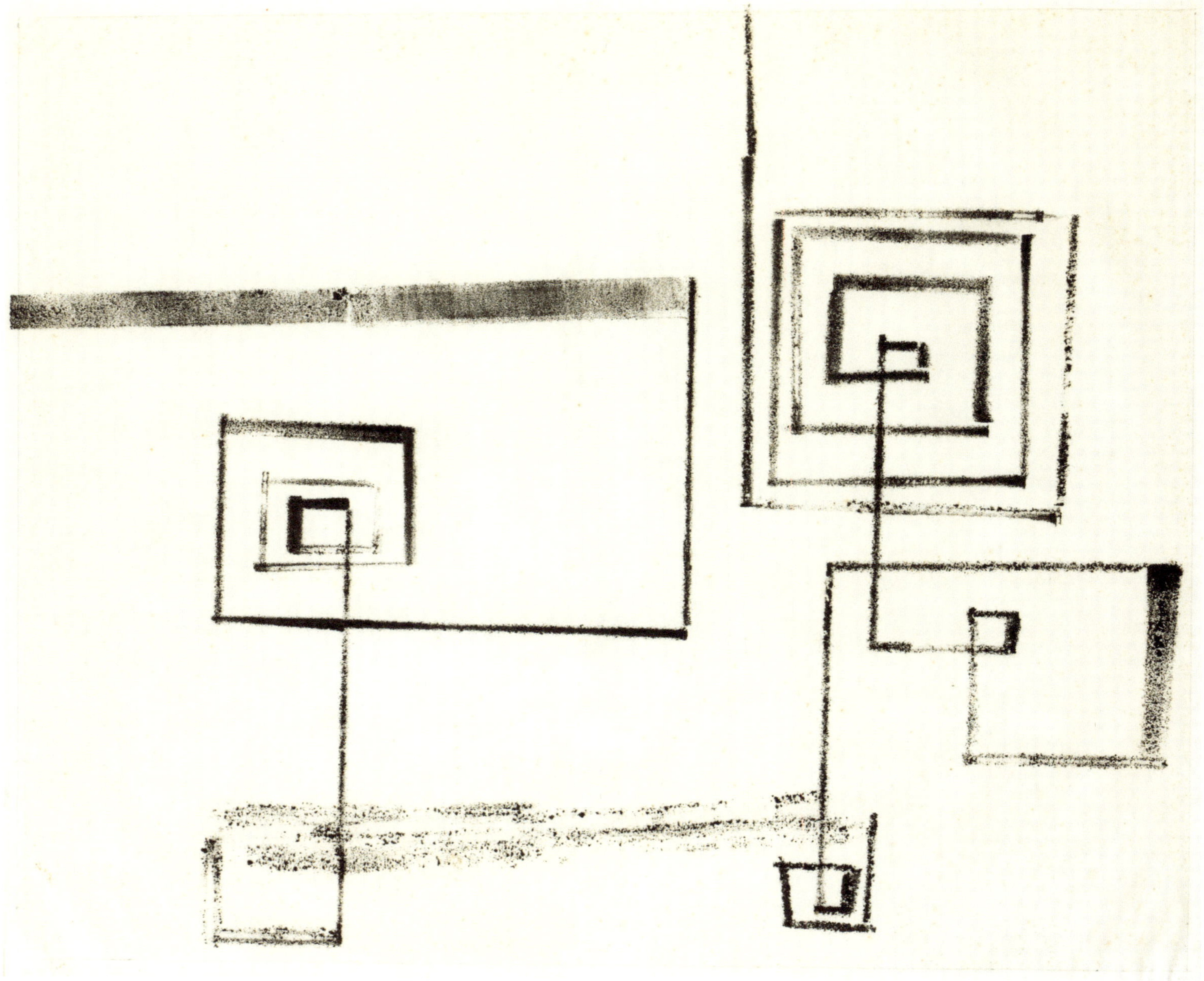

Untitled, 1960
Ink, watercolour on paper, 32 × 48 cm

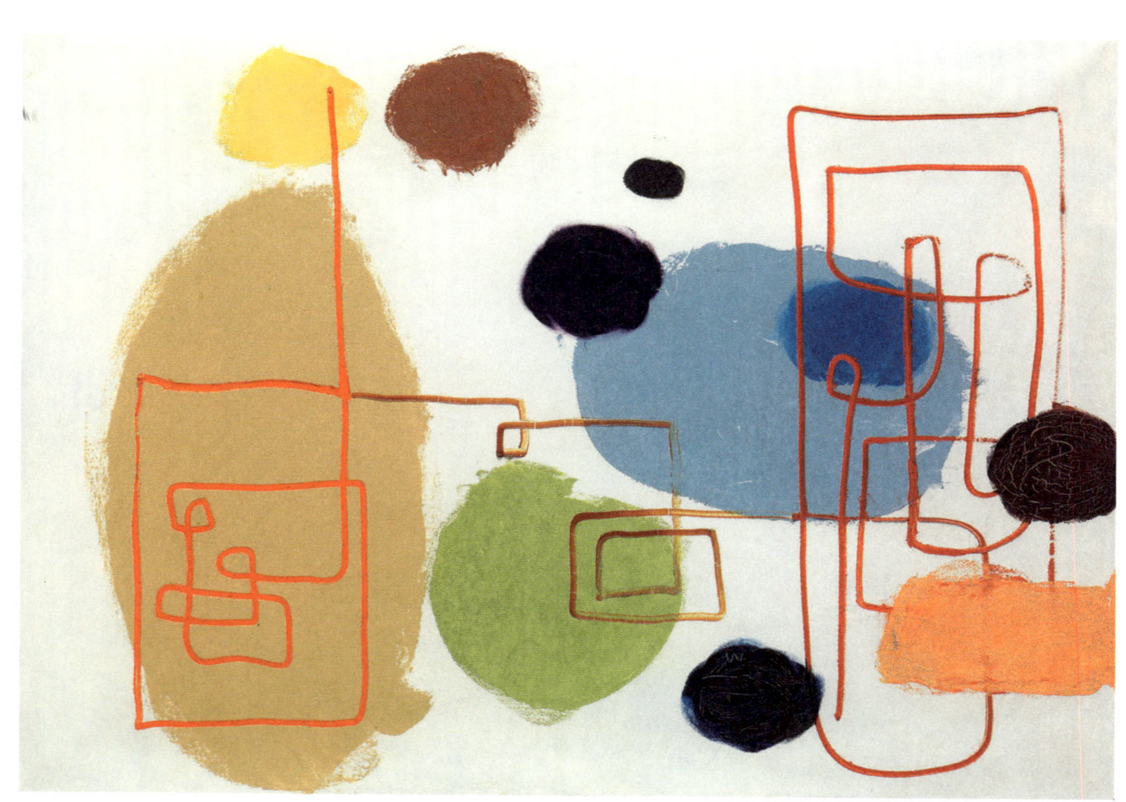

Untitled, 1962-63
Oil on canvas, 67 × 96 cm

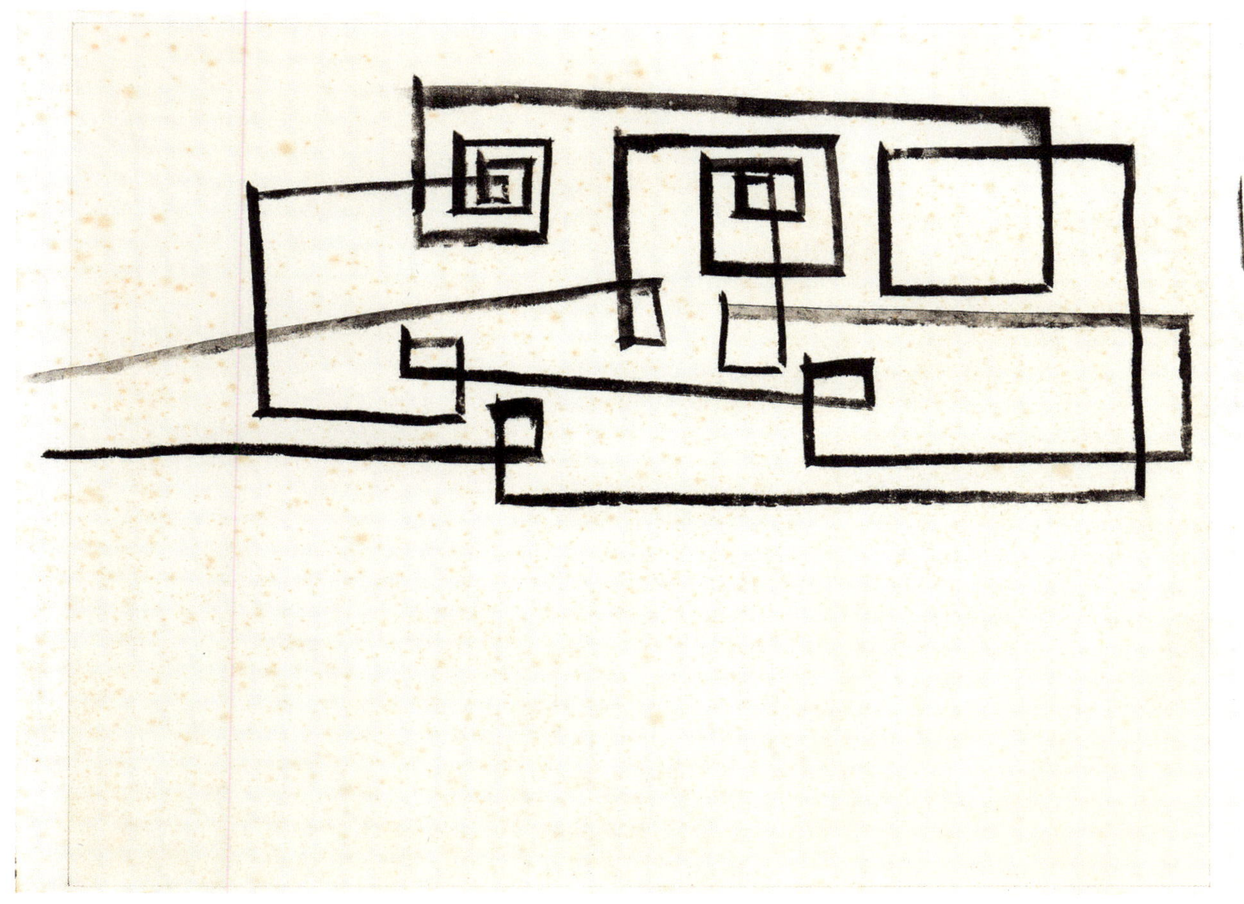

Untitled, 1960
Ink on paper, 32 × 48 cm

Untitled, 1971
Offset on paper (printed on a sheet together
with another work),
19 × 19 cm

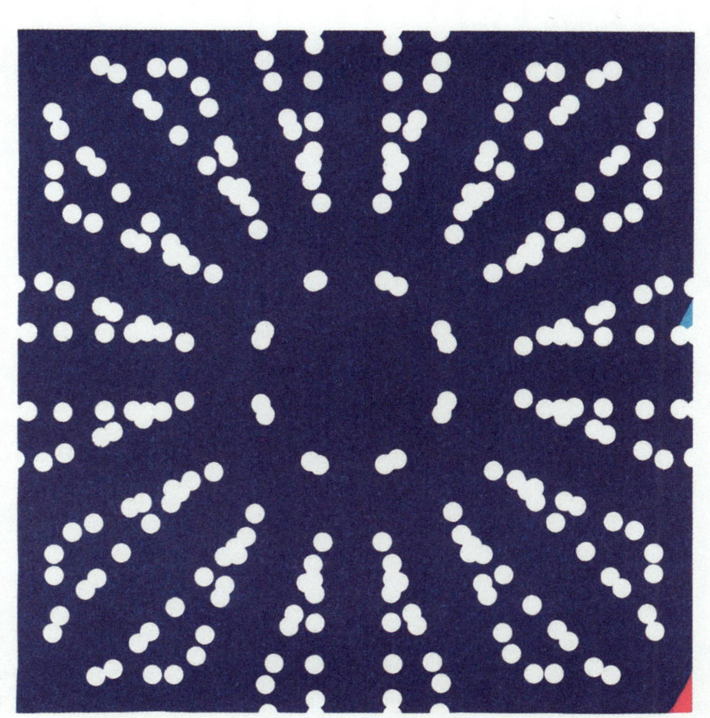

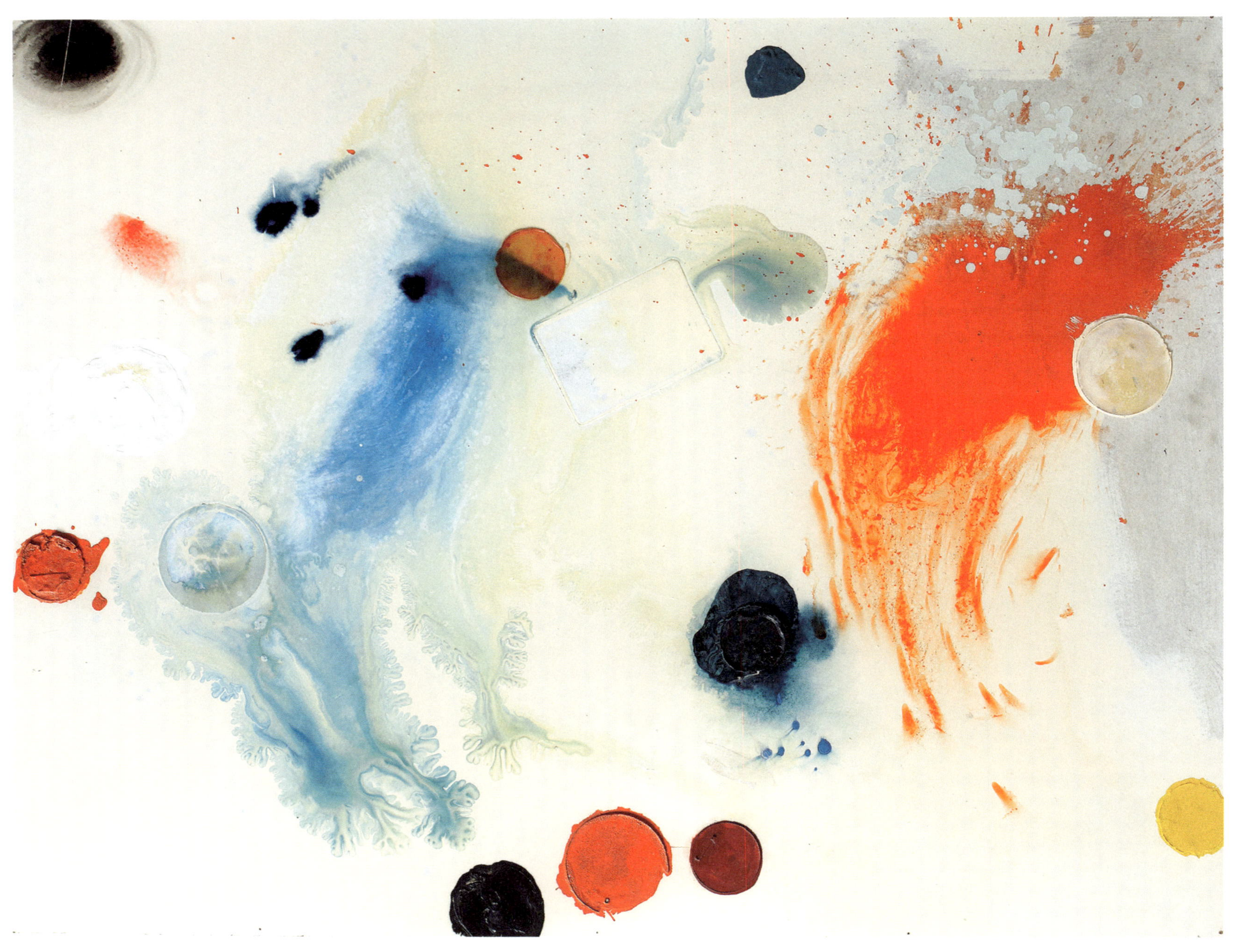

Untitled, 1962
Enamel on masonite, 91 × 122 cm

Untitled, 1962
Oil on canvas, 60 × 75 cm

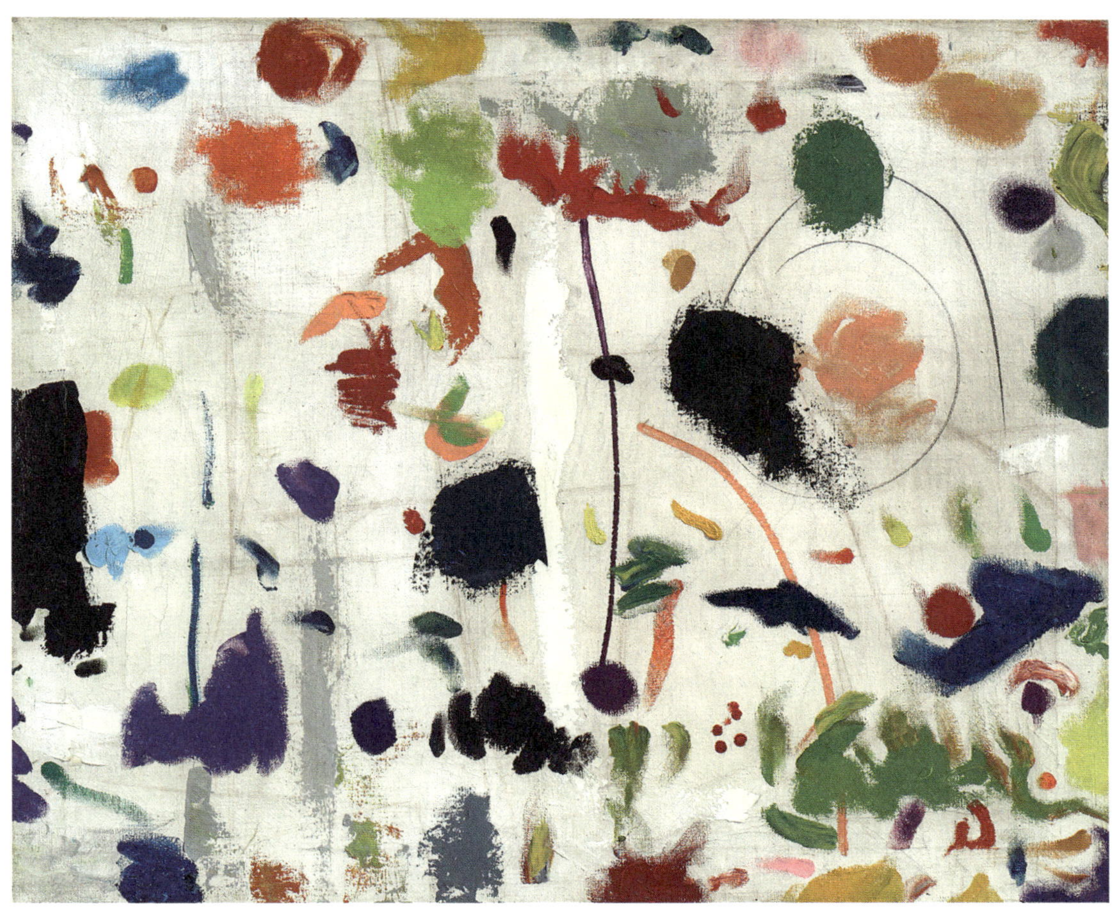

Untitled, 1962
Oil on canvas, 67 × 57 cm

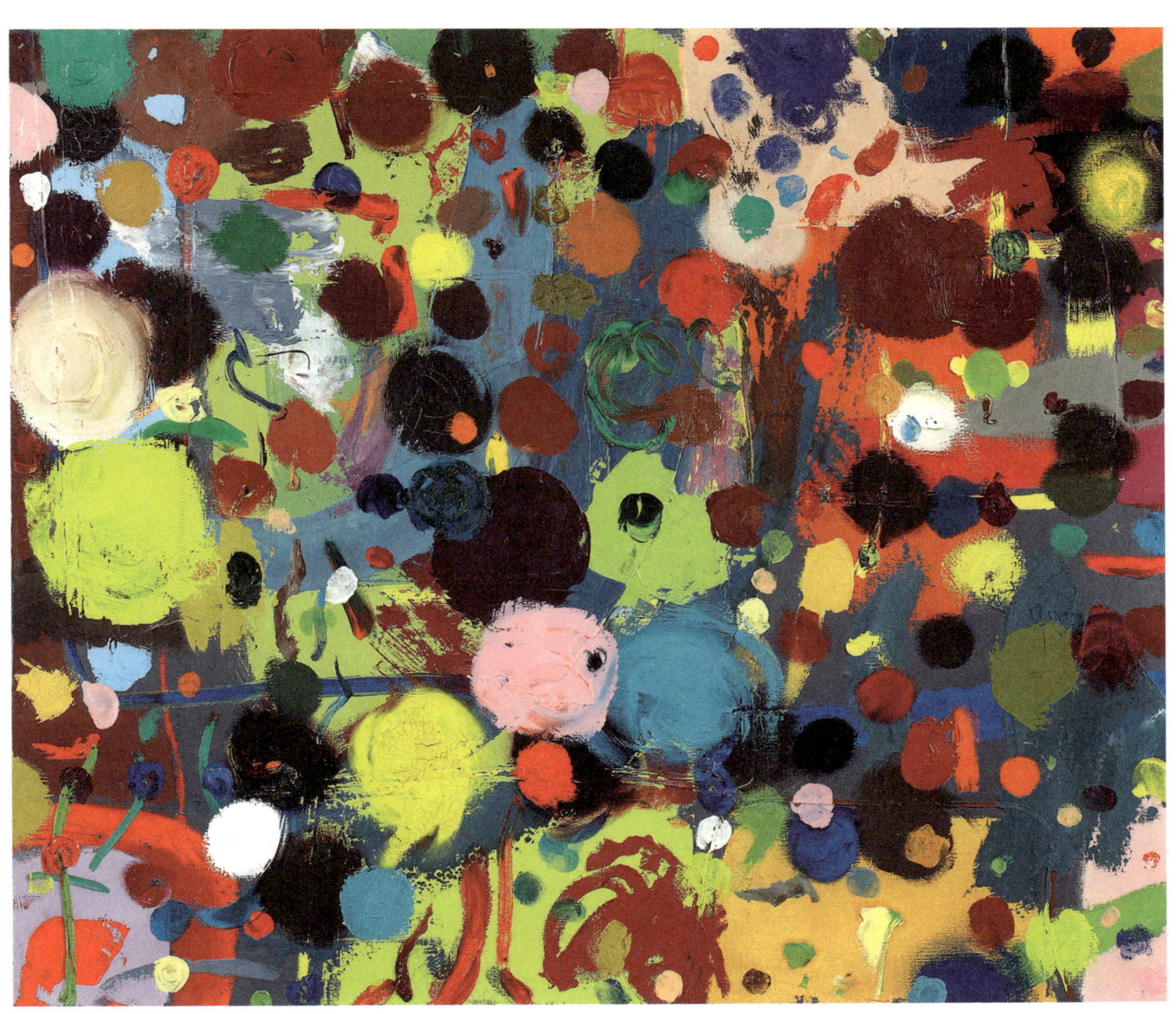

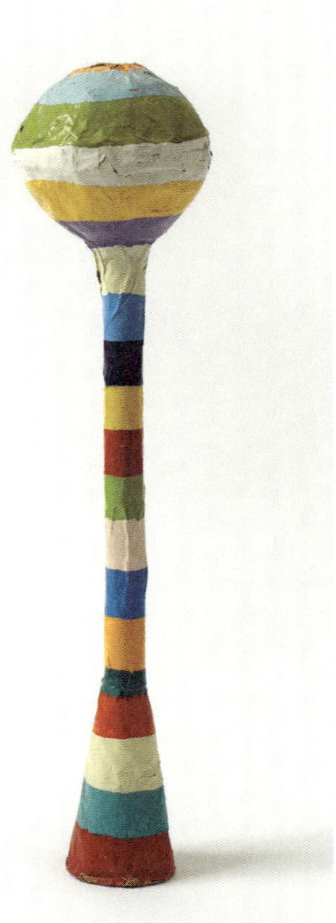

Study for colour scheme for water
tower in Ängelholm Municipality,
Sweden, 1972-73
Architecture model, enamel on papier
maché, 63 × 15 × 15 cm

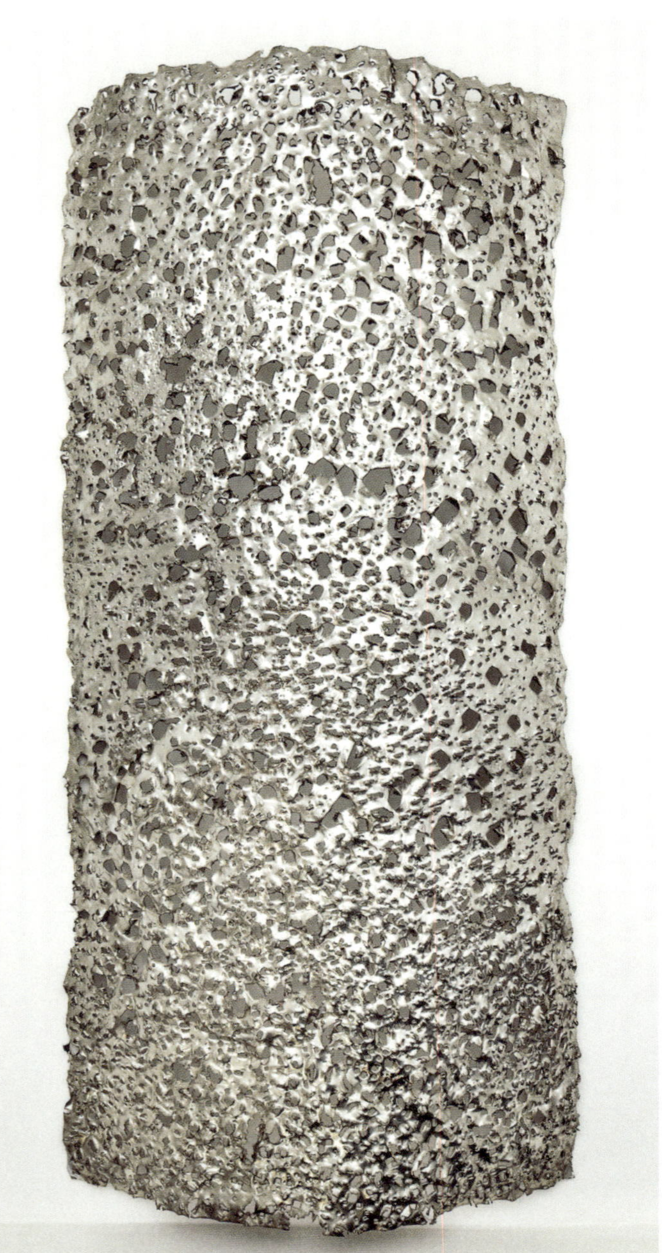

Untitled ("The Grater"), 1962
Curved aluminum relief,
pierced, 200 × 100 × 20 cm

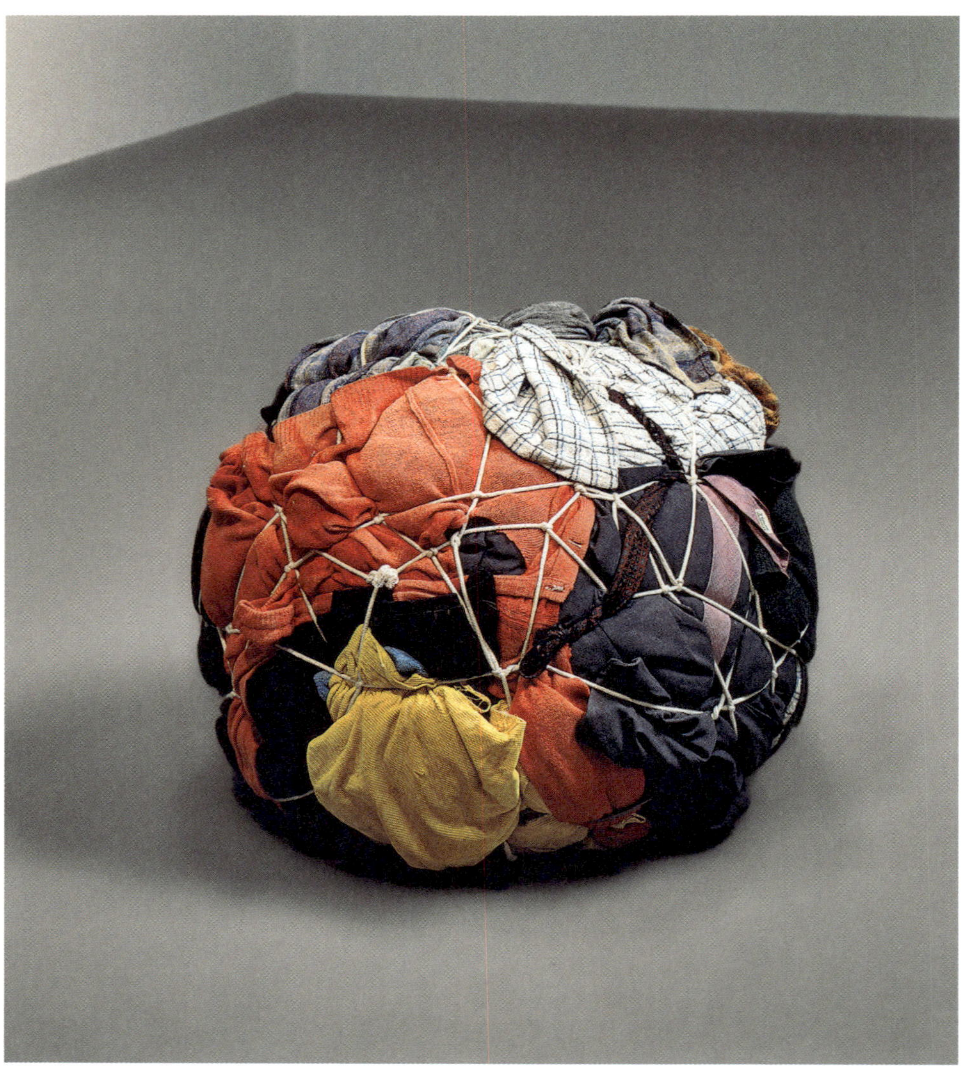

Untitled ("The Cloth Ball"), c. 1962
Clothing items, rope, 59 × 82 × 82 cm

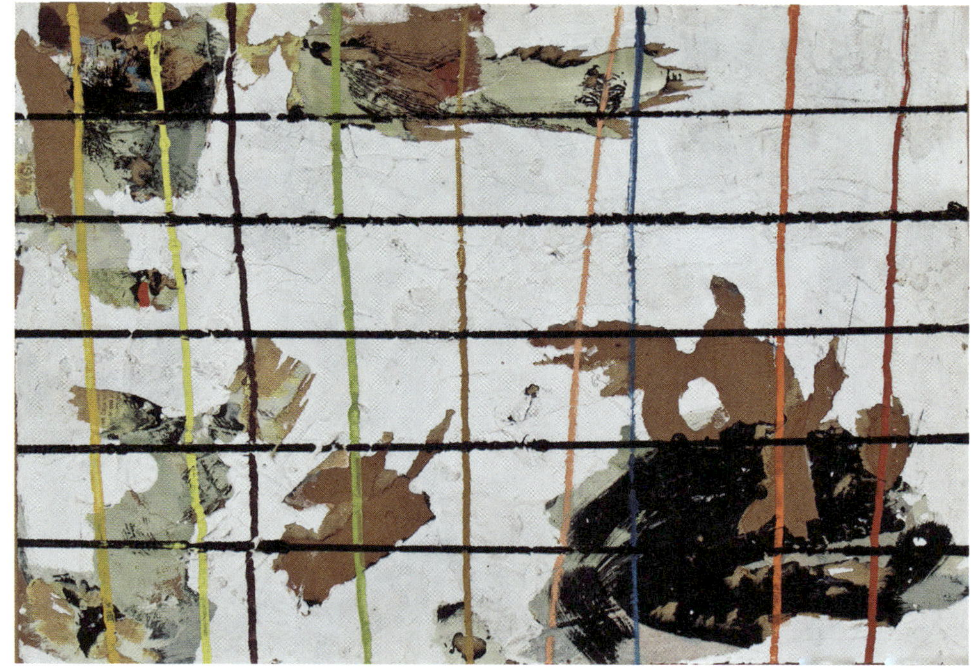

Untitled, 1962
Oil on masonite, glued
painted paper, 42 × 60 cm

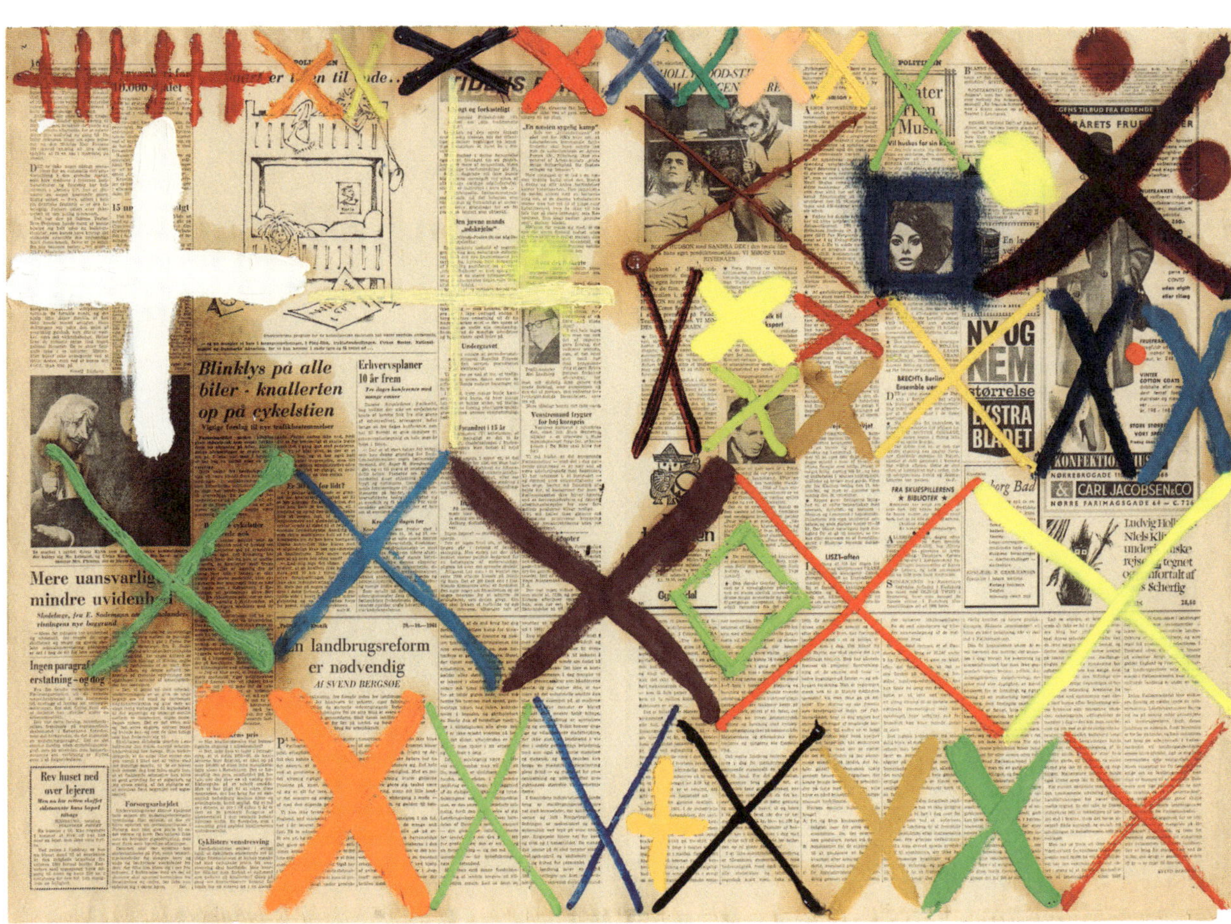

Untitled, (1961)
Oil, collage on newspaper,
56 × 79 cm

Untitled
("Tyre Imprint from Bus 29 at Kgs. Nytorv"),
1962
Etching, 51 × 64 cm

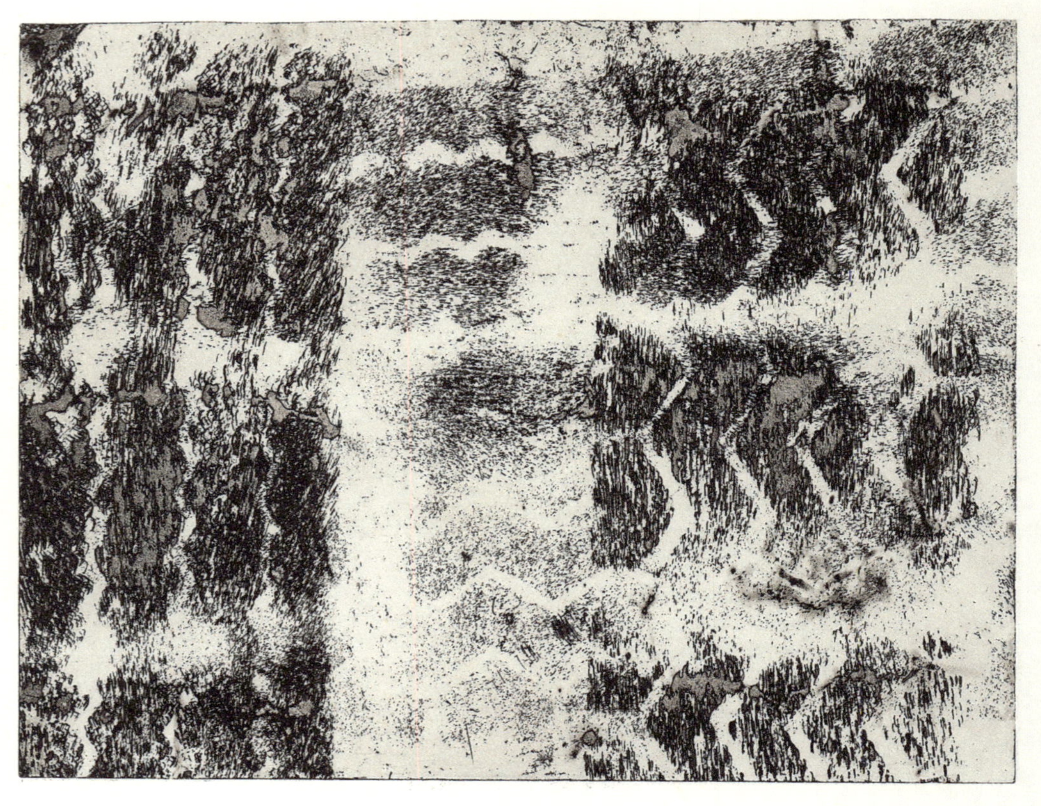

Untitled
("100 Blows with a Hammer"),
1962-63
Etching, 64 × 75 cm

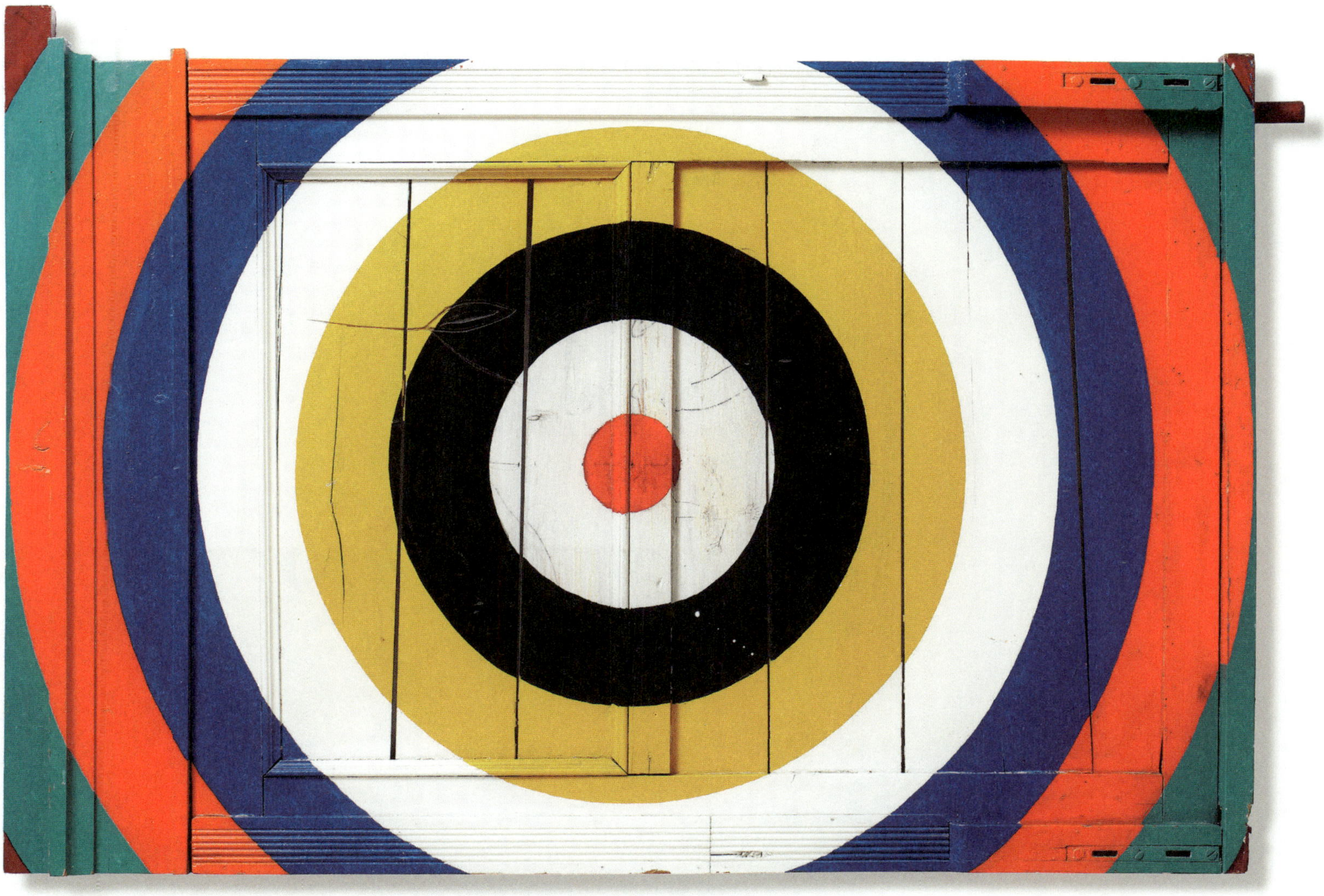

Untitled, 1962
Enamel paint on wood (Bedpost)
90 × 130 × 9 cm

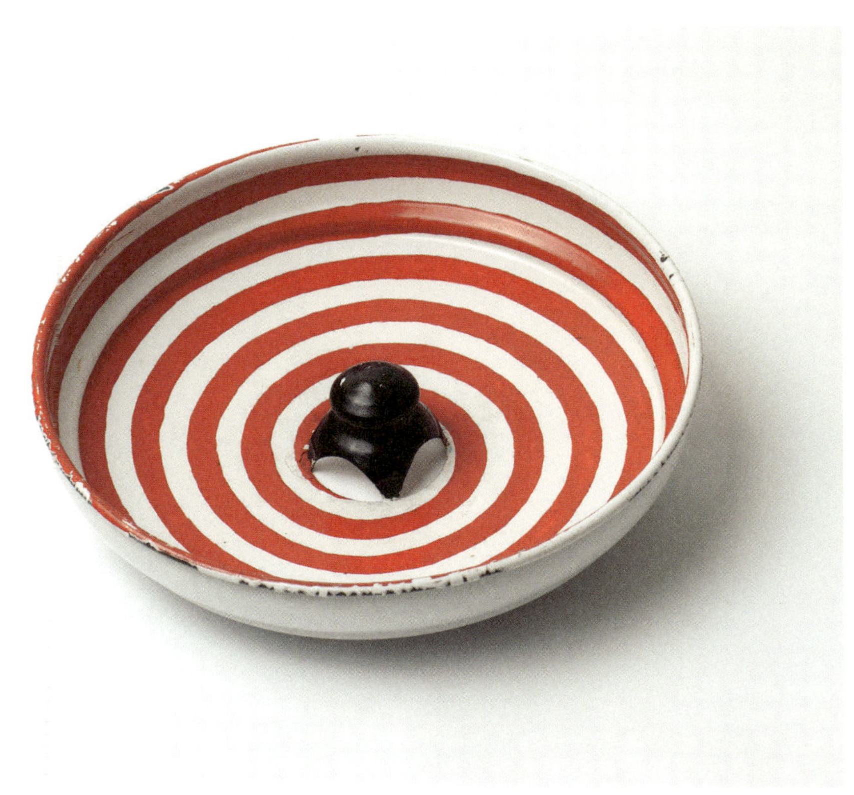

Untitled
("Lid for Toilet Bucket"),
1960-62
Enamel paint on metal, dia. 31 cm

fig.1

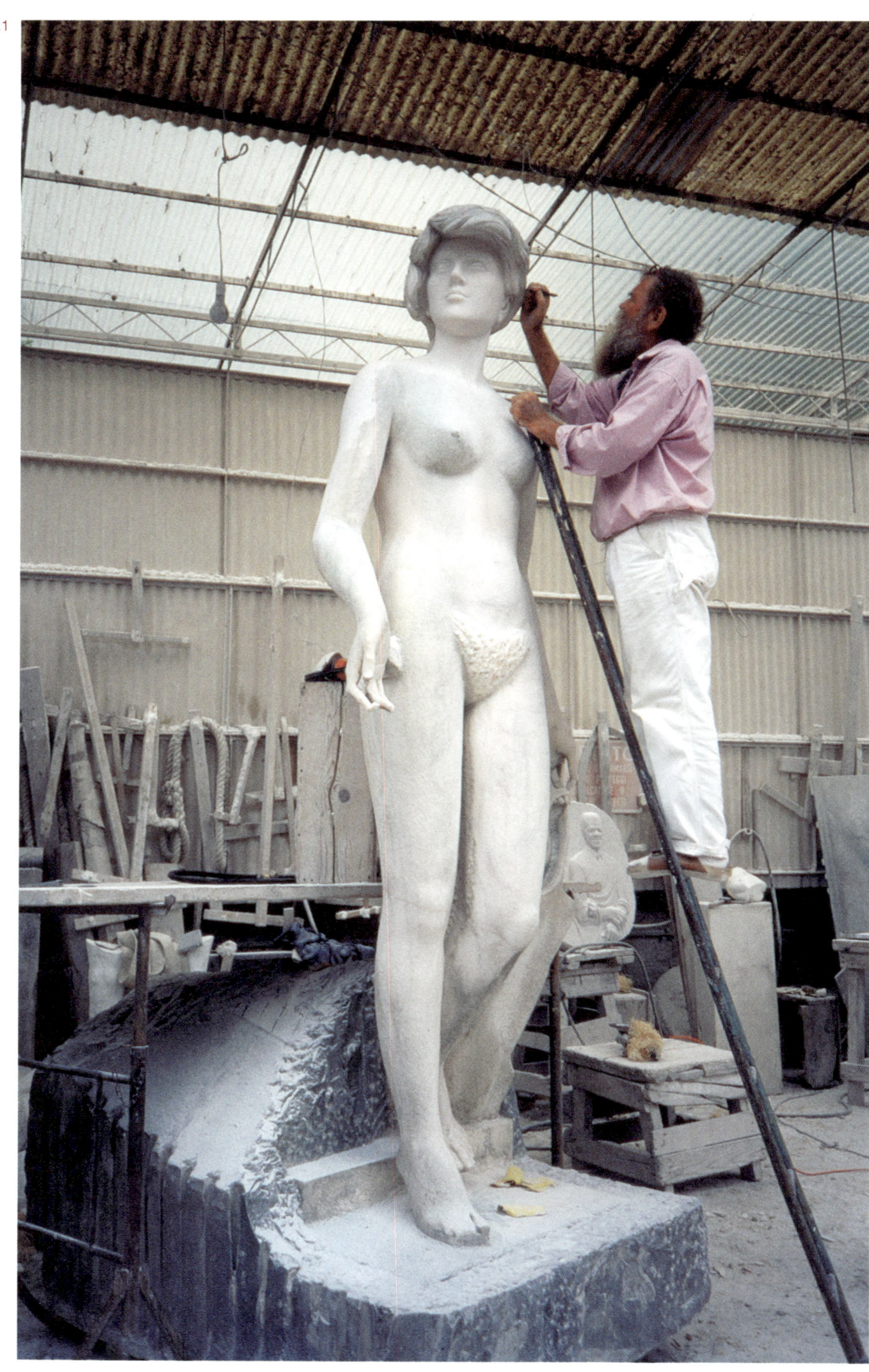

Big Rosa
A sculptural story

By Anders Krüger

Anders Krüger (b.1960) is a sculptor and professor. Has taught at University of California San Diego, Columbia College Chicago og the Art Academy at Umeå University. He lives and works in Stockholm and in Copenhagen, where he since 2016 has worked as a sculptor at the Agency for Culture and Palaces.

fig. 1 Poul Gernes working on *Big Rosa* in Pietrasanta, Italy
Big Rosa (The Princess – The Prince – The Artist's Trousers), 1980-96
Pink Portuguese marble and grey Italian marble, h: 350 cm

"The princess, the prince and the artist's trousers" is inscribed on the plinth of the sculpture *Big Rosa*, which was to be Poul Gernes' last work. The 320 cm tall sculpture, weighing a good six tons, was completed in Pietrasanta in Italy shortly before Gernes died in March 1996. For an artist who, with uncompromising consistency, had devoted the last 25 years of his life to colourful and decorative public comissions, it may seem remarkable that his last great artistic achievement was something as old-fashioned as a figurative monumental marble sculpture.

Big Rosa's character as a solitary, classically inspired sculpture differs radically from Gernes' other production, but the words inscribed on the plinth may provide us with some clues to the work. And the fact that the trousers that the nude woman holds in her left hand look like a pair of traditional bricklayer's trousers of the same type as Gernes himself often wore gives us a hint of what is going on. That the face and expressively ornamented hairstyle bear clear resemblances to a young Aase Seidler Gernes – Poul Gernes' wife and collaborator throughout his life – underpins the narrative and autobiographical dimensions of the work. In the interplay between the anachronistic marble figure and the subtlety of the carved words, a story begins to take shape – a story that moves freely between the classical iconography of the sculpture, the traditional dramaturgy of the saga and the artist's private biography.

But what is actually the relationship among the three actors of the story – the princess, the prince and the artist's trousers? The princess undoubtedly plays the main role. The frog that sits crouched on the massive plinth behind the female figure is of course the prince. The trousers – are they a trophy that the amazon-like princess has won? In that case the artist is introduced here in his absence – literally with his trousers down. Or has he been transformed by the princess's kiss into a frog? Humour and self-irony are rare ingredients in the long history of the figurative marble sculpture – but *Big Rosa* is a unique exception.

Big Rosa has a twin sculpture on a smaller scale – Little Rosa – executed in pink Portuguese marble. Gernes began the work on both sculptures back in 1980, but because of health problems they were left unfinished at the quarry in Pietrasanta and only completed in 1996.

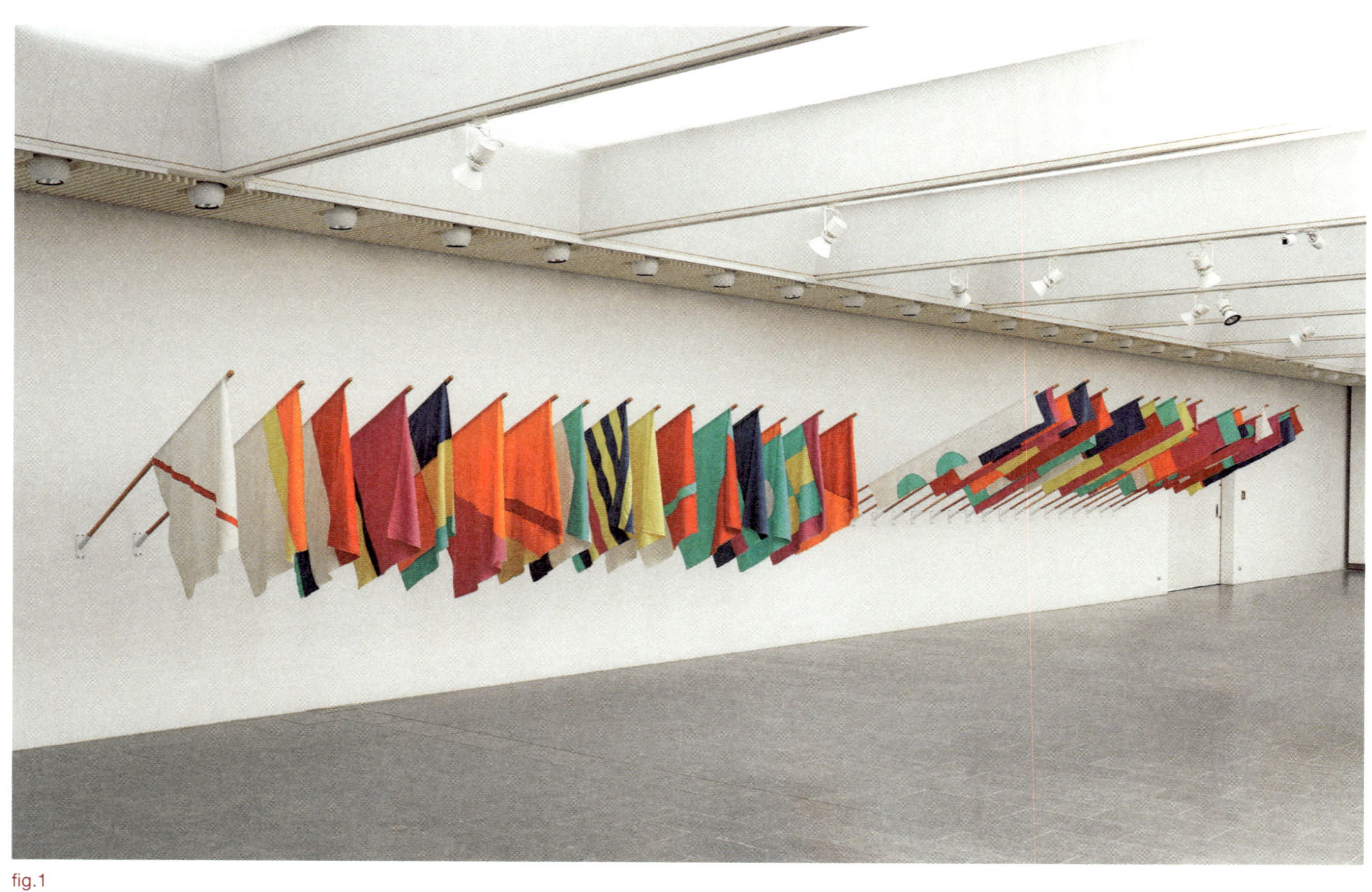

"I know that work, although I didn't know it at all"
A Conversation between Paul Smith and Hans Ulrich Obrist about Poul Gernes

By Anders Kold

fig. 1   Poul Gernes' flags in Louisiana's
          collection, installation view from 2013

fig. 2   Paul Smith's flag shirt

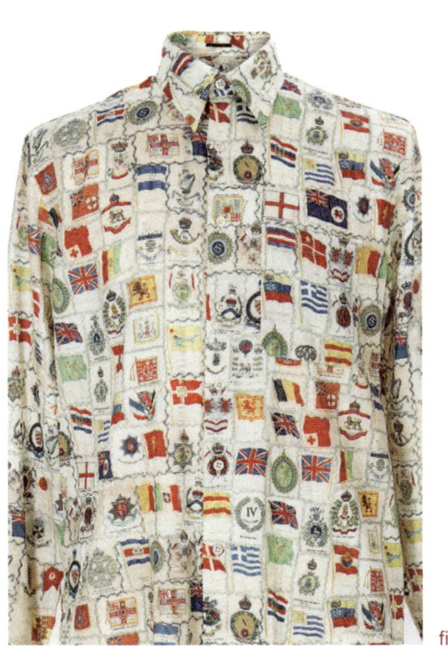
fig.2

Hans Ulrich Obrist: When I visited you at your office last time, I introduced you to Poul Gernes and we had a fascinating conversation. I was wondering if you can reconstitute what you thought when you first saw Gernes' work?

Paul Smith: I thought "I know that work," although I didn't know it at all. It was the use of colour and the use of simple polka dots and stripes that was so familiar to me because it was very much part of my era. If you look at some of my work you realize that there are a lot of parallels.

HUO: Gernes felt that the art world was kind of too narrow – he wanted to reach out to more people.

PS: That's so Paul Smith, too.

HUO: In the early 1970s Gernes more or less left the art world. He walked out of Louisiana in February 1970 from a show together with Joseph Beuys and Per Kirkeby and other contemporaries. After that he didn't want to work with galleries and museums and for eight years he was involved with decorating a hospital (Herlev Hospital), thereby cunningly staying out of the art world. You opened your shop the same year Gernes decided to leave the art world and go toward something more accessible, and in a way it must have something to do with the spirit of that moment. Can you recall that?

PS: What was so strange and what's so interesting is that there are quite a lot of parallels – also the fact that I started my first shop in October 1970. I think that we just wanted to reach out to and try things. My shop was called Vêtements pour Hommes – I mean, in Nottingham in the middle of England – just *anything* to do something that was odd or different or special. We wanted freedom of expression. In my shop there was a David Bailey film that was banned by the BBC; I had an Andy Warhol soup can signed by Warhol in my shop for sale; later on in 1974, I had David Hockney's work for sale in a little gallery in the basement of the shop called Pushpin Gallery. It was a dirty, smelly cellar but I painted it white – it was still smelly; I also had prints by Guy Peellaert. So it was just anything – all this energy you wanted to push out.

HUO: What were the first objects you made?

PS: Union Jack handkerchiefs and narrow ties, made on my mum's machine that you work by hand. I bought handkerchiefs and then I made the screen with the different colours and then silkscreened them, then I did T-shirts.

HUO: What's interesting with the Union Jack is that in a way it's Pop.

PS: It's actually quite relevant to the subject we're talking about, because people like Jasper Johns did the American flag and he was very famous for all his flags – his white flag and so on, which was sensational at the time.

HUO: Johns of course is also about the targets and provides a link to both you and Gernes. When was the first time you used targets and dots and stripes? When did that enter your world?

PS: Very early on, because at the age of 18 I'd encountered all these people from art school by chance because of a pub I went to. What was amazing then was this world that opened up to me, because people were talking about something called the Bauhaus, and I thought it was maybe a house nearby or something – I didn't realize that it was actually a movement – and then Kandinsky, then later on Pop art. I hung out with all the young artists and the graphic designers and photographers. That's how I discovered the world of fashion. Suddenly everything was changing and everybody was trying to make their own stamp. A lot of the art students weren't necessarily doing things from their head, but had some little thread they could find occasionally: "I've got this book on this guy called Rauschenberg." Now it's on Instagram, but back then New York was a long way away. Photography was more classic at that time, but the art world especially was very experimental, as was music and as were clothes. At the time I did a target T-shirt, I did a flag T-shirt, I did a sort of Jim Dine oil paint splatter. I did things that on reflection were just expressions through effort.

HUO: I grew up in Switzerland and obviously there are also stripes and geometric shapes with the Concrete artists, but the Swiss Concretes worked with very dogmatic systems that were kind of more closed systems. What seems interesting is that you're here in 1970 and both you and Gernes seem to work with open systems. For me it's interesting how you have a basic shape – I wouldn't know if you could call it systematic – kind of pressing it to its limits – but you take it very far and in that sense, it's like losing a bit of the control.

PS: Paul Smith is an independent company, so we don't have to think about all those things I loathe – brand image, shareholder pressure or anything like that. So when we opened the shop in Los Angeles, the bright pink one, I just said "Let's do it in bright pink," and there was nobody we had to ask.

HUO: With all these alternating basic patterns you provide space for the viewer, for the person who can feel his or her particular relationship with some pattern and it's not controlled.

PS: Yes, and that's my job in a way. When I have my assistant designers around here, I say "I'm going to say 20 things, they are probably all going to be stupid or not relevant, but – you know what? – my job is to be brave enough to say them." So I say them and one of them just might stick.

HUO: With regard to Gernes' variations on stripes – and the same thing is true for the dots – there are also random elements. Chance seems to play a role – yet there is repetition and difference. Can you talk a little more about the idea of endless repetition and difference? Is there a moment or point where it comes to a conclusion or can there always be the next one?

PS: It's always the next one, it's always a progression, especially in clothes design, because we work in seasons. One of the problems I have is that I have too many ideas. They're all saying "Stop." … The thing about using colour is that, when I'm making stripes for clothes, first of all I always make them in actual yarn because when you actually have depth then they reflect on each other, the colours reflect on each other. If you look at a print-out it's so flat with no energy, whereas if you look at the yarn it's got this energy about it.

HUO: That's exactly what Gernes would say: he wouldn't send it to some industrial plant like the American minimalists to get it sharp and cool, like "LA fetish finish." Gernes would take on your yarn thing – only he would do it with a brush, because he believed in energy and the energy is in the material, too. Can you talk about that – what is energy?

PS: The energy is the love of life, I think – that and the inbuilt feeling that you want to make everything as good as you can. When I started to do stripes, this was the only way I could to do it. You know, just by literally doing it … Sometimes I think that we over-intellectualize things, because just

the use of colour and the use of circles and the use of squares and the use of stripes is something that we're surrounded by – vertical and horizontal lines in this room and circles and playing with colour and how you see colours together and how colour can change so much. How you feel about something. If you put orange and red together it's electric and exciting and if you put navy and white together it's very smart and clean and clear and fresh.

HUO: But then there's obviously also the idea of "as found." I wrote a text recently with Gerhard Richter on his colour charts. Now he does it digitally, but at the beginning when he did colour charts he found them in painting supplies stores, so they were a kind of ready-made. What's the rule about this "as found" in your work?

PS: The joy of the studio downstairs is: yes, of course we work on the computer – but also I still encourage drawing and painting because I think it's the thrill of the mistake that I like. When you just put something in and you didn't expect it, that's such a nice thing. For example with Josef Albers, when you look at his colours and how he put the colours together, they were all just done with bits of paint on little cards, just playing with the colours together.

HUO: But Albers had a kind of a colour theory in the earlier 20th century, and so of course did Runge, the Romantic age and Goethe with his colour theories, but it seems to me that Gernes didn't really have a colour theory, and you don't either?

PS: Not at all.

HUO: In connection with the work he did at the hospital he did say – as if he was a monk abstaining from the established art world: "Colour will heal you. I can make you well."

PS: Absolutely, colour is very healing. My pink shop in Los Angeles is one of the most Instagrammed buildings in all of California and it's because of the pink, because it's so flattering and it makes everybody look lovely.

HUO: That's another link, because you bring colour into architecture, and that's what Gernes did as well. He brings it into the architecture – the famous example is the cinema in Copenhagen.

PS: Did you see the Land Rover Defender I designed as well? I drive one of these, which Land Rover knew, so as an homage they asked me to make one. The Land Rover is built for the farmers or for the military and the idea was that if you have a crash here or you have a crash here, everything comes apart. Now in a modern car it's all one. So what I did was 27 colours, so you could have lots of crashes, so each bit could be replaced but with a colour that's incorrect.

HUO: That may lead to a design beyond your control and I think that's something that Gernes would have embraced – that you bring in chance, that you bring in life. There is a quote by Gernes, which is the title of the show at the Louisiana: "I cannot do it alone – want to join in?" Now obviously the 60s and 70s were also a moment with a kind of DIY in art, art with instructions and so on. Gernes' gesture in asking us to join in was that he didn't believe in the role of an authoritative artist, and in that sense his work is about being anti-authoritative, and if your major work then ends up in a hospital healing other people, I guess you've taken it out of a closed art system and into something different.

PS: Yes, sharing it with everyone.

HUO: As you've told us about your very first shop in Nottingham, it has never been only about your

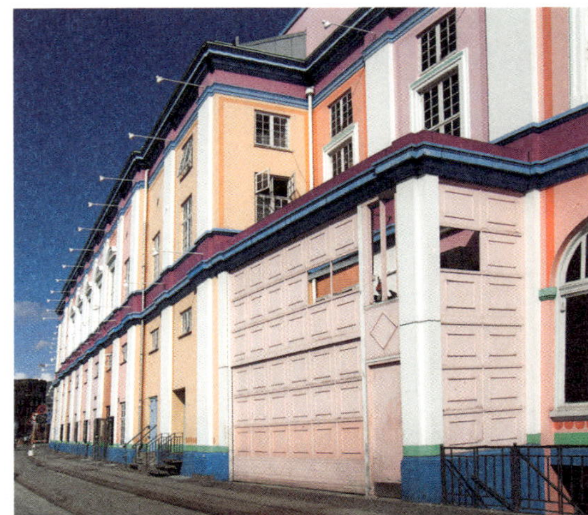

fig.3

fig.4

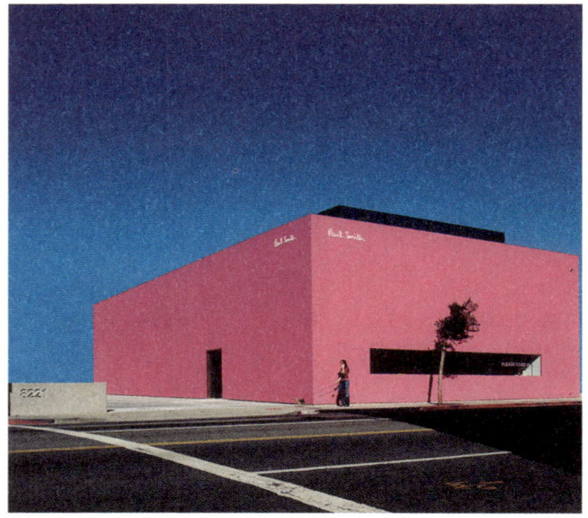

fig.5

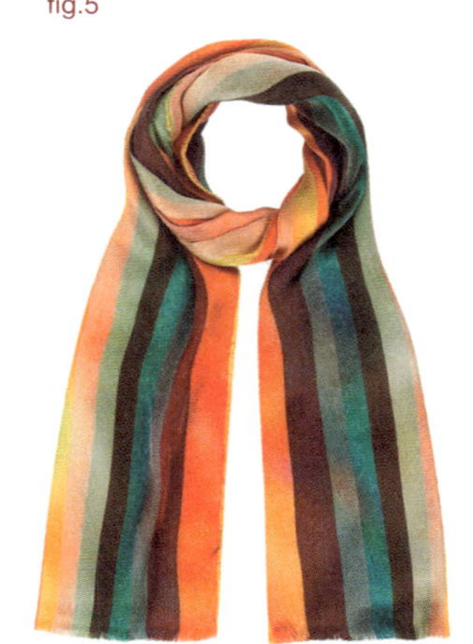

fig.6

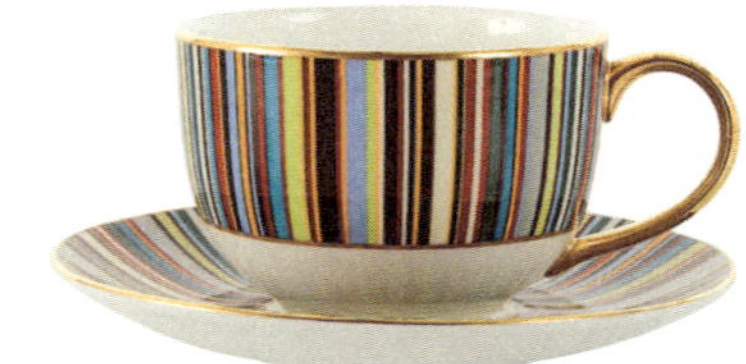

Paul Smith (b. 1946) is a British designer.
He showed his first menswear collection
in Paris under the label Paul Smith in 1976.
He opened his first store in Nottingham
in 1970 and now has more than 300 shops
worldwide.

Hans Ulrich Obrist (b. 1968) is Artistic
Director of the Serpentine Galleries, London.
Prior to this, he was Curator at Musée d'Art
Moderne de la Ville de Paris. Since his first
show *World Soup (The Kitchen Show)* in
1991, he has curated more than 300 shows.

fig.7

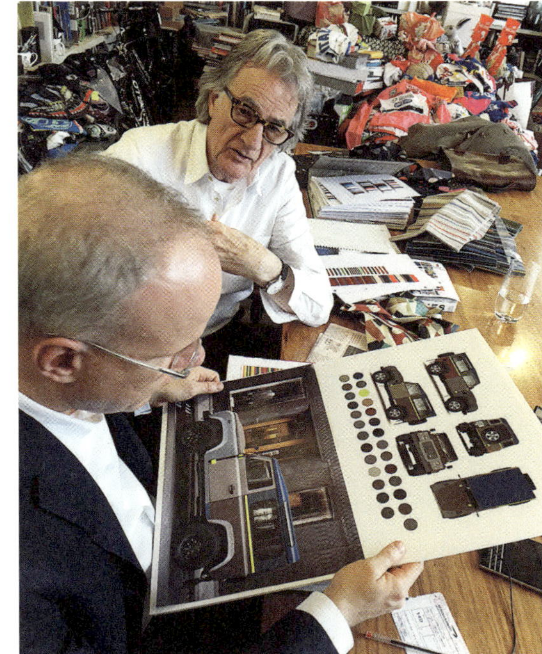

fig.8

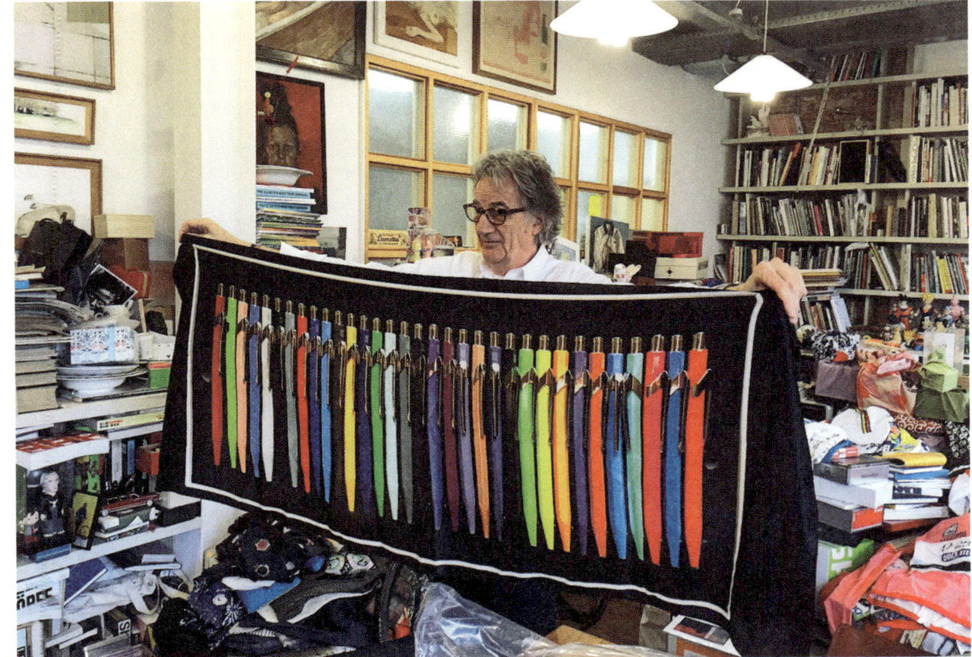

own products; there was always a lot of popular
culture, a lot of art, a lot of design, almost like a
mini exhibition. And that's interesting when we talk
about Gernes' connection with popular culture.
PS: That's the point about the democratic aspect
to it. That little first shop, which was 3 metres
square, you would walk in and you were close to
me, so immediately I was not a confrontational
person, and I always wanted to say "Oh have you
seen this, I was in Paris." It was a way of breaking
the ice, making people relax, and then, without me
realizing it, that became very, very appealing to
anybody – to a 12-year-old and to a 90-year-old,
to anybody.
HUO: You bring in these things – you curated it,
in a way.
PS: And everything has been chosen with my
eyes and that's quite unusual in today's very busy
world. I see everything, there's nothing I don't see.
HUO: There seems to be an interesting connection between Gernes and you with regard to your
relation to folklore – a folkloristic element. Can
you talk about this? How you connect to the
folkloristic.
PS: In my shop I've always had things I've seen
from around the world. So in that sense it's maybe
like folklore, is this what you mean?
HUO: When you have insisted over time on adding
little signs for bikes or cufflinks that adhere to the
hot and cold taps, I would say that's basically
everyday folklore, great basic design that runs
through your work.
PS: What's so interesting in an interview like this is
it makes me realize there are aspects of what I've
done which are thought about in different ways,
but I've never thought about it in a different way,
I've always just done it.

fig.9

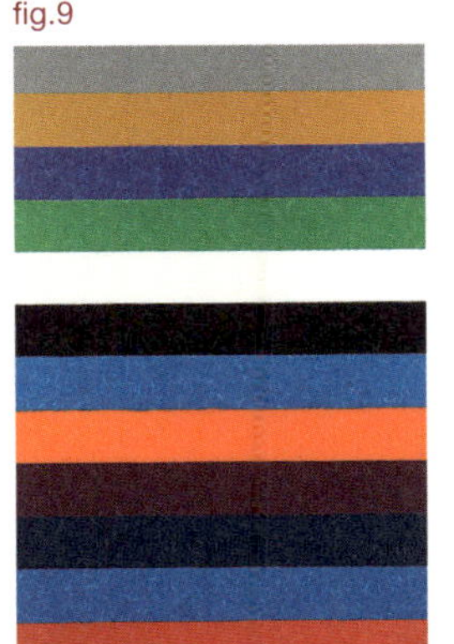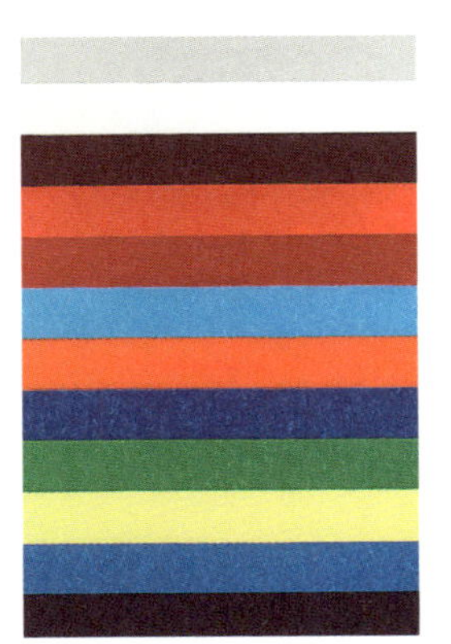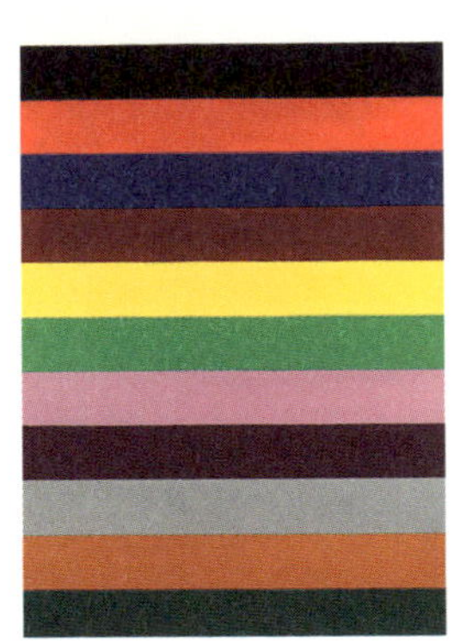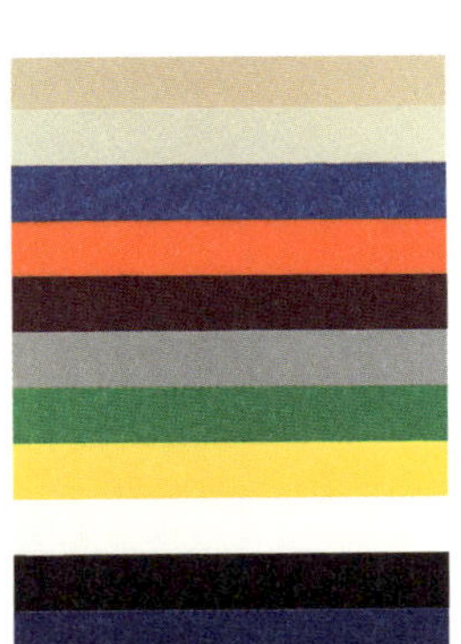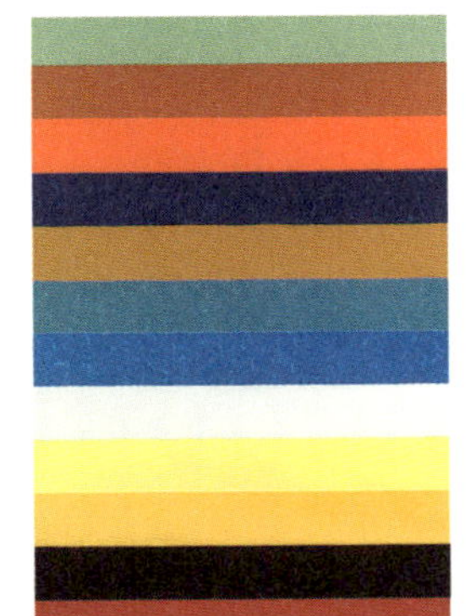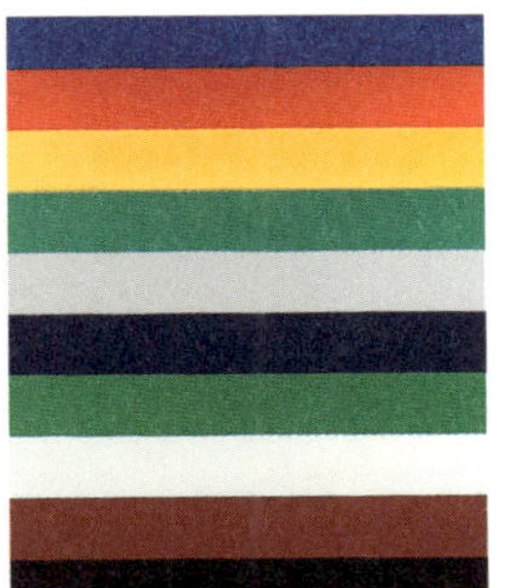

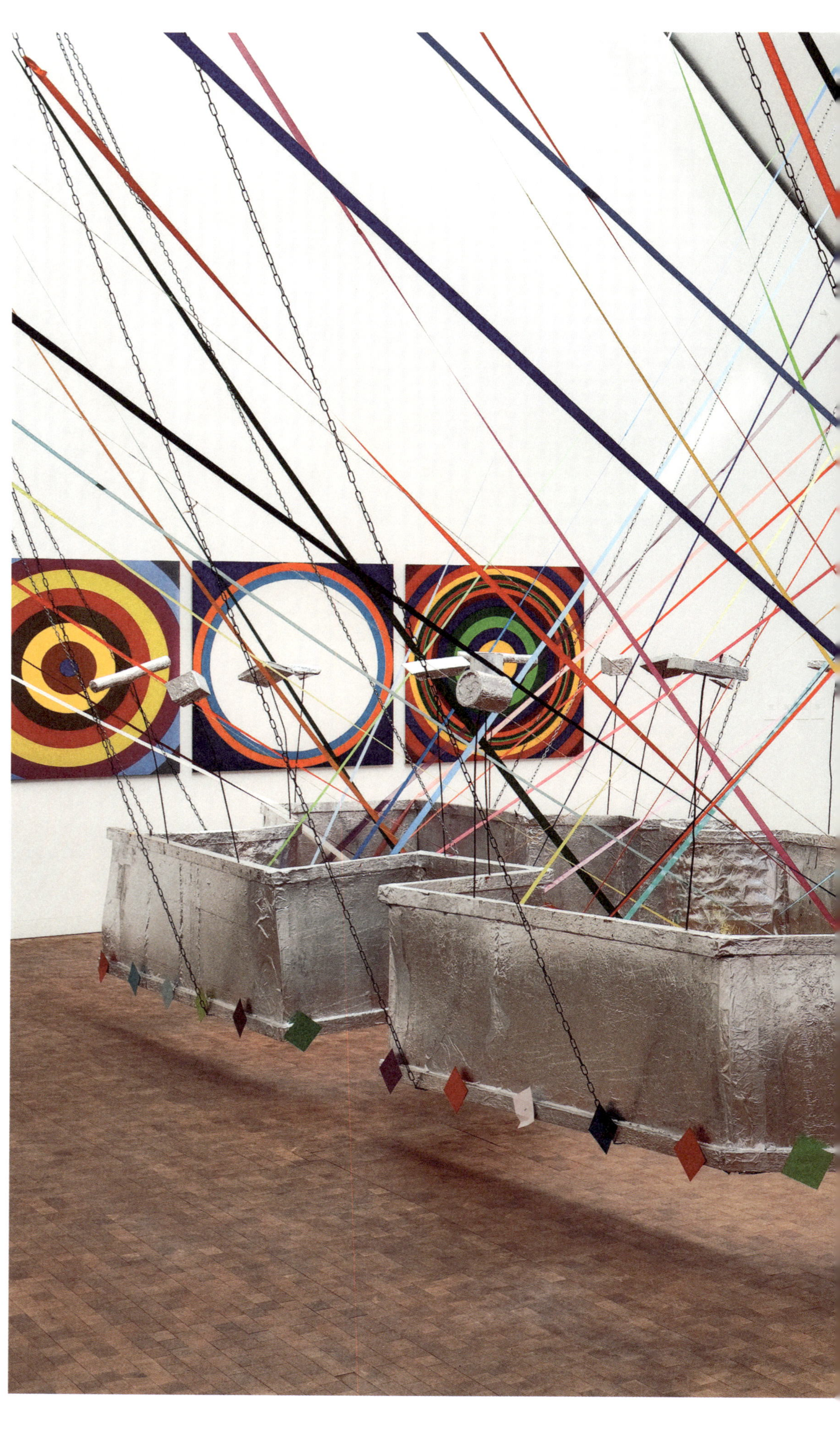

Untitled ("The Dream Ship"), 1968
Mixed media, variable measurements
Installation view from Sorø Kunstmuseum,
2015

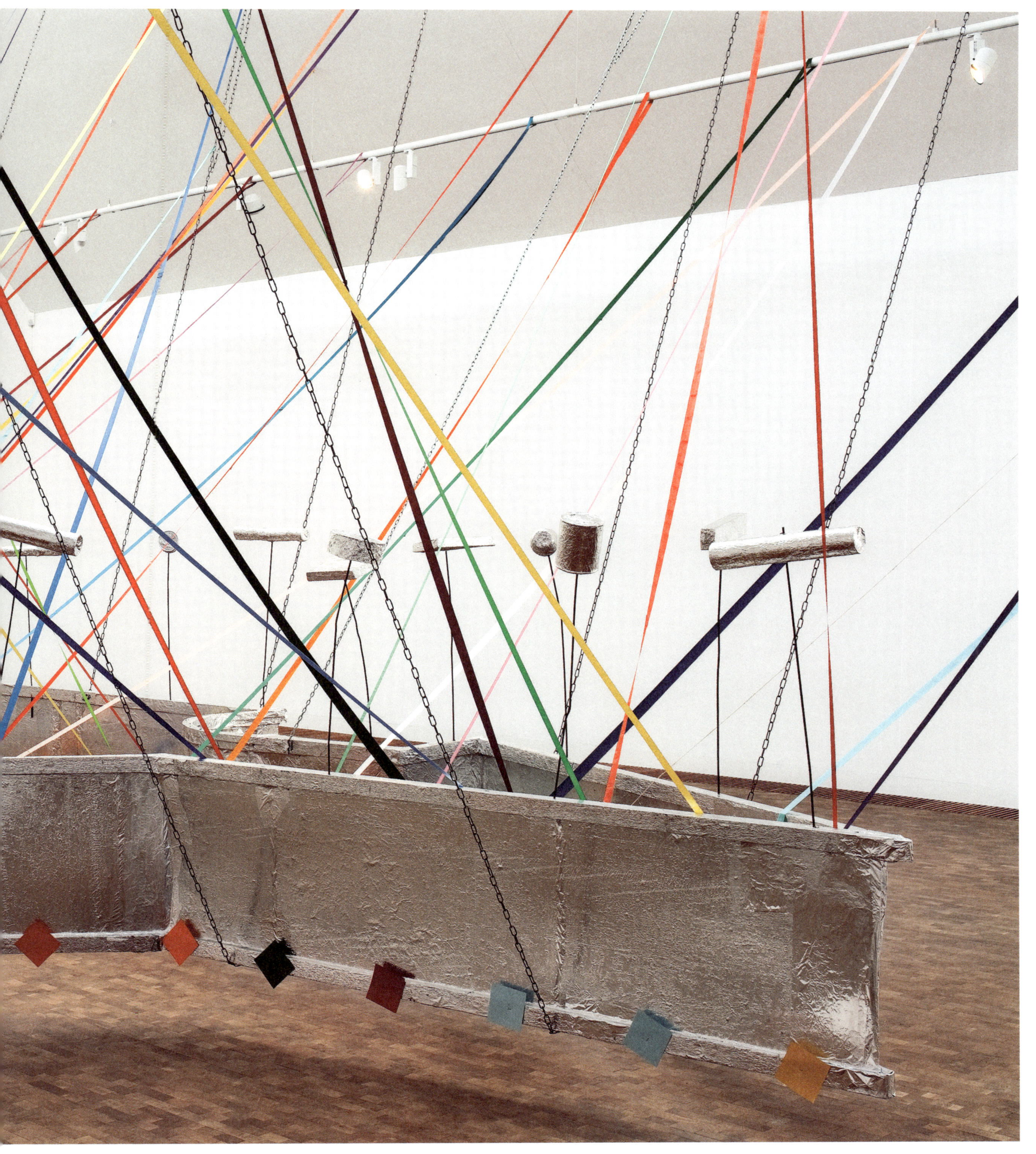

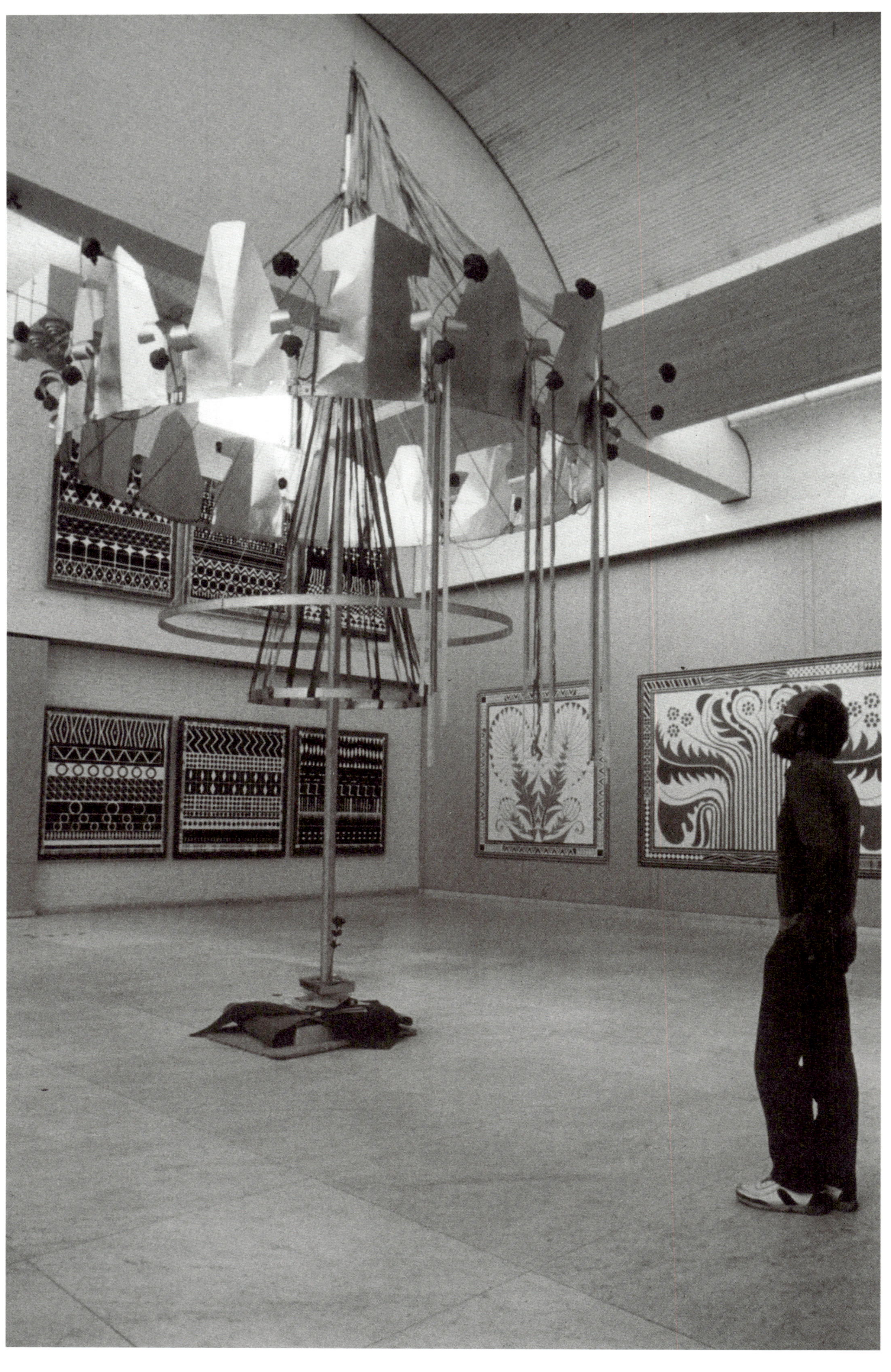

Maypole, 1978
Mixed media
Installation view from Nordjyllands
Kunstmuseum, 1983

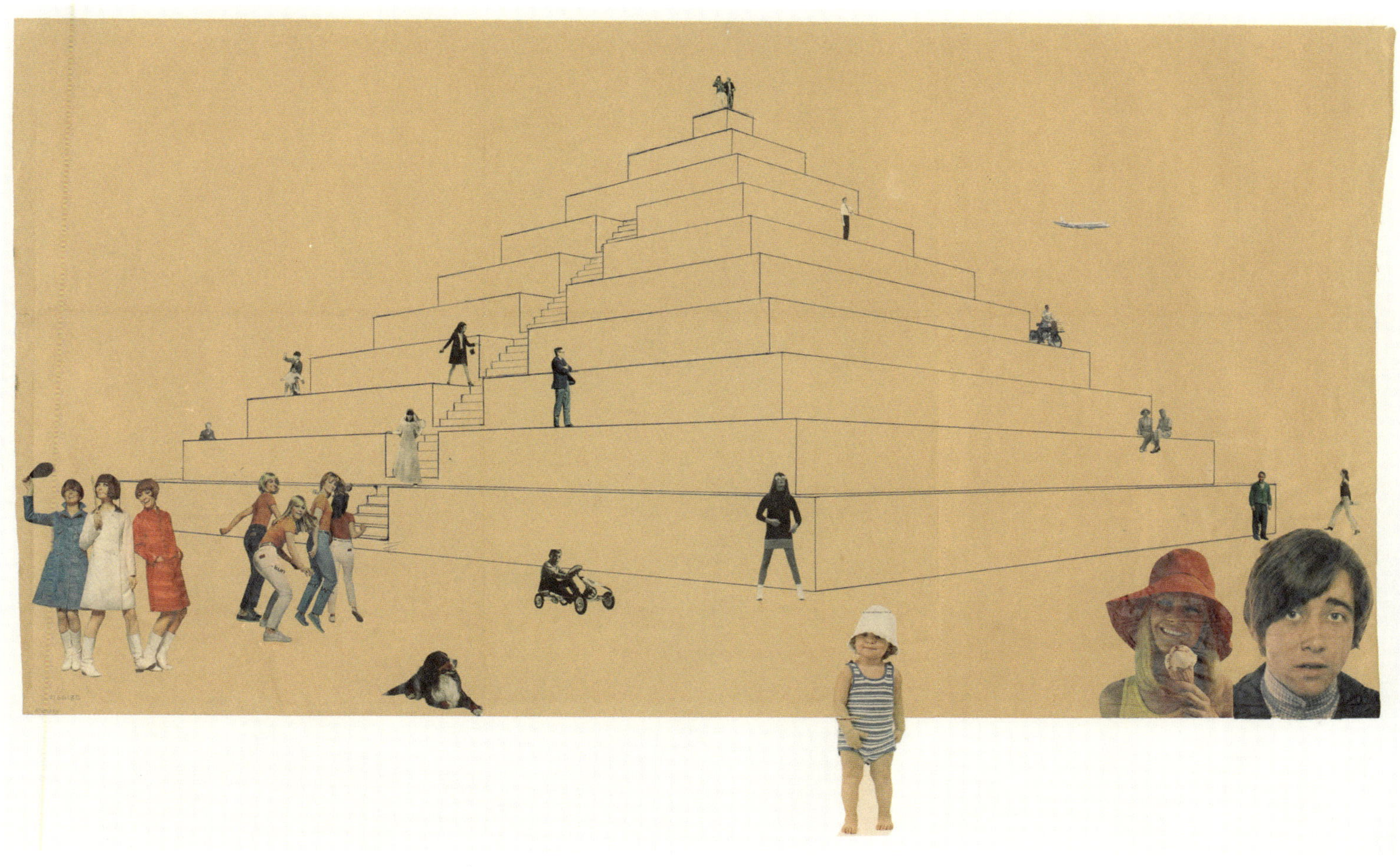

Sketch for Sculpture for Israels Plads,
Copenhagen (not realized), 1967
Pen, collage, 94 × 187 cm

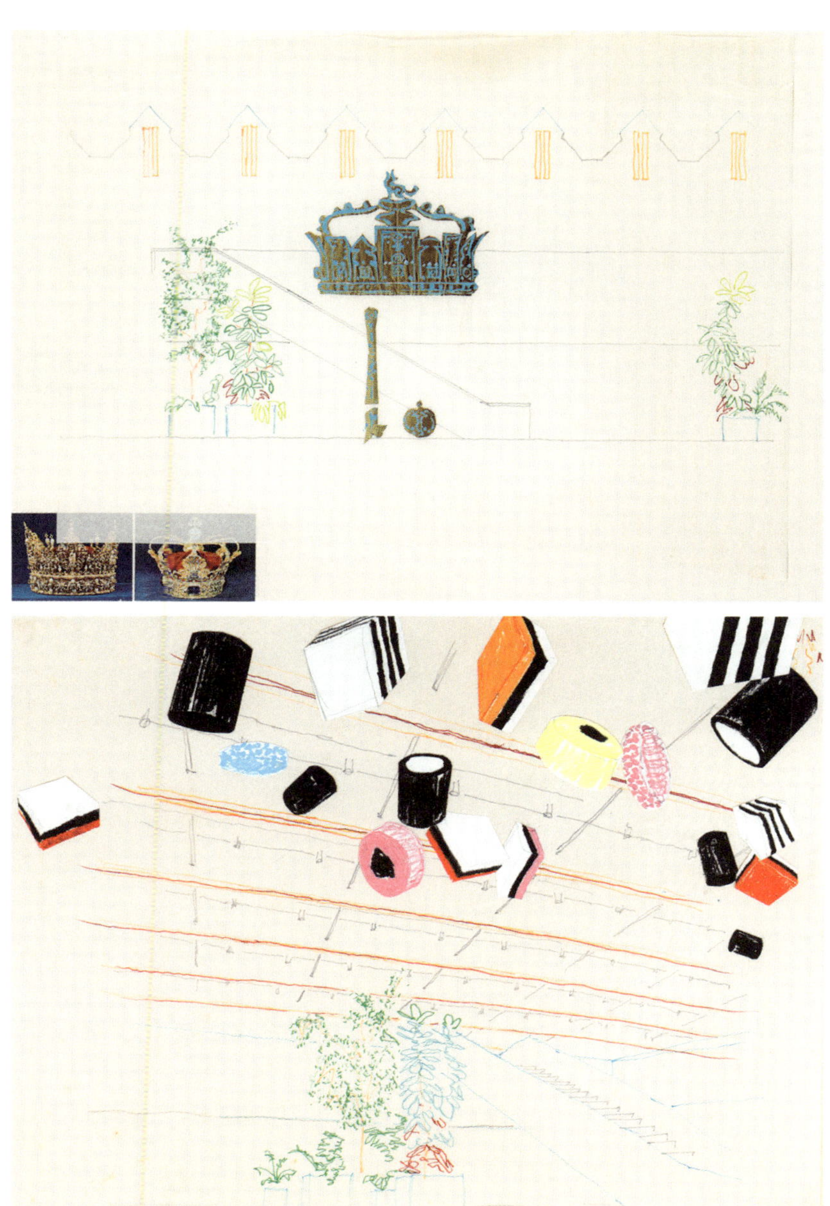

Untitled , 1978
(Sketch for decoration, Esbjerg Seminarium)
Felt pen, collage on manifold paper,
70 × 100 cm

Untitled , 1978
(Sketch for decoration, Esbjerg Seminarium)
Felt pen, collage on manifold paper,
70 × 100 cm

Pyramid, 1967/2016
Scale model of public commission
(not realized) for Israels Plads, Copenhagen
Wood, 6 × 12 × 12 m
Installation view from Louisiana Museum
of Modern Art, 2016

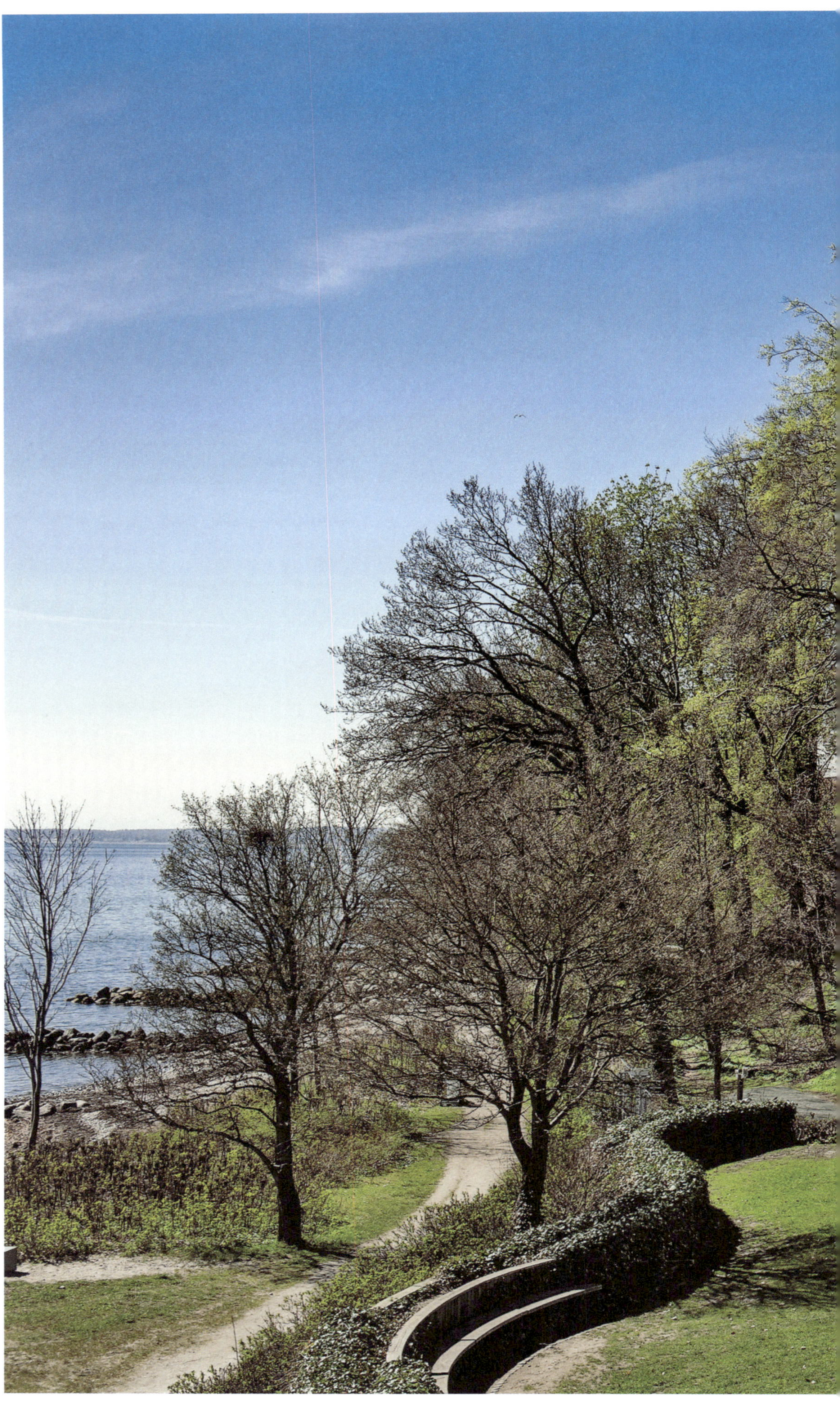

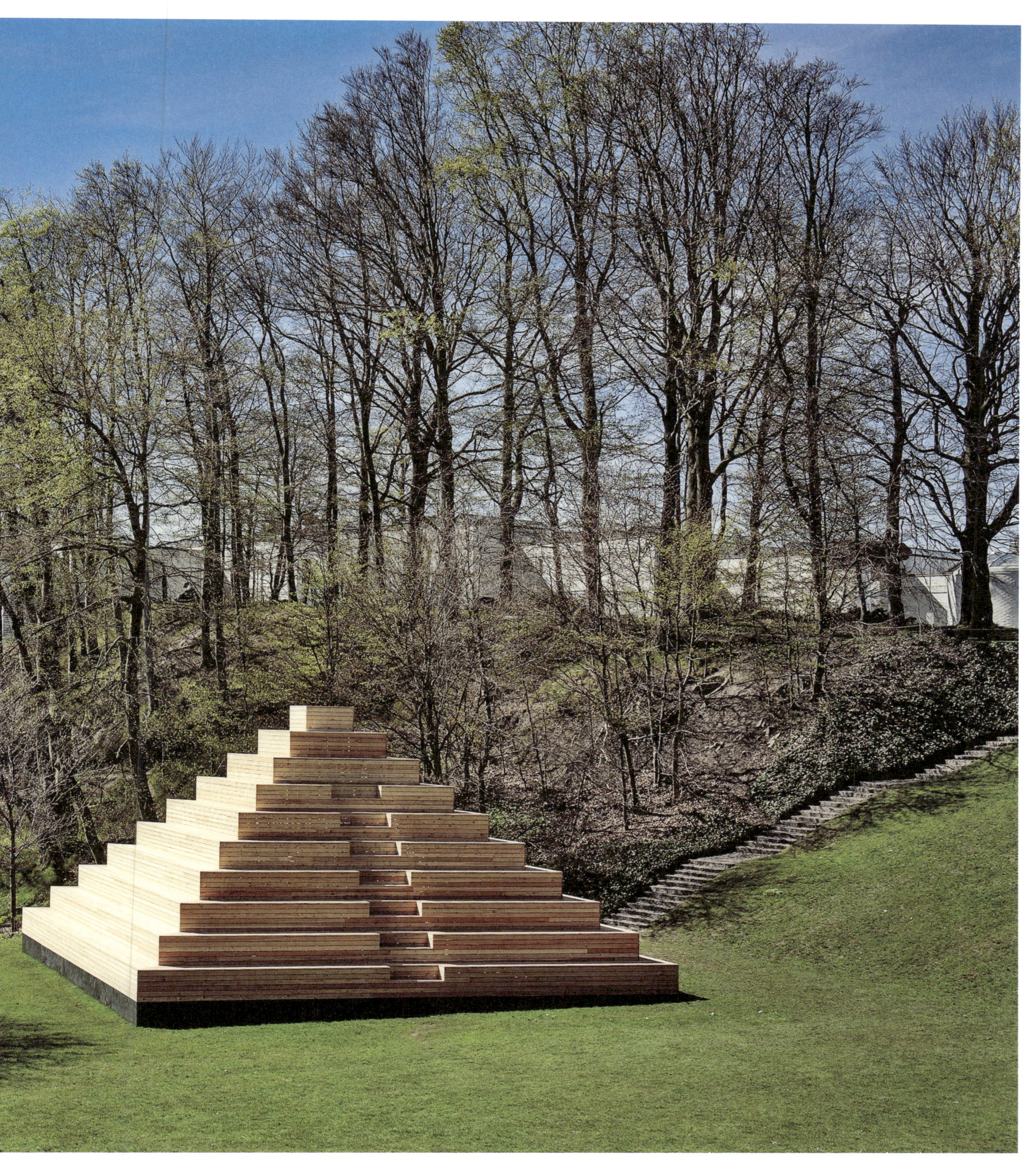

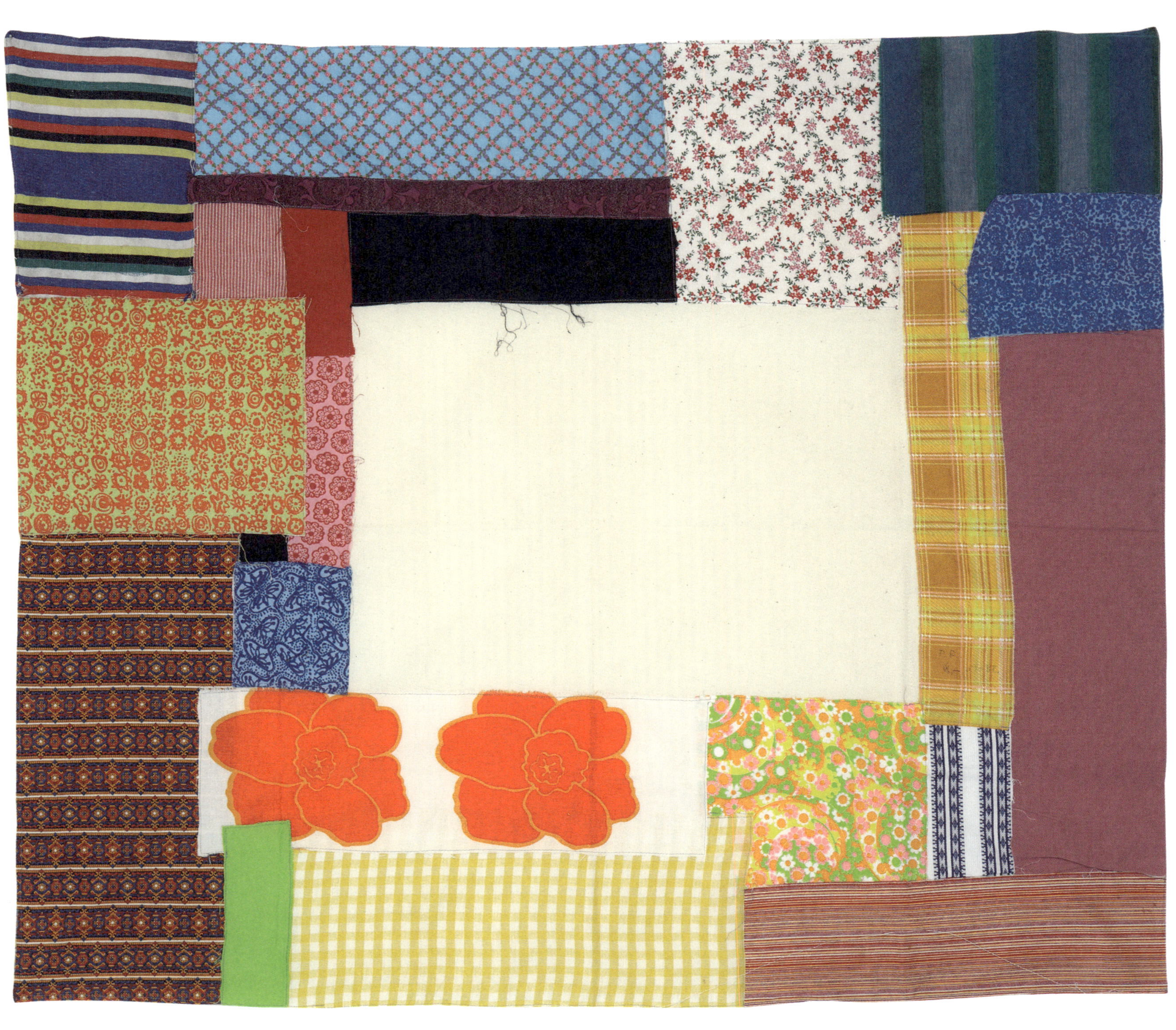

Untitled
("Suggestion for a European
Common Market Flag"), 1972
Flag, textile, 115 × 136 cm

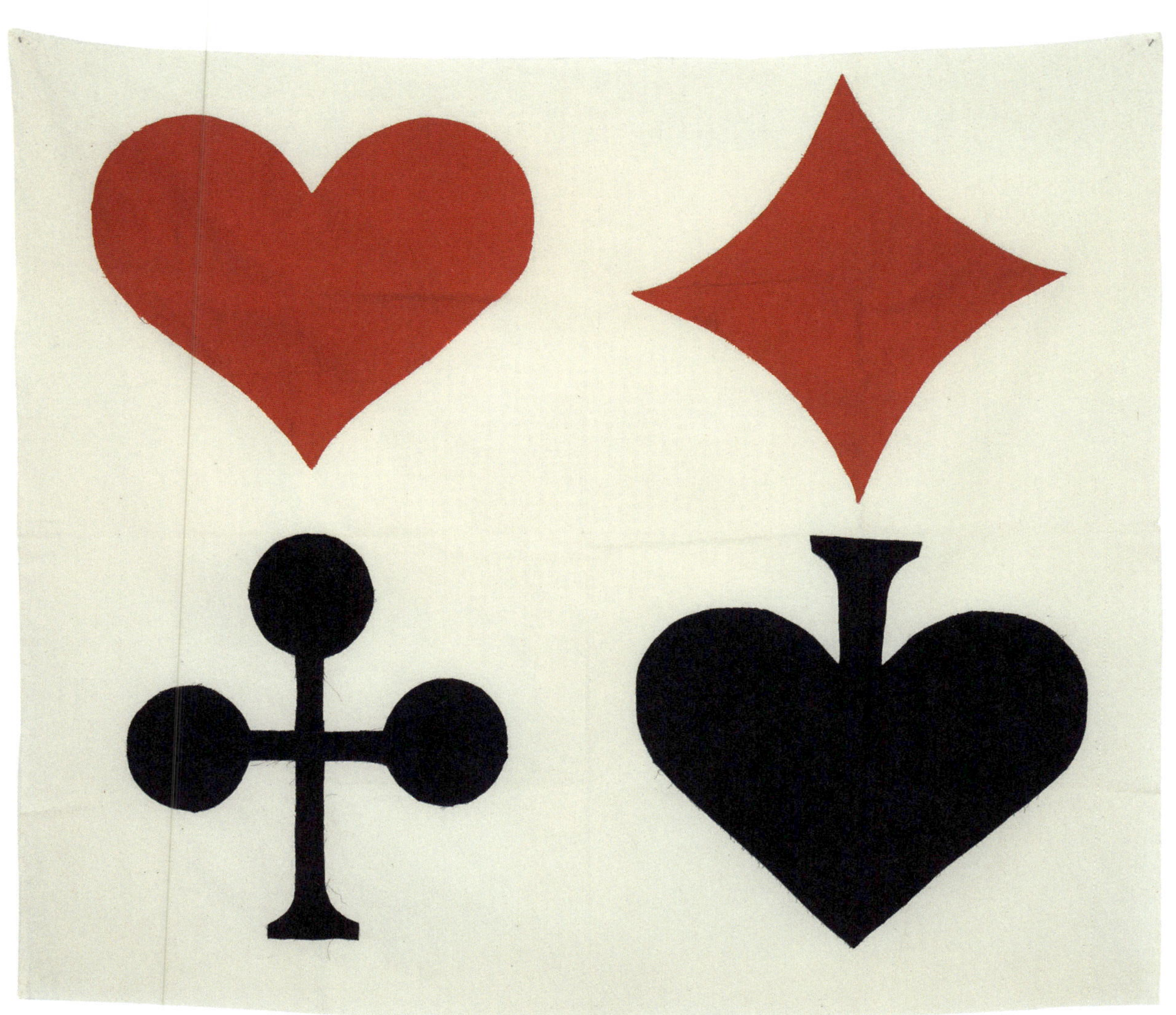

Untitled
("Suggestion for a European
Common Market Flag"), 1972
Flag, textile, 112 × 134 cm

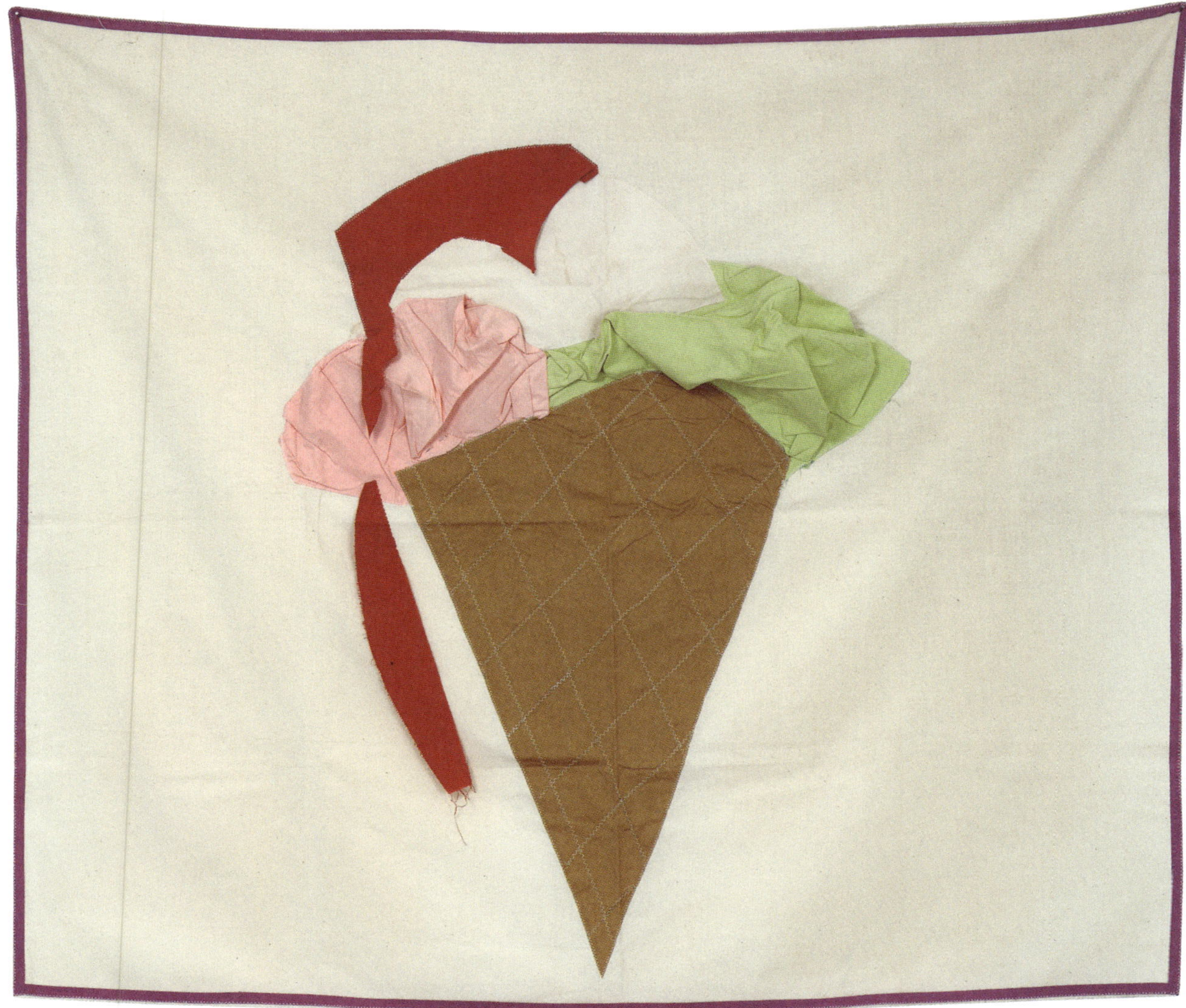

Untitled
("Suggestion for a European
Common Market Flag"), 1972
Flag, textile, 110 × 135 cm

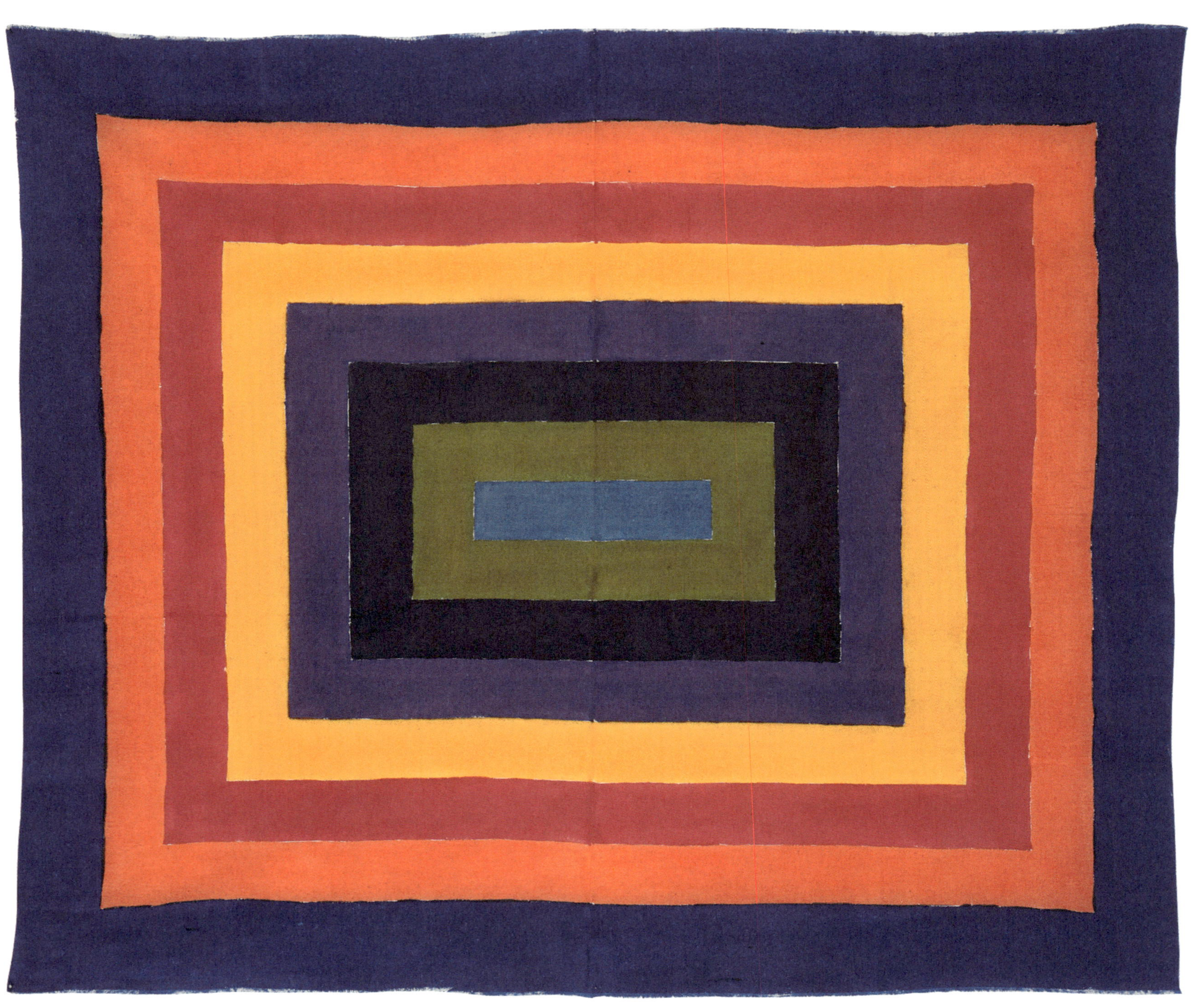

Untitled
("Suggestion for a European
Common Market Flag"), 1972
Flag, textile, 108 × 133 cm

Untitled
("Suggestion for a European
Common Market Flag"), 1972
Flag, textile, 110 × 131 cm

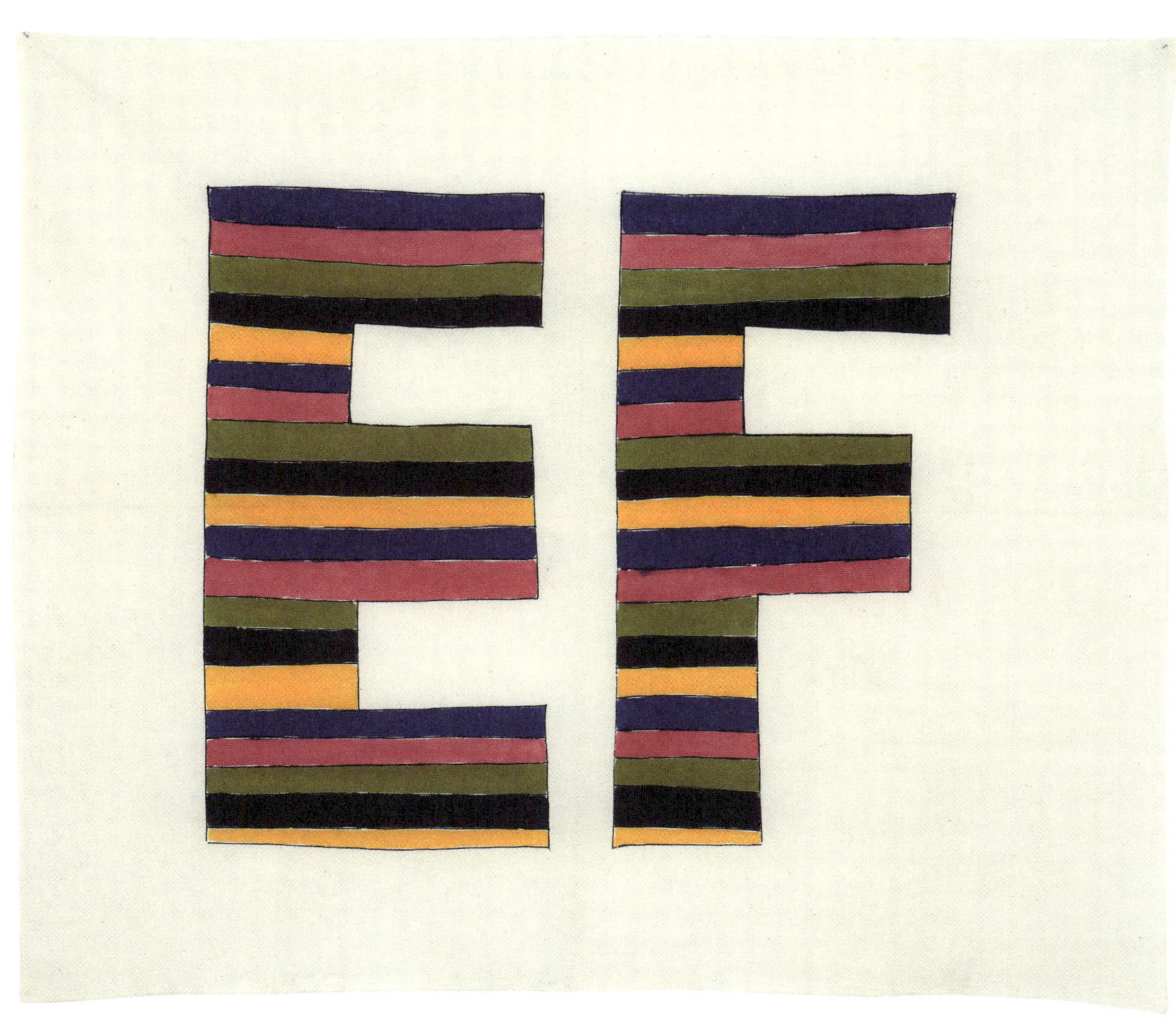

Untitled
("Suggestion for a European
Common Market Flag")
Flag, textile, 110 × 131 cm

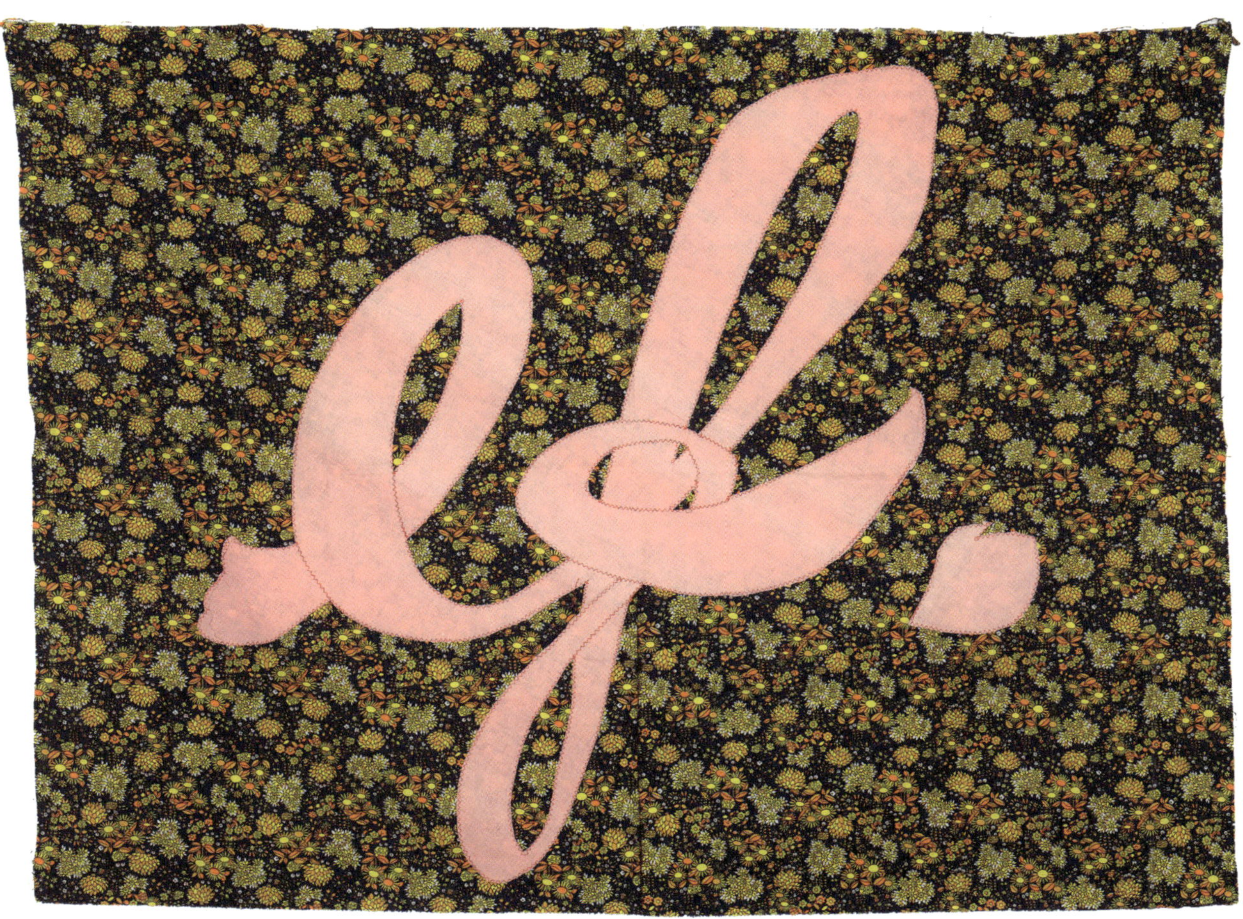

POUL GERNES. I CANNOT DO IT ALONE – WANT TO JOIN IN?
© Louisiana Museum of Modern Art and the contributors

Edited by Lærke Rydal Jørgensen and Anders Kold
Graphic design: Rasmus Koch Studio
Photo Editor: Sidse Buck
Translations from the Danish: Glen Garner (Poul Erik Tøjner/Anders Kold, Helle Brøns, Anders Kold
and Lene Bøgh Rønberg), James Manley (Kristian Handberg, Anders Krüger, Kathrine Rasmussen)
Proof Reading: James Manley
Articles by Helle Brøns, Anders Kold and Lene Bøgh Rønberg are peer reviewed
Front cover: Top: Poul Gernes, 1977-78. Photo: Steen Møller Rasmussen. Middle: Self Portrait (5), 1965.
Linocut, 24 x 16 cm. VejleMuseerne – Kunstmuseet. Bottom: Poul Gernes, 1965
All works by Poul Gernes © Gernes Estate
Printed by Rosendahls
ISBN: 978-87-92877-68-0
Printed in Denmark, 2016
www.louisiana.dk

This catalogue is published on the occasion of the exhibition
Poul Gernes. I cannot do it alone – want to join in?
2 June – 16 October 2016

Curator: Anders Kold
Curatorial Assistant: Kathrine Rasmussen
Curatorial Coordinator/ Registrar: Marianne Ahrensberg
Exhibition Architect: Jens Kamp
Graphic Design: Marie d'Origny Lübecker
Conservator / Exhibition Producer: Børge Igor Brandt

Photo:
Anders Krüger: p. 80; Anders Sune Berg: p. 8 fig. 1, p. 9, p. 11 fig. 7 og 8, p. 12 fig. 12, p. 15, p. 25
fig. 4, p. 28 fig. 10, p. 31-32, p. 36-38, p. 49-61, p. 71-74, p. 77-79, p. 89, p. 92-95; Asger Sessingø:
p. 6; Erik Hagens: p. 68 fig. 10; Finn Thybo Andersen: p. 28 fig. 11; John Davidsen / Bjørn Nørgaards
Arkiv: p. 27 fig. 9; Jørn Freddie: p. 24 fig. 2; Katrin Rother / Galleri Kaufmann: p. 13 fig. 15; Kim Hansen
p. 90; Leá Nielsen p. 12 fig. 11, p. 86; Museum Jorn, Silkeborg: p. 16; Ole Hein Petersen: p. 8 fig. 2,
10 fig. 4 og fig. 6, p. 30, p. 76; Paul Smith Studio: p. 83, p. 84 fig. 4-6; Polfoto: p. 88; Polfoto / Magnus
Holm p. 43 fig. 4; Poul Buchard / Brøndum & Co.: p. 7, p. 10 fig. 5, p. 11 fig. 9, p. 33, p. 35, p. 39,
p. 72, p. 82, p. 85 fig.9; Scanpix / Egon Engmann: p. 66 fig. 4; Scanpix / Jørgen Jessen: p. 27 fig. 8;
Scanpix / Mini Wollf: p. 26 fig. 6; Skissernas Museum – Museum of Artistic Process and Public Art,
Lund, Sweden: p. 89; Steen Møller Rasmussen: p. 23, p. 13 fig. 13, p. 34, p. 42, p. 43 fig. 5, p. 45 fig.
9, p. 47 (photo reconstruction), p. 84 fig. 3; Thomas Hommelgaard: p. 40; Thomas Seest: p. 43 fig. 3,
p. 45 fig. 9; Troels Andersen: p. 5, p. 65 fig. 1, p. 67 fig. 5 og 6

The Exhibion is supported by:

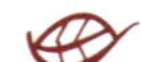 15. Juni Fonden

Louisiana's Main Corporate Partners:

REPUBLIC OF **Fritz Hansen**®

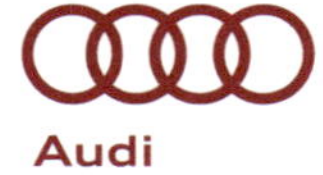
Audi

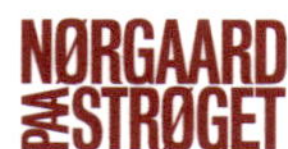

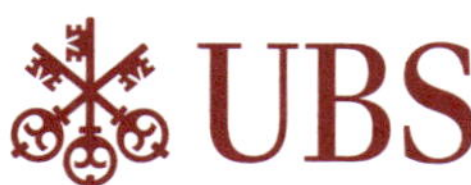

supports programs and exhibitions at Louisiana

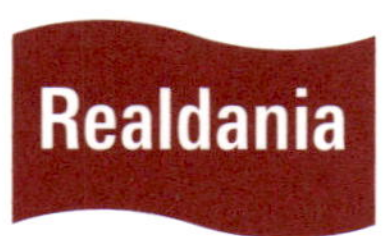

supports Louisiana's architectural exhibitions